Reunion:

How We Heal Our Broken Connection to the Earth

Reunion:

How We Heal Our Broken Connection to the Earth

By

Ellen Gunter and Ted Carter

Chauncey Park Press
Oak Park, Illinois

Reunion: How We Heal Our Broken Connection to the Earth
© Ellen Gunter and Ted Carter

www.reunionthebook.com

Published in the United States by
Chauncey Park Press
Oak Park, Illinois 60302
www.chaunceyparkpress.com

Inside Design by Suzanne Austin Wells
Chauncey Park Press

Cover Design by Katherine Baronet
www.kbaronet.com

Photo credits:
Photos for covers of title pages of Chapters 2, 4, and 6 are by the authors.
Photo of Ellen Gunter by Suzanne Austin Wells
Photos for covers of other chapters purchased from www.123rf.com

*While all the website adddresses included in this book were checked and verified before
publication, due to the changing nature of information on the internet, some addresses or
links may change over time.*

For every copy of Reunion sold, the authors will plant a tree. Join us in replenishing
our forest, rebuilding habitats for wildlife and helping to reverse CO_2 build up at
www.americanforests.org (our favorite tree-saving source) or your preferred group.

Library of Congress Number: 2010924362.
ISBN: 9780966780871.

1. Environment 2. Spirituality 3.Self-Help

For Johnny and Miles,
the bookends of my life

For my daughter, Valeria, and her generation

TABLE OF CONTENTS

FOREWORD

THE TITLE OF THIS BOOK holds the heart and soul of its message: To provide individuals with a guidebook through which a relationship of *reunion* with nature and this environment could be established. *Reunion* is a book that could not have been written other than at this time for only at this present moment in history do we find ourselves at odds with our own environment. Such a phenomenon is a first, a genuine anomaly among living creatures—to be hostiles within our own environment. And yet, we have become exactly that—the aggressors against nature and all the systems that sustain life. That many of us do not overtly participate in crimes against nature does not lessen the seriousness of our environmental crises as we must ask ourselves: How much did I do to prevent this situation in the years leading up to this moment?

As I prepared my notes for writing the Foreword to this remarkable book, quite an awesome thought occurred to me: When did we become "outsiders" to our own world? When did we start referring to nature as "out there", a place somewhere in the woods as opposed to everywhere? When did the word "environment" become essential to our vocabulary as the term needed to communicate the "great outdoors" and all the integral systems of Mother Nature? And how is it that most people assume that the word "environment" means "way out there" and not their own backyard, their own neighborhood, their own urban area, and their own corner park? When and how did we become so unfathomably detached from everything outside our front door, so much so that we had to find new words and even create new psychological syndromes to identify so-called symptoms of lack of contact with nature? What has become of us?

That is why *Reunion* is a book that should be required reading for every single person. Something radical has changed in us and it's not good. We have strayed from our fundamental nature and we must find our way back to our primary rapport with the earth and our own life instincts before we lose sight of those precious instincts entirely. By that I mean, for example, that it is instinctive, a type of inherent common sense, to know how to garden. To say this differently, it is natural for us to grow our own food. We may start off awkwardly as we first put our hands into the rich earth, but believe me when I tell you that you are born with an instinct to understand the cycles of nature because *you* live according to those same cycles. You are governed by the very same cycles of nature that bring seeds to maturation as fruit-bearing trees or vegetables. We are made of the same stuff.

That fact makes a separation from that "same stuff" all the more remarkable – how did that happen to us? When did we lose contact with this place called Earth? Because the truth is, we could not have lost contact with the "environment" had we not first lost contact with our own inner nature and its need to stay in contact with the simpler rhythms of life. I recall, for instance, that I walked to and from grade school each day and then when I got home, all the kids on the block headed outside to play. We were not attached to Ipods and computers and other electronic gizmos. We were attached to our bikes and to racing around the block and to playing tag; simply put, we were attached to our bodies and to how far and fast we could push them before we collapsed from exhaustion – or had to come in for dinner.

I don't recall any of us ever feeling "ungrounded" or needing to go elsewhere to "get in touch" with nature. We came into the house covered with nature – dirt, insect bites, rain-drenched – you name it. And we thrived.

Somewhere between those blissful days and now, however, values shifted. As we discovered the world of technology and convenience, we, and the world around us gradually morphed into society requiring that we come up with technical names for everything, including what used to be just "outside". Now this place that is foreign to so many is formally called the "environment". In this new world, what I used to think of as "walking" has been relegated to the category of "exercise". As a measure of how far we have drifted off course in terms of what it means to be a grounded human being, guided by common sense and an inherent understanding of how to live in harmony with our natural timing and pace, consider this all too common scenario: After we figure out what to call "where" we are (aka, the inner or outer environment), followed by a strategy to motive ourselves to "exercise" our bodies as basic walking is no longer just "walking", next we have to recall how to "nourish" our bodies with wholesome food. We've even forgotten how to properly feed ourselves. This is a summation of the modern day person and such a description encapsulates why this book is essential reading. When did we become so out of touch with our essential nature and how can we come back to ourselves and to wholeness once again?

Author Ellen Gunter poured two years of her life into meticulous research as she formulated what information to include in *Reunion*. Her selection of information, given that vast amount that she accumulated, came from a combination of necessity and wisdom, intuition and vision. In one chapter, Ellen gives the reader an historic perspective built upon our relationship to oil – and that is an eye-opener. This chapter falls under the category of "necessary" information and it is astounding. And then she leads the reader into a mind-boggling chapter on seeds – and it is just that – mind-boggling. From the metaphor of the mustard seed to the crimes of the Monsanto Corporation (and others) in their efforts to own patents on all of the seed from which the globe's food is grown, this chapter is a must read if only because your body is literally a product of these facts. But this is just a sample of what awaits the reader in this masterpiece.

As someone who has been in the field of human consciousness and environmentalism for decades, I have come upon many self-help books offering suggestions for people, next step ideas, as it were. Ellen has done the best job of this task of any author I have ever come upon. In the chapter entitled Reunion, she presents more than one-hundred of the most common sense ideas that I have ever read for how to achieve the book's purpose—to heal our broken connection to the earth—and to that I say, "Well done, Ellen."

While Ellen Gunter was the writer and main researcher in this gallant book, the vision was born from Ted Carter, the "soul" author of *Reunion*. Ted is a landscape architect by day. By night, Ted is a Nature-Mystic, a man devoted to protecting Mother Nature. It was Ted who first envisioned writing a book to give voice to the numerous crises confronting our Earth but in addition to the crises – made all the more familiar through Al Gore's wonderful work – Ted's vision included his wanting to communicate his deep love and passion for nature. Ted speaks "nature" fluently. He is someone who can look at a plant or tree and sense its health or what it needs to return to balance. He gardens in his bare feet and communes with nature spirits as working companions. He is a marvel to watch.

Reunion is a book that carries a sacred message as well as a practical one: We must find our way back to our own nature as well as our way back to a rapport with this Earth because we are one and the same system of life. That is not a mental bit of information – it is a mystical truth.

Caroline Myss
Oak Park, IL
February, 2010

INTRODUCTION

We are the consciousness of the earth.

—Joseph Campbell, *The Power of Myth*

REUNION IS ABOUT WAKING UP to the world we live in but can no longer see. It's about how we have ruptured something precious and basic to each one of us—our connection to the earth we all come from—and how each of us can begin to heal that disconnection. It requires retraining ourselves to see with more than our eyes and beyond our stubborn polarities.

Tielhard de Chardin pointed the way—that there's more to us than meets the eye—when he said, "We are not human beings having a spiritual experience. We are spiritual beings having a human experience." It's our inability or unwillingness to access our own natural spiritual acumen that is at the heart of our disconnection.

To be able to add a spiritual lens to our eyes, however, we have to look differently—first inside ourselves, then outside ourselves. And that requires a discipline that's deliberate and courageous, and requires mindfulness and discernment. It's this discipline that helps us finally begin to look at the loss of what Daniel Smith has called our "heart's ease,"[1] our separation from a deeper way of seeing what surrounds us.

As we look around at the condition of our air, water and food, the disappearing glaciers and the poisoned landmasses, we have to ask, *what could possibly get so many of us to engage in behavior that is sure to kill us?* At the heart of this question lies our reason for writing this book. What has brought us to this environmental precipice isn't just greed and power.

We are not just physical beings who love to acquire and conquer. We are also beings of mystery who crave connection and meaning in our lives. While we can see the physical manifestations of what is happening to our environment, how do we understand how we got to this place, measure what we have lost and find our way back?

That's what *Reunion* sets out to do. First, it looks at what we are made of and where we are, the snapshot of us at this moment in earth's history. Second, it examines how we got here and how our current attitudes toward the earth's resources endanger generations to come. Finally, it offers us numerous ways to help our eyes see with a heightened spiritual awareness, to literally *envision* new ways of living and being, as others around us are already doing.

Reunion grew out of a chance meeting. Ted Carter and I crossed paths for the first time in a hotel classroom in Chicago in early 2003. We had both come to attend the first "Sacred Contracts" class being presented by author and teacher Caroline Myss through her new institute, CMED. During the two years we met for the classes, we often found ourselves paired up together in work sessions and at meals and coffee breaks on those intense weekends. I noted that Ted always arrived for the classes earlier than the rest of us. Besides attending as a student, he was in charge of dressing the stage with plants, trees, and season-specific earth elements, setting a mood and tone that acknowledged Mother Nature and added a sacred aspect to the room.

The class days were long, beginning early and seldom ending before 10:30 p.m. (The evening's lesson was a film—presented by faculty member Jim Curtan—that always managed to parallel the day's work and offer startling synchronicities.) Afterwards, Ted and I, plus my husband and the many others we grew close to, sat up into the wee hours of the morning, exhausted and over-stimulated, but unable to give up to sleep— talking, postulating and listening—trying to understand what it was that was happening to us.

Because in fact all our lives changed. Going on a spiritual exploration—inviting the sacred into your life—makes everything shift. It changes the lens on your eyes so that nothing ever quite looks the same again. Life takes on a different character and tone. Many of us kept in touch by phone and email and reunited for advanced classes in Chicago. Deep, cherished friendships took root. We had shared a common and unique experience that each of us found hard to discuss with anyone besides our classmates, because what we shared wasn't material, it wasn't measurable or definable in any logical or cognitive sense. It was experiential and, being experiential, it defied description.

The information and insights we were blessed with during those magical years put us on a path toward understanding some of what we were doing here on earth for this short period called a lifetime. And it has a way of demanding some form of accountability—and service.

"You don't think," Caroline asked more than once, "that the universe is going to let go of a well-trained soul, do you?"

In other words, our old lives, the ones we had fought tooth and nail to keep safe and secure, were over. Ooops. Guess she forgot to tell us that. Because what we did by saying yes to that class was to say yes to a changed life.

There is a Zen saying about going on a spiritual quest that goes like this: If you're not going to finish the journey, it's best you never start. Because there is no going back, no unscrambling of the egg. Making that commitment ignites a fire that alters the axis of your life's orbit. And when that axis shifts, it can begin as such a gentle touch that you don't have the slightest conscious clue that your life has just taken a 180-degree turn.

Ted and I hatched the idea for this book during just such a gentle shift in the summer of 2007, when my husband and I were visiting him and other friends in Maine. We had often talked by phone well into the night about what was happening to the earth. What could we possibly do, we asked ourselves? We were just two people. One day I joined him on a visit to some of the places he and his firm had done landscape design for. As I looked around at the beautiful properties we walked through, "landscaping" didn't fit what I was seeing.

"How would you describe what you do exactly?" I asked.

"I help create sacred spaces in people's homes and yards," he said, "and I teach them how to see and hear how the earth speaks to them."

While he explained further, and as we began to talk about working together on a small book that would help others perform the magic he did routinely at his client sites, a bigger truth began to emerge. This, we learned, is the way the cosmos reveals itself, gently drawing you in one direction, then almost imperceptibly taking you someplace you had not imagined. That bigger truth became this book.

Until I met Ted, my idea of a landscaper was someone who threw plants into the ground in strategic places and sent you a bill. But what he did was profoundly different. His artistry and reverence for the earth were evident everywhere in his work. Walking around some of the properties he had transformed just felt good. There was a magical sense to each space, a sort of aliveness in the air that turned up the senses. For him, working with the earth isn't a job, it's a calling—something he does with reverence and respect. To Ted, the earth is an extension of himself.

Here was common ground we shared. We had both grown up with a distinct reverence for the earth, a deep sense of wonder about its mystery and majesty. I had spent much of my childhood in Miami, Florida in the mid-1950s. Violent weather patterns—particularly hurricanes—were a fact of life. A short time after a hurricane passed, the DDT trucks would drive through and douse the neighborhoods in thick clouds of insecticide to keep mosquitoes from hatching out of the pools that lay stagnant after a storm. All of us kids would go out and play hide and seek in those foggy plumes. Nobody knew about anything being wrong with that then. In fact old public service ads from those days show people sitting on the beach getting blasted with a cloud of DDT and everyone acting as though it was as refreshing as bath powder. No worries—that was the message.

There was no talk about eco-consciousness then. The term had yet to be invented. A few years later my sister shoved a copy of Rachel Carson's *Silent Spring* into my hands and I was astounded, not only at the news it conveyed about the devastation being done to the planet and to all of the species that inhabit it, but also how obvious it was after the book's publication that many of the people at the center of the controversy about pesticide use—the government agencies, farmers and particularly the chemical companies—wanted to keep things just as they were.

Nobody wanted to admit that anything was wrong despite the overwhelming evidence Carson presented. I was stunned to find out that the government was doing such a poor job of protecting us and I was appalled at the way Carson was subsequently demonized and characterized as unqualified, a scaremonger who wanted to erase all the progress made by American farmers since the end of the war. In fact, she was a highly esteemed biologist and had taught at Johns Hopkins and the University of Maryland and then was editor in chief of publications at the U.S. Department of Fish and Wildlife. Before *Silent Spring*, she had written two other acclaimed best sellers about the biology of the sea.

She had criticized the regulatory agencies of the government for basically carrying water for corporations like Monsanto, the manufacturer of DDT, failing to warn the American public of the potential dangers and unknown long-term effects that these chemicals would have on the earth, and ultimately on us, our genes and, as a result, our children. There was, she pointed out, no mechanism of accountability, no sense of responsibility, and seemingly no concern about the American public remaining out of the loop. She quoted French biologist and philosopher Jean Rostand, "The obligation to endure gives us the right to know." And she thought that we should do better than just endure.

As I was awakening to the horrors of the slow poisoning of our planet, Ted's parents were patiently ensuring that his education included an abiding respect for the earth. His mother fed the family from her extensive organic garden, years before growing vegetables without chemicals had gained prominence. She took turns with the neighbors working in co-op stores, helping to unpack crates and wait on customers for a share of butter, eggs and milk from local farms. Shared acts of community like this in the 1960s were nuances in the cracking open of the modern consciousness, the first whispers to us that the closer we stayed to our food sources, the better.

Eventually his mother's passion for good, safe, fresh food would inspire Ted's family to start a successful company that specialized in fresh fruit juice products. Their line, called Fresh Samantha (named for Ted's niece), was a favorite on the U.S. East Coast in the 1990s.

"Having parents who showed me how the earth works and how to work in the earth formed me. And it ignited my imagination. When I think of children today, I wonder how they learn to leave their physical spaces and create things with their hands, how they learn to be at home outside in nature instead of inside the spaces that wall them off from those experiences."

Unfortunately, recent studies indicate that attendance at national parks has been declining steadily since the early 1990s (hopefully Ken Burns' stunning 2009 PBS series on the national parks will help change that). During that same time period the number of hours children spend playing video games has steadily risen, as has the incidence of childhood obesity.

Author Richard Louv, whose book *Last Child in the Woods* looks squarely at a condition he calls "nature deficit disorder," says that this isn't good for the species as a whole, but it's especially harmful for children.

Throughout human history and prehistory, he says, "children spent much if not most of their developing years either working or playing outside." In less than three decades, "we're seeing the diminishment and perhaps the disappearance of that."

There is a theory called the biophilia hypothesis that says that for all our modern technological savvy, at a biological level we are still hunters and gatherers. "At some level that we don't fully understand, we need direct involvement with nature, and when we don't get that, we don't do so well." [2]

Where did Louv get his love for the outdoors? "From my parent's own enthusiasm for nature," he said. Modern parents, take notice. Modeling a love of and respect for nature is an important building block in a child's upbringing. It nurtures them as surely as food and a safe and loving homelife.

One of the goals of this book is to show the earth as something more than the raw materials we gather from it, to see it as the fount of life, what British research scientist James Lovelock called *Gaia*, a giant living organism. To be so disconnected from it as to have no sense of its presence everywhere in our lives is to lose one of the most primal balancing components of our bodies and spirits.

We live in an age of hyper-consumerism. The contents of our meals travel an average of 1500 miles before reaching our plates. We take for granted being able to make trips in an afternoon that would have required weeks of laborious, dangerous travel barely a century ago. We talk and text with people around the world on devices that didn't exist a decade ago. Some experts estimate that we consume more energy in five minutes than our cave-dwelling ancestors did in an entire year.

We used to be an agriculture-based culture. Now giant combines do the work our hands used to do. Technology has made the job of raising and transporting our food much more efficient. But this efficiency has come at a high cost: not only has it compromised and exhausted our soil and water resources, it has also polluted our air and land with staggering quantities of toxins and unknown change agents. Some experts believe it has disoriented, exhausted and poisoned the very bees we count on to pollinate our food crops. The effect on our own bodies and DNA is, quite literally, unknown.

In an endless Mobius of cause and effect, this industrialization of farming has also made us lose touch with what we come from. We have become removed from the earth, blind and deaf to her cries. Today we live in a totally new paradigm, often many stories above the earth in a hermetically sealed room with no access to fresh air or any way to feel what is beneath our feet.

In 2005, the Dalai Lama spoke at a weekend conference on healing in Washington, D.C. His topic was the growing convergence of science and spirituality, how practices like meditation naturally dovetail with healing. The audience was filled with immunologists, psychologists, cardiologists, neurologists, and others from the global, medical and scientific community. During his talk, His Holiness referred to a graph that showed that as the U.S. Gross Domestic Product—the traditional way we measure our economic health—has risen in the last 50 years, it has been mirrored by a corresponding increase not only in depression but also in the use of the drugs that treat this ailment and the conditions related to it. In other words, as consumption—our material measuring stick of success and progress—has gone up, our levels of contentment have headed in the other direction. Our endless pursuit of more and more is getting us less and less. As we devour more, we are not only *not* satisfied, we are more starved. How can this be? It's a question that defies simple explanation.

What the Dalai Lama talked about is rampant. We are in what could be called a crisis of *un*consciousness. Today the U.S., which manufactures most antidepressants, accounts for two-thirds of their prescriptions. Growing numbers of Americans find that smoothing the edges and staying unconscious—with one of the thirty different types of antidepressants on the market—is an ever easier path. According to Charles Barber's book, *Comfortably Numb: How Psychiatry is Medicating a Nation*, in 2006 alone, more than 227 million antidepressant prescriptions were filled in the U.S. (up by *30 million* since 2002) and although prescriptions for antidepressants used to be disseminated strictly by psychiatrists, it's increasingly true that family doctors, not mental health care professionals, now prescribe these drugs to patients.

That's not accidental. According to Barber, pharmaceutical companies spend roughly $25,000 per year *per doctor*, tracking what each physician nationwide prescribes, a bit of data mining that helps Big Pharma maintain pinpoint precision on what the best markets are and how to better shape their messages.[3] Meanwhile, as more and more of us are seeing just how dire the problems are, nobody seems to know how to get us out of the mess we have gotten ourselves into on our planet.

What's wrong with this picture? Everything. Rather than sleeping, it's time for us to awaken to the challenges, the promises, the responsibilities and the exciting opportunities that await us. We not only have to wake up, we also have to open our eyes wide to what is happening to our planet, our country, our cities, our neighborhoods—and inevitably— our bodies. One of the purposes of this book is to outline the steps to that awakening—through a somewhat different lens, one that not only acknowledges the problems we face as 21st-century beings, but also offers a new way of looking at the solutions they require.

Why? Because for all that's wrong, there is also much that's right. This companion truth—that we can undo this great harm we have all contributed to—is also part of our birthright as earthlings. Our real nature is to find a way to share and live in community, not just to compete. Andy Lipkis, president and founder of Tree People, a nonprofit that rescues and rebuilds decimated landscapes, says that research shows that T cells, the immune system boosters in our bodies, rise when people volunteer and help. *We are designed to reach out and lend a hand.* It is one of the legacies of being human. Helping is a creative act that creates a feedback loop. Creative energy is spiritual energy, and those energies feed the longing for connection to one another that plagues our hearts. It all goes back, as the Dalai Lama suggests, to our starving hearts.

Want proof? Point to yourself. Literally, take a moment and do this physically. Did you point to your stomach? Your head? Probably not. Most people point to their chests, the homestead of the heart. We all know where we live. And *Reunion* is all about how to excavate your way back to that vital core of your being.

This distancing is not just physical, because we are more than mere bodies. We are also spiritual beings, energy beings, with aspects that are invisible but quite real. Anyone who has ever studied a martial art or been treated with acupuncture knows about the energy meridians in the body, how heat can be concentrated and drawn through it, focused for healing or even combat.

Before Caroline Myss wrote the pivotal book *Sacred Contracts* which drew us to her coursework of the same name, she wrote about the body's energy systems, called *chakras*, in her book *Anatomy of the Spirit*. These seven energy centers were first identified and explained by the mystics of India, but she describes them metaphorically as little revolving hard drives, loaded with memories and purpose. Running along the spine to the top of the skull, the lower three include the area from the tailbone to the solar plexus. They deal with our survival needs: acquiring food, drink, shelter, protection, material things, solidifying our connection with family and earthly roots. The upper three, from the throat to the crown of the head, regulate the needs of our minds and spirits: choice, speech, logic, reason, intuition, connection, meaning, destiny. The fourth, between the waist and the throat, mediates the upper and lower chakras and is the seat of emotion. It is called the heart chakra.

Symbolically speaking today, while our lower three chakras are devouring (obesity is at epidemic levels), our upper three are starving (ditto depression and a sense of hopelessness). Our heart's task is to find the happy medium so that our upper and lower energy systems can be congruent. It's a monumental task for our stressed-out, overworked hearts. Notice how many television commercials feature medications aimed at treating heart disease, high blood pressure, and high cholesterol. The pharmaceutical companies know what ails us even if we don't.

The template of the body's seven chakras illustrates the wisdom of our own unraveling, how we have much to learn from what our own bodies are telling us if we will only listen. There is healing in that listening and in that effort to reconnect ourselves to the global life force we are all a part of. Reestablishing a connection to the earth reunites us to our hearts. Working with the earth is intrinsically healing and heart based. Earth is at the center of our existence; we are born from her and return to her at the end of our lives. She connects us as human beings like one body with nearly seven billion movable but integrated parts. What happens to the earth happens to us—we are not separate from one another. Once we begin to see that, the way we look at our own lives can shift, opening a whole new world of possibility to each of us.

Our first chakra is the one closest to the earth when we sit on the ground. Our seventh resides at the top of our skull. A break in the first chakra means that there can be no congruence for the whole, no feedback loop for the system. Because of our broken first chakra connection and the wounding and disconnection of our fourth, people are starving for connection and for meaning.

Anyone who turns on the television for five minutes or scans the titles of books, magazine covers or Internet blogs knows the truth. Something has to change and it has to happen quickly. It's time to wake up from our stupor and acknowledge that waiting for someone else to step up and make the first move isn't the answer. The people we've been waiting for are already here. It's us—concerned citizens, neighbors, fathers, mothers, siblings, professionals, the young and the wisdom holders.

You know—earthlings.

Ted once reminded me of a trip he had made to visit a Yaqui shaman friend of ours named Lench Archuleta, with whom he had studied nature and earth spirituality in the Arizona desert.

"One afternoon we sat on a bluff overlooking what appeared to be a distant dust storm. It wasn't. The bulldozers cutting deep swaths were making space for yet another new subdivision. As we watched, Lench told me his tribe has a name for us. They call us *termite people* because we are eating the earth's flesh. And by doing that, we are literally eating our future, our world. It is, he said, a form of madness, of suicide."

We are guests on Planet Earth. Most of us learn as children to be respectful of the places we visit, to leave them clean, as we would hope others would do for us: a sort of Golden Rule of earthly manners. We have not been worthy of our host. In fact, we've been very poor stewards, misbehaving on a horrendous scale, so much so that we have changed the planet's very chemistry, altering its biosystems, its topography, even its geographical structure.[4]

In an age when truth is at a premium and most members of the media are too frightened to offend their sponsors or owners, it is incumbent upon us as citizens to investigate and broadcast the truth. Just as most of the people who fought for our independence from England were citizen soldiers, today's leaders in the movement to save the Earth for future generations take their authority from the right to breathe clean air and eat uncontaminated and available food. At an award ceremony in 2008, in which ordinary citizens were being acknowledged for their work in truth-telling, the award-winning journalist Bill Moyers said that "the most important credential of all is a conscience that cannot be purchased or silenced."[5]

Understanding the depth and scope of the ecological crises before us is not easy. If we are to understand the issues swirling around us—from global warming and climate change to skyrocketing resource costs, to the state of our soil and seed, to disappearing water resources, to food riots around the world—we have to understand that they derive from one simple but telling truth. We have numbed ourselves to what is happening around us. On some level we sense what we are losing—that most basic connection to the earth that is an ancestral birthright of our species. And it is a loss that must be healed.

In the many decades since Rachel Carson first shocked the world into the realities of the killing power of toxic pesticides like DDT, the environmental movement has been missing a key ingredient—a spiritual sensibility. As Rabbi Michael Lerner says, "The Environmental movement cannot just teach about the scientific facts. It has to talk about a new spiritual vision."[6] It is not possible to see a complete picture of what is happening to us and the earth we all share without examining it through a lens of spiritual consciousness.

That vision Rabbi Lerner is talking about is creating what would have previously been seen as unlikely alliances. Nobel laureate and director of the Center for Health and the Global Environment at Harvard Medical School, Dr. Eric Chivian, met for lunch one day in 2005 with Rev. Richard Cizik, a leader of the National Association of Evangelicals, to discuss their shared concern for the growing human impact on the earth's resources. Together they formed the Scientists and Evangelicals Initiative. "Whether you believe God created life on earth, or that it evolved over billions of years, it doesn't matter. We all feel that life, however it came to be, is sacred," says Chivian, "And it is our shared duty to protect it."[7] In May 2008 the environmental movement's odd couple was named to *Time Magazine's* list of 100 most influential people.

Reunion is not a diatribe against technology, nor is it a call to go back to the ways of 18ᵗʰ-century farmers. Rather it is an examination of what is happening in our world and how we can fix it collectively and individually by reconnecting with the earth that nurtured us on a spiritual and not just a physical level.

When *Silent Spring* exposed the growing widespread use of chemical pesticides and fertilizers and its attendant dangers, Rachel Carson was describing an unfolding national health crisis. Now we face it on a much grander planetary scale with a much larger cast of characters, part of a drama called global warming—a modern tale of our indifference and neglect—the consequences of our separation from our link to the earth. We stand half a century later in the future Carson warned us about, asking the same questions, wondering why the accountability is still lacking from the same institutions—the government, the corporations, and the conventional agriculture community.

But this time we know something we did not know then—that saving our planet and ourselves is up to us. It's our responsibility to, as Gandhi said, "be the change you want to see," to stop waiting for others to come to our rescue, but rather wake ourselves up instead—open our hearts and learn how to listen to the call of our spirits. As the popular catchphrase tells us, "We are the ones we've been waiting for." So let's get busy. There's no time to waste.

How this book is organized

The book is divided into six chapters and a bibliography.

- *Chapter 1* examines the threats to the planet's health through the lens of the human energy system known as the chakras, clarifying how the broken first chakra affects our human and planetary spiritual anatomy, and relates to our disconnection from our biosphere.
- *Chapter 2* describes how our current environmental crises represent severe, even suicidal, manifestations of our disconnection from the earth.
- *Chapter 3* shows how the preponderance of oil in our culture—especially agribusiness—compounds this disconnection, from our dependence on other countries for our energy to the dumbing down of our agricultural polyculture.
- *Chapter 4* explains how the most basic building blocks of our nourishment—seeds—are being compromised and weakened

and how that is adversely affecting the stewards of the earth—the farmers—whose sacred connection to the land has in many cases been severed.

- *Chapter 5* describes the ways in which we as individuals can begin to wake up to what the book has presented, that being connected to the earth is an age-old tradition practiced in every major spiritual and religious tradition. The chapter includes specific activities that you can use to implement change and heal your own connection to the earth. By learning and practicing ritual and understanding the earth's rhythms and seasonal rites of passage, each of us can find unique ways to heal our own connections and help others heal theirs.

- *Chapter 6* looks at stories of how others in our world are responding to a deeper inner calling of the self, of finding new ways to be generous, to be innovative and work hard—all parts of our innate spiritual DNA—and how those are exactly the individual grass root traits our nation and our planet need now.

- The *bibliography* provides bibliographic information and a list of resources you may want to consult to learn more.

Tread softly. All the earth is holy ground.

— Christina Rossetti

Endnotes

1. Daniel B. Smith, "Is There an Ecological Unconscious?" *New York Times*, January 27, 2010.
2. NPR, Morning Edition interview, May 25, 2005.
3. Charles Barber, *Comfortably Numb, How Psychiatry is Medicating a Nation* (New York: Pantheon, 2008), xvi.
4. Thomas Berry, *The Dream of the Earth* (San Francisco: Sierra Club Books, 2006), 12.
5. http://www.huffingtonpost.com/bill-moyers/on-journalism_b_95444.html; Bill Moyers' Remarks on the Occasion of the 5th Annual Ron Ridenhour Prizes.
6. From an interview in the 2007 documentary, *The 11th Hour*, produced by Leonardo deCaprio and Warner Brothers Films.
7. Billy Baker, "Saving 'God's creation' unites scientist, evangelical leader," *Boston Globe*, May 1, 2008.

PART ONE

We snooze. We lose.

The fault, dear Brutus, lies not in our stars,
but in our selves.
-- Julius Caesar, Act 1, Scene 2

CHAPTER 1

Understanding what we're made of

*Everything alive pulsates with energy
and all of this energy contains information.*
-- Caroline Myss, *Anatomy of the Spirit*

W<small>E ARE ENERGY BEINGS</small>. If we trace our history back to our earliest myths and history, from the Big Bang theory to the Bible's description of the birth of light on earth, to the age of nuclear energy and the silent power of the Internet, it is clear that our epoch as humans has an energetic framework.

When it comes to analyzing and coping with our world, our brains defy description and understanding. Paired with our hearts, they are the dynamic duo—with often opposing agendas—that we rely on to resolve our most familiar dilemmas. Thinking and feeling, hearts and minds, the above and below of us. They are our sources of power and mystery. No one can really explain why a heart starts beating and goes on for decades, nor how a brain finds a cure for a disease, much less how it knows to warn us that someone is untrustworthy or why it finds solace in prayer. These are our mysteries. They are ideas that are too big to be described literally with words. That's why we have to resort to the symbolic language of literature and art to explain them to ourselves. As each generation passes into the next, we leave our best efforts in our wake like a trail of bread crumbs hoping someone along time's path can decipher what we could not.

What is happening to our planet and to ourselves—our external and internal worlds—cannot be explained or healed with data or warnings alone. So this book will not resort simply to statistics, pleadings to common sense or threats of extinction. The scope and gravity of what is going on with our earth requires a deeper context, a more tender and three-dimensional picture that appeals not just to our hearts and minds but also to our very souls. It calls for a perspective that is not often combined with information on the environment.

Rather than looking at the crises we face as issues to be checked off of a to-do list, we need to see beneath the words to the real messages trying to get through to us. We as a culture are unmatched at assembling facts and events into a mosaic of a condition-at-large and taking it on with hard work and a can-do attitude. We have giant hearts and giving and compassionate natures. Why isn't this enough to motivate us to look more deeply and make sense of this and demand change of our leaders and ourselves?

To begin to answer this, we need to understand how different this challenge is from anything we have ever faced before, to see this as a call to our spirits to awaken and look at the earth and our relationship to her differently and to understand where things have come apart, where we are broken and why and how we can fix ourselves, each other, and the conditions that are harming our planet.

We must add a spiritual lens to our eyes and then look inside as well as outside, not just at the material, intellectual, and emotional worlds—but at our spiritual insides too. While the ability to reason got us out of the dark ages and into the age of enlightenment, the mere copious application of that genius to invention, technology, speed, wealth, and sheer determination cannot heal us. Reconnecting to the earth also reconnects us to our spirits and a fuller recognition of what life is meant to be about. And that is the reunion that can heal us.

A STROKE OF GOOD FORTUNE

It's common knowledge that we use our left brains to understand the data and sensation that come at us and the right brain to intuit their symbolic importance. The scientist James Lovelock likens our left-brain genius and the computers and modes of communication it created to the nervous system of the earth's body, connecting us as an energetic whole. As with a computer, sometimes your software needs updating and it's time for a download, but if you're disconnected, as so many of us are these days with our full schedules and stressed-out lives, no downloads can get through. When that happens, it occasionally requires a timely lightning bolt to bypass those disconnections.

That's what happened to neuroanatomist Dr. Jill Bolte Taylor when she had a sudden stroke at the age of 37. Her stroke opened a window on life that she could not have seen any other way. Taylor had decided early on to devote her career to understanding her brother's schizophrenia, why his circuitry ends up in delusions while her brain is able to give her the life she wanted, so she began studying brain circuitry in Boston at the Harvard Department of Psychiatry, learning how differently brains communicated at the cellular and chemical levels. She and her colleagues were "mapping the micro-circuitry of the brain, which cells are communicating with which cells, with which chemicals, and then with what quantities of those chemicals. So there was a lot of meaning in my life because I was performing this kind of research during the day." [1]

On a December morning in 1996 she awoke with a pain behind her left eye. She ignored it and began her morning ritual of workout and shower. Within minutes she realized something was wrong. Her limbs did not look right to her and as she walked to the shower, she realized her mental processes had slowed. She had the peculiar sensation she was outside of herself watching what was going on inside. But still she ignored it. She was way too busy to have a stroke and her left brain efficiently kept her locked into her morning routine. There were all those to-do lists to complete.

In the shower she lost her balance and as she propped herself against the wall, she realized she could not tell where her hand left off and the wall began. The whole thing was just one big field of molecules. Everything had melded into a single pulsating field of energy. At that moment her left hemisphere went offline and with the brain chatter off, she experienced what many have sought but few Westerners have achieved: a silent brain. Rather than finding herself listening to the usual inner prattle centered on job stresses, the endless task lists of everyday life, or the emotional baggage she had accumulated over her lifetime, she found something else: euphoria.

As she made her way out of the shower, her right arm became paralyzed and in that instant she realized she was having a stroke in the left hemisphere of her brain. At the same time, the pragmatic, functioning scientist in her was delighted. "How many brain scientists have the opportunity to study their own brain from the inside out?"

Just as a loose connection can occasionally make a light sputter sporadically, her left brain would periodically come back "on" and using these moments, she slowly made her way to her desk and devised a method for calling for help. She could not remember her number at work but could see a picture of her business card in her mind's eye, so she painstakingly went through a stack of cards until she found the shape that matched her inner picture. Finally she was able to match the shapes of the numbers on her business card to the same shapes on a phone pad. When her left brain would go offline, she would forget what she had done and have to begin again, so she began to cover each number with her paralyzed arm as she dialed and using this system as she went in and out, she was finally able to get through to her office, initiating her eventual rescue.

From the stroke's onset, it would be four hours before she could negotiate an SOS. During those hours she was able to witness the slow disintegration of her ability to rely on reason for survival. Curled into a fetal position during the ambulance ride to the hospital, she thought she would die and said goodbye to her life. She remembers floating expansively in a space that was definitely outside of what she now saw was her very tiny body. She called it Nirvana. When she realized she wasn't dead after all and was not only still experiencing this, but suddenly aware that everyone could experience this, a clarity came over her. "I realized what a tremendous gift this experience could be, what a stroke of insight this could be to how we live our lives. And it motivated me to recover."

Surgery to remove the golfball-sized blood clot from the left side of her brain would save her. It would take her eight years to fully recover. What she discovered in those first moments standing in her shower watching herself merge with all matter, was key—that if this was true for her, it could be true for anyone at any time. This is a place each of us can choose to visit. It's ready and waiting. Nobody has to have a stroke to get there.

Twelve years after her stroke, Taylor described what happened to her in a lecture. Holding a bisected brain in her hands, she talked about how the two sides of the brain think and care about very different things and process information differently. "Our right hemisphere is all about this present moment. It's all about right here right now. It thinks in pictures and learns kinesthetically through the movement of our bodies. Information in the form of energy streams in simultaneously through all of our sensory systems. And then it explodes into this enormous collage of what this present moment looks like, smells like and tastes like, what it feels like and what it sounds like. I am an energy being connected to the energy all around me through the consciousness of my right hemisphere. We are energy beings connected to one another through the consciousness of our right hemispheres as one human family. And right here, right now, we are all brothers and sisters on this planet, here to make the world a better place. And in this moment we are perfect. We are whole. And we are beautiful."

The left hemisphere, on the other hand, is designed to take the right hemisphere's messy wisdom and organize it. "Our left hemisphere thinks in language. It's that ongoing brain chatter that connects me and my internal world to my external world. It's that little voice that says to me, 'Hey, you gotta remember to pick up bananas on your way home, and eat 'em in the morning.' It's that calculating intelligence that reminds me when I have to do my laundry. But perhaps most important, as soon as my left hemisphere says to me 'I am, I am,' I become separate. I become a single solid individual separate from the energy flow around me and separate from you."

"Right here, right now, I can step into the consciousness of my right hemisphere where we are—I am—the life force power of the universe, and the life force power of the 50 trillion beautiful molecular geniuses that make up my form. At one with all that is. Or I can choose to step into the consciousness of my left hemisphere, where I become a single individual, a solid, separate from the flow, separate from you. These are the 'we' inside of me."

For Taylor, the slow stroke she endured enabled her to shut down her logical left brain to harvest the insights and soul-connectedness of her right side. In losing her balance in the shower and then seeing herself as an energy being seamlessly connected to all other beings and the source of life itself, she regained a much more important balance that changed her life.

This is so often the way the universe reveals its secrets. Using her brilliant left brain, Jill Taylor went looking for ways to understand how to connect with her brother's thinking process. What she found instead was how her equally brilliant right brain was waiting for her with the gift of a lifetime, a key to how we can all learn to connect with each other and see the magnificence of what we are all a part of.

We are living in times that are moving too fast for us to see them if our rational minds are all we rely on. In almost no time at all on the cosmic clock, we have spun out of a place we can understand in a meaningful physical or emotional context. "The Internet consists of a quintillion transistors, a trillion links and a million emails per second."[2] A quintillion is a 1 followed by 24 zeroes. (To put that in perspective, a billion has nine zeroes.) If it took you two seconds to read that last quoted sentence, just think how much transpired in that tiny space of time. Now add this: in a single second, our bodies have blown through ten times more processes than there are stars in the universe.[3]

The point is that, like Jill Taylor, we have to open ourselves to see everything differently. What our right brains are trying to tell us is that we can no longer live just as analytical thinkers. We have to see our own hands on the shower wall, how we and what's outside of us are all one. We have to try seeing what our left brains would tell us is not there, because our right brains know otherwise.

Luckily, we are built to do just that.

OUR SPIRITUAL SKELETON

In 1996 author Caroline Myss wrote a best-selling book called *Anatomy of the Spirit*, which explains that we not only have a physical skeleton but also a spiritual skeleton whose existence is easily confirmed by the basic tenets of nothing less than Christian, Judaic, Hindu and Buddhist thought. As a medical intuitive Myss also speaks authoritatively about how our actions, thoughts and belief systems impact not just our physical and emotional selves but also create a direct feedback loop with our spiritual lives.

"The universal jewel within the four major religions is that the Divine is locked into our biological system in seven stages of power that lead us to become more refined and transcendent in our personal power."[4] Presenting a modern reinterpretation of the ancient theories of the seven chakras, Myss describes these power centers as an "energy spinal cord through which the life force or prana flows into our physical body."[5] Together they make what could be called the framework of our spiritual anatomy.

Via those energy centers, our spines serve as conductors of energetic impulses and data. Learning the vocabulary of the chakras helps clarify that our physical, mental, and spiritual bodies are not only *not* separate entities, but together actually speak a mutually reinforcing language.

If you have ever been treated with acupuncture, or studied yoga, tai chi chuan or chi gong, you have probably heard some of this vocabulary and perhaps felt the rush of heat, power and even calm that coincides with your energy centers being lined up or cleared. Arranged vertically along our spines from our tailbones to the tops of our heads, these centers, while they have no material form, carry very real packets of data about us. Myss encourages us to envision them as separate little whirring hard drives of energetic and biological information that work in tandem. What registers in one chakra registers in all, speaking to us in the language of the spirit with a unique chakra-specific message.

Each chakra can be matched with specific body parts and emotional states of being. Each also honors a unique spiritual challenge. If we ignore the emotional and spiritual lessons that go with each chakra, which is always connected to some version of waking up our consciousness, we can often see the results in our bodies in the form of unrest, stress or illness. Conversely, if we understand that illness can be a call to spiritual awakening, we can begin to heal ourselves by honoring the lessons the chakras lay out for us, whether they are about ridding ourselves of guilt, blame, or victimhood, standing up for ourselves, being honest about where we sabotage our relationships, opening up our creativity or finding the calling that feeds our lives.

Understanding how the chakras work gives us a vast new toolset that can help us as we seek solutions to our problems. Because these teachings cross religious and cultural boundaries, they can work globally. Although this chapter deals primarily with the first chakra, what affects it affects the other six, so it helps to understand how all seven work as a whole. The following table explains where the chakras are and each chakra's corresponding emotional and spiritual lessons.

TABLE 1. THE CHAKRAS: THEIR LOCATIONS, ISSUES, AND LESSONS[6]

Chakra	Physical Location	Body organs, related conditions	Emotional strengths and challenges	Spiritual lesson
7	Top of skull; soft spot at birth	Skin, skeletal and muscular systems. Energetic disorders, mystical depression (dark night of the soul), heightened sensitivities to light, sound, pollutants in food, air, water, soil, other environmental factors.	Intuition, doorway to divine, faith, spirituality. Ability to trust life and see larger pattern; values, ethics, courage, selflessness, inspiration, devotion. Realm of visionaries and humanitarians. "Thy will be done." and... "I have a dream."	Our connection to heaven. Transformative experiences; spontaneous healings, mystical compassion; developing a spiritual backbone, ability to surrender to Divine. Your container for grace.
6	Area above and below eyes	Brain, eyes, nose, ears, pineal and pituitary glands, nervous system. Brain tumor, hemorrhage, stroke, blindness, deafness, spinal problems, learning disabilities, seizures.	Mind, intellect, intuition. Truth, self evaluation, feelings of adequacy, attitudes, beliefs, openness to ideas of others, emotional intelligence. Realm of inventors and philosophers. "I think, therefore I am." and..... "Trust the force, Luke."	Spiritual wisdom and maturity. Comfortable with inner power.

Chakra	Physical Location	Body organs, related conditions	Emotional strengths and challenges	Spiritual lesson
5	Throat and mouth	Throat, thyroid, teeth, mouth, gums, trachea, neck vertebrae, esophagus, parathyroid, hypothalamus. Chronic sore or raspy throat, mouth ulcers, TMJ, scoliosis, laryngitis, swollen glands, thyroid problems.	Choice, addiction, truth, will, regrets, passage of lies and deceit, judgment and criticism, faith and knowledge, following one's dream, capacity to make decisions; the place where desires of heart meet with wisdom of mind. "I swear to tell the truth, the whole truth and nothing but the truth." and ... "My name is Bill and I'm an alcoholic."	Healing of addictions; standing in authentic self, truth. Choice through enlightened self knowledge.
4	Heart area	Heart and lungs, circulatory system, shoulders and arms, ribs, breasts, thymus gland. Congestive heart failure or heart attack, mitral valve prolapse, asthma or allergies, lung or breast cancer, upper back, shoulder issues, bronchial pneumonia, high blood pressure, depression.	Love, forgiveness, compassion, hatred, resentment, vengeance, grief, anger, loneliness, commitment, hope and trust. Realm of poets, mystical expression. "How do I love thee? Let me count the ways." and... "I'll get even with you if it's the last thing I ever do."	Not compromising emotional well-being. Transcending self for others, doorway to soul.

Chakra	Physical Location	Body organs, related conditions	Emotional strengths and challenges	Spiritual lesson
3	Waist (gut)	Upper intestines, stomach, liver, gallbladder, kidney, pancreas, adrenal glands, spleen, middle spine. Arthritis, ulcers, colon or intestinal problems, indigestion, anorexia, bulimia, obesity, liver or adrenal dysfunction, diabetes, pancreatitis.	Ego, personality, self esteem, need for applause, integrity, shame, pride, arrogance, dignity, fear of humiliation, gut instinct, personal power and identity, self empowerment. Honor code formed here. "You'll never amount to anything." and… "You're the best thing that ever happened to me."	Empowering others. Humility, liberated from arrogance. Not dependent on opinions of others.
2	Genitalia, lower hips	Sex organs, large intestine, lower vertebrae, hip area, pelvis, appendix, bladder. Chronic pelvic or lower back pain, ob/gyn issues, sexual impotency, urinary problems.	Sexuality, job, physical desire, competition, power, creativity, money, seat of betrayal, partnerships, "weapons room." "Want to race to the corner?" and… "I made him an offer he couldn't refuse."	Having creative, physical, financial resilience. Living in integrity and intentionality.
1	Tip of tailbone, root chakra	Legs, bones, base of spine, feet, rectum, physical body support, immune system, sense of smell, connection to earth. Chronic lower back pain, sciatica, varicose veins, rectal tumors or cancer, depression, immune system disorders.	Material world. Rootedness and feeling at home; family first, groups, tribes, gangs, organizations, religions, political parties, values, beliefs, superstitions, entitlement, genetic inheritance, sense of home, fight or flight. Filter of every transaction. "My country 'tis of thee." and… "We're number one."	Honoring root connection to earth; leaving the tribe to individuate and expand and strengthen its wisdom; connecting to global consciousness. All is One.

Why the first chakra is important

The first chakra, the seat of our rootedness, drives everything in our lives. It is the filter of every transaction, the gateway to the rest of the chakras. It tells us whether we fight, flee or relax when someone or some task approaches. It tells us who to trust and when we're safe. It also tells us when we are in danger. It's no accident that the sense of smell is tied to this chakra. In the millennia before fire departments, civil defense warning horns and The Weather Channel, we had to be more alert to smell approaching fires and sense changes in weather.

Physically the first chakra is our structure, foundation and elimination system—bones, tendons, ligaments, skin, feet, and rectum. It's also home to our immune system, our social connections (tribe, family, home, country, the Earth), and our emotional connections (personal and family security—knowing whether to flee or fight—and our mental health). At the first chakra, all of these connections merge with our primary connection to the Earth itself. When that connection is broken, we are out of balance at a very basic level of survival, safety and sanity. We literally do not know who we are as humans. We are un-conscious. The truth of this chakra, says Myss, is All is One. This is reflected in the Christian sacrament of baptism which blesses the newborn (Catholicism) or the one reborn into belief in Christ (Protestantism) and Shekinah in Judaism, which is "symbolic of the mystical community of humanity."[7]

Because it's part of our spiritual architecture, it's always there for us to connect to. It's part of our fiber and fabric. It's what Jill Taylor experienced not just as a mental exercise but as a physical fact as she stood in her shower watching it unfold before her eyes. For her soul, those precious moments of clarity were the equivalent of what Galileo saw that moment he first realized that the sun, not the earth, is at the center of the universe. It's not us at the center of the giant wheel of creation we all belong to, but God.

Our chakras always point the way for us, like signals to watch and listen for. Understanding how they work helps us make sense of the mysteries in our lives. Our first chakra ties us to the earth, to nature. As Chapter 4 describes in more detail, we used to be closer to the land for all our needs. That passed with the coming of the Industrial age as our urban and suburban areas began to fill and sprawl, with much of our remaining rural areas put under the knife of giant corporate agrifarms. As we live increasingly busy and distracted lives, detached both from the source of the food we eat and the land that nourishes us, we have become numbed to the havoc being wreaked on our planet and the illness that is slowly suffocating her.

This is how our broken first chakra affects us and plays out in the environmental crises we find ourselves surrounded by. The issue is not that we must race to fix the world to save it. If the world burns up in a global warming skillet and we all perish, the earth will recover quite nicely. It doesn't need us, as Alan Weisman points out so chillingly in *The World Without Us*. Rather, we need the earth. What must change is us and the way we view and honor the earth we live on. "It is the world view we are trying to heal, not the world."[8]

To heal that view, we have to heal our broken connection to the earth.

THE EARTH IS AN ENERGY BEING TOO

Just as we have a two-sided brain, we also have the capacity to speak to and listen to two worlds simultaneously. Our outer worlds are constantly receiving messages from our inner worlds through all sorts of signs: synchronicities, chance meetings, coincidences, thoughts that won't go away, and sheer "aha" moments. As Wendell Berry said, "We receive more information from the environment than ever enters the limelight of our conscious awareness."[9]

Our lives break down when we try to give our outer worlds more authority over us than our inner worlds. We all know people who spend their lives in jobs they hate or relationships that no longer work because they cannot see past their fears of what might happen if they left.

Just as we have to look at our own physical and spiritual energy, we have to begin to look at earth energy in a different way too. This is where understanding a bit of how other people view the world can help us Westerners look at ourselves in a new way. In director Ang Lee's first film, *Pushing Hands*, he gives Westerners insight into just how this energy can work. Retired tai chi master Chu leaves Taiwan to come to New York to live with his son and daughter-in-law. He ends up as a humble dishwasher at a Chinese restaurant where, at the film's end, a cultural collision pits the small 70-year-old master against more than a dozen assailants whose goal is to remove him from the restaurant by force. Pushing, pulling, lifting, shoving, even throwing their bodies against him en masse do nothing; he is immovable. While this amounts to an entertaining scene, it depicts

FEELING IS BELIEVING

We feel the way the chakras work in us all the time. If you have ever been to a baseball game, here's how your chakras likely reacted.

When you stand up and pay your respects as a band or singer performs *The Star Spangled Banner*, what you feel is resonating in your tribal and patriotic first chakra, accompanied by a rush of feeling in your heart-centered fourth. When your team gets a home run, you cheer from the seat of competition: your second chakra. When your team lets a five run lead disappear and loses in extra innings, we feel it in the gut, the site of third chakra's center of self esteem. And in a moment of tribal angst we use the strident voice that emanates from our fifth chakra throat to perhaps question the umpire's heritage.

Later you may analyze what happened and make sense of it all with your analytical sixth. That leaves the seventh. An avid sports fan might argue that that's what you connect to on the rare occasion when you see your team come from three games behind to take the World Series in the bottom of the ninth inning in the seventh game. What else could be at play here but divine will?

an absolute truth. Such a person who is rooted in his first chakra earth energy is immovable beyond rational explanation. Equally true, when you are *un*rooted, you are powerless. That's what it means to be disconnected, to be separate from the earth's energy.

We are living in an age when we have to acknowledge and embrace unseen power and wisdom such as this, to retrain our minds to take in information we have sensed but never articulated before. Information about the chakras has been traced to Hindus writings from more than two thousand years ago. Today their names and locations are a common part of the vocabulary in exercise classes where the alignment of breath and movement is stressed. Understanding the way the human energy anatomy works is one way to see how our inner and outer worlds relate together as body, mind and spirit because the chakras have not only physical aspects but emotional and spiritual aspects as well.

They take the form of the powerful hits we feel when we lock onto something connected to our spirits and souls: the aha moments, when we jerk at an insight uncovered in a therapist's office, that a friend reveals in anguished confidence, that we hear in our meditations, or see in a film or read in a book that speaks to us. It's that something that "hits a nerve," when an undeniable truth suddenly drops down into our consciousness and reveals itself. We react almost instinctively, physically jarred from the buzz. This too is part of our spiritual natures. It is through this vortex of energy, this swirling tunnel of light and storm, that we connect to our potential as humans, and they are very real and tangible steps in our soul's journey. These are the often palpable little hits to our very conscious sixth chakra selves, the exchange of information between the intuitive spirit-connected right brain and the rational linear left brain: Hello over there in rationalville, anybody listening? This is where those thoughts and insights must invariably find purchase, fertile soil, where the left brain accepts them, rolls them over and, using right brain intelligence, languages them.

This is another reason why connecting to the land is so critical. Sitting on the energy of the earth, we can receive healing signals too. Think of the way nature calms you. The next time you are able, go find a quiet place outside. Sit down and close your eyes. Sooner or later you will sigh. This is our rational side letting down the bridge to our interior by breathing in a surge of breath, what the Hindus call *prana*. This is how we can plug in, become more whole, at one, in touch with our natures, with nature itself.

The energy of the earth has called to people for millennia. There are reasons why sacred places like the Pyramids, Stonehenge, the statues of Easter Island, the cathedral at Lourdes, Machu Picchu, the Temple of Heaven in Beijing, Delphi and countless others exist where they do, and why, as feng shui master Bob Longacre says, for millennia building projects began with a sacred ceremony to recognize and honor what was being birthed and given a home in this new construction. They possess a unique spiritual energy that called to their builders: this is the spot. And they still call to the pilgrims who visit them every day.

OUR COMMON IMMUNE SYSTEM

The earth has an immune system every bit as real as our own. And we are connected by every element in our environment. What happens to the earth happens to us. And the way we treat one another is also mirrored in the way we treat the earth. What is happening to the earth is damaging its immune system from every aspect: air, water, soil, food, and beauty—

from the ground beneath our feet to the polluted skies which block the stars above us. As Chapter 2 shows, if we open our eyes, we can see the consequences of our disconnection from what is happening to all of us. As we sit in our heated and air conditioned homes with stocked refrigerators and hundreds of TV channels to keep our minds occupied, what's going on in the outside world may seem just fine, but we sense otherwise.

While the typical idea of what an immune system does is usually tied to a kind of military language describing invading viruses and medicines that can overwhelm any infection, environmentalist and author Paul Hawken suggests that the earth's immune system is designed as a response to a need, rather than a call to battle. "The ultimate purpose of a global immune system," he says, "is to identify what is not life affirming and to contain, neutralize, or eliminate it."

"Because a lot of people know we are sick and want to treat the cause, not just the symptoms, the environmental movement can be seen as humanity's response to contagious policies killing the earth, while the social justice movement addresses economic and legislative pathogens that destroy families, bodies, cultures and communities. They are two sides of the same coin because when you harm one, you harm the other."[10]

In *The Botany of Desire*, Michael Pollan asks whether we choose to admire the flower or is it that the flower makes itself so irresistible that we are seduced into looking at it and perhaps eating it or planting it in the garden to help perpetuate its own species? Hawken asks the same question: Are we motivating ourselves or are all the non-government organizations (NGOs) popping up all over the globe (he estimates there may be as many as two million of them worldwide) actually a part of the earth's attempt to get us moving before it's too late? If we are part of the earth, isn't it possible that we are behaving the same way we would if our brains were having a stroke and, like Jill Taylor, we were getting a warning shot over the bow in time to save ourselves and help us appreciate along the way the universe we are a part of? If so, it is just as feasible that at this juncture we are sharing the earth's sense of danger and acting as co-creators of mutual healing of our common immune system.

NATURE AS THE CURE TO OUR DISCONNECTION

According to author Paul Devereux, what's required is a reinstatement of what he calls an "ancient sense of our relationship with nature." He believes that in an ecopsychological sense, it's the mind that needs healing and modern mentors and therapists use nature to accomplish that, reflecting a nod to old times. "Traditional and archaic peoples actually saw the world in animistic terms."[11]

Yaqui shaman Lench Archuleta, for example, takes clients into the Arizona desert to "get their spirits back," stressing quiet, contemplation and time spent alone in nature. "One of the first things I do is make people take their shoes off and wiggle their toes in the earth. They've lost that connection to Mother Earth and they need to get it back. It usually takes them a day or two to detox from the stress they left behind. Once they get used to the quiet, things begin to open up in them. They become alert in ways they did not know they could be. That's because being in nature gently forces you to use your five senses."

It's a simple thing, to take your shoes off, but it's also very powerful. It makes you keenly aware of how different the earth feels on your skin. We walk on the earth all the time without having any sense of its texture and temperature. As you walk around, he encourages you to name what you see. Naming things is another small but powerful act. When you name something, you have to look at it and acknowledge its existence. Naming objects is one of the first lessons we teach our children. It's how we connect them to their world, how they identify its component parts and grow familiar with their surroundings. It gives them a sense of home.

It's the same with nature. The problem is that our disconnection from nature is a manifestation of our blindness to what we are doing to it. As Rachel Carson said, mankind's war against nature "is inevitably a war against himself." When *Silent Spring* was published in 1962, the chemical companies making the pesticides that the book took to task used a spokesman, a scientist named Dr. Robert White-Stevens, to destroy Carson's credibility. His main weapon was fear, saying that if we couldn't control pests in the fields, in short order we would "return to the dark ages" and within a few years Americans would be spending most of their income on food.

"Miss Carson maintains that the balance of nature is a major force in the survival of man," White-Stevens said, "whereas the modern scientist believes that man is steadily controlling nature."[12] The hubris in that statement betrays how we got to this point in the first place—by believing that our intellects are the only worthy guides. But it was and is a point of view that works for the best interests of those who benefit most from an absence of dissent. C.S. Lewis once noted, "What we call Man's power over Nature turns out to be a power exercised by some men over other men with Nature as its instrument."

"We *are* nature," says Hawken. We live in community, not alone, and any sense of separateness that we harbor is illusion."[13]

Awakening to this lack of separateness offers us a chance to stretch ourselves, to expand beyond our egos. "Through nature, the species is introduced to transcendence, in the sense that there is something more going on than the individual. Most people are either awakened to or strengthened in their spiritual journey by experiences in the natural world."[14]

Sadly, many studies indicate that in the last 50 years, and especially the last 20, the practice of encouraging children to spend time in nature has declined tremendously. One of the painful results is that children recognize the component parts of nature less and less. The discouragement of natural play stems from several sources. In *Last Child in the Woods*, Richard Louv explains that there are many causes: a marked increase in the amount of television children watch each day, the rise in personal computer and Internet usage, the increase in organized play versus unsupervised play and of course the huge popularity of video games and personal music players.

Shrinking greenspaces and the preponderance of lawsuits that now make playing outside a high-cost risk, even the pervasive use of air conditioning are also part of the problem. The end result is the same. Children as well as adults have less and less of an understanding of what nature is all about. Not knowing nature's vocabulary limits our understanding of our place in it. It also limits its preciousness to us. You cannot value what you cannot name.

When we saw pictures of our planet from space, the famous big blue marble shots sent back by the astronauts, it shocked and delighted the whole human race. The picture became so ubiquitous that psychologist Jean Houston reported seeing it pinned on the walls inside huts in remote tribal villages. "It went into our minds—we psychically internalized our planetary home."[15]

We believe what we see and hear, and nothing makes that as real to us as nature does. The stewardship we need to invest in is ultimately not for the Earth's sake but for our own. We can never again risk the hubris of believing ourselves masters of nature, even if it's under the guise of healing it.

A MARRIAGE MADE IN HEAVEN

A 1995 report published by MIT found not only an "increased environmental consciousness" over a twenty-year period (largely due to the clarity of Rachel Carson's message in *Silent Spring* and the corresponding outgrowth of pro-environment cultural messages) but also found that when respondents focused their concern for the environment in terms of what was best for their children and subsequent descendants, environmental awareness took on a sacred cast. Nature was a sacred and spiritual connection not necessarily tied in with religious teaching of a particular stripe. "The consideration of the right of future generations to God's creation—with its formative and restorative qualities—is a spiritual act, because it looks far beyond our own generation's needs. This spiritual argument, made on behalf of future children, is the most emotionally powerful weapon we can deploy in defense of the earth and our own species."[16]

Modern theologians could not agree more. Any attempt to envision solutions to what ails us and the earth must come not just from a scientific or economic set of needs but from one which speaks to our souls. Rabbi Michael Lerner says that this is what the environmental movement has been missing. "What they haven't been adequately sensitive to is the need to help people understand the spiritual crisis in the society that makes them feel so despairing about the possibility of changing the world. And basing it on love, on caring, on generosity and on awe and wonder of the universe. The environmental movement can't just teach about the scientific facts, it has to also teach about a new spiritual vision."

Imam Feisal Abdul Rauf, founder and CEO of the American Society for Muslim Advancement, says the same is true in Islam.

"The Koran is very specific. We are custodians of the earth. Islamic law has some very specific things. We are prohibited, for example, under Islamic law from polluting bodies of water. We are prohibited from destroying trees. I can see in the context of the desert climate of Arabia where the prophet Mohammed was born, lived and died, polluting a well or destroying a tree was really destroying a resource which was the common property of not only all of humanity but all of the animal kingdom. Certain parts of the earth are the common property of not only all of humankind but all of the animal kingdom as well. And we have to be observant of not only our rights but the rights of other tenancies which exist on this earth."

By using a spiritual connection to the environmental crisis, Rabbi Lerner says that one key fear can be addressed that doesn't usually show up in most discussions, the fear of being first. The environmental movement also has to address this notion that "if they take the first steps towards love, caring, generosity and environmental sensitivity, that they will be the ridiculous ones, the fools, the adolescents, the people who have lost all touch with reality."

What we need, he says, are some Daniel Boones. "It's so critical right now for there to be people who are willing to be the pathfinders, the first people out of the closet as spiritual people, saying yeah, I really believe in the voice of hope. I'm not going to settle anymore for a politics that's a politics of compromise, I'm not going to go for the lesser evil anymore, I'm not going to settle for political candidates whose environmental sensitivity never leads to the dramatic steps that are necessary to save the planet. I'm going to stop all those compromises and go for my highest vision." It is time, he says, for us to step out of the fears that have plagued us for so long and which the media have helped perpetuate, to get beyond the "I" consciousness of the isolated individual, "and actually form a group of people working for a higher purpose together."[17]

How we start healing

The way we start is to look squarely at the problems we confront, to learn, and to take in the scope of what is going on. We do it in small steps and we do it together. We risk being the first ones, the pathfinders, the ones others may shake their heads at in disbelief. We risk all of this because it's worth it and it's the right thing to do. Once awake, you can no longer pretend you're still asleep. You must own what you know. As Wendell Berry said, "One must begin in one's own life the private solutions that can only in turn become public solutions."[18]

In other words, we become the leaders we've been waiting for.

Endnotes

1. The full video and transcript of Dr. Jill Bolte Taylor's story is available at www.Ted.com; it is also described in her book, *My Stroke of Insight*, New York: Viking, 2006.

2. Paul Hawken, *Blessed Unrest*: *How the Largest Social Movement in History Is Restoring Grace, Justice, and Beauty to the World*. New York: Viking, 2007, 143.

3. *Ibid*, 170.

4. Caroline Myss, *Anatomy of the Spirit, The Seven Stages of Power and Healing*, New York: Random House, 1996, xiii.

5. Caroline Myss, *Sacred Contracts, Awakening Your Divine Potential*, New York: Random House, 2001, 165.

6. Information about the chakras and details in the chakra table was compiled from readings in books by Caroline Myss, including *Anatomy of the Spirit*, *Sacred Contracts* and *Entering the Castle* as well as lectures at her educational institute, CMED.

7. *Anatomy of the Spirit*, 73.

8. Paul Devereux, *Re-visioning the Earth: a Guide to Reopening the Healing Channels Between Mind and Nature*, New York, Simon and Schuster, 1996, 44.

9. Wendell Berry, *The Unsettling of America: Culture and Agriculture*, San Francisco: Sierra Club Books, 1981, 35.

10. *Blessed Unrest*, 144-145.

11. *Re-visioning the Earth*, 14.

12. "The Silent Spring of Rachel Carson," *CBS Reports*, 1963.

13. *Blessed Unrest*, 171.

14. Richard Louv, *Last Child in the Woods*, Chapel Hill: Algonquin Books, 2005, 296.

15. *Re-visioning the Earth*, 15.

16. *Environmental Values in American Culture*, by William Kempton, James S. Boster, and Jennifer A. Hartley (Cambridge, MA: MIT Press, 1997), Chapter 1.

17. Quotes from Rabbi Lerner and Imam Rauf from *The 11th Hour*, produced by Leonardo DiCaprio, directed by Nadia Connors and Leila Connors Peterson, Warner Bros., Los Angeles, CA, 2007.

18. *The Unsettling of America*, 23.

CHAPTER 2

The Bed We Have Made

Out of the south cometh the whirlwind.
— Job 37:9

AROUND THANKSGIVING OF 2004, Beth LeBlanc, a resident of the Lakeview neighborhood of New Orleans, noticed water seeping into her front yard on Bellaire Drive. The seepage soon morphed into a pool 80 feet long, 10 feet wide, and half a foot deep. As it grew, it poured into her next-door neighbor's yard. It would be three months before the city's Sewerage and Water Board sent someone out to determine the source of the leak, to see if it was drinking water or sewage from a broken pipe, or even water from nearby Lake Pontchartrain. The investigator told LeBlanc it looked like the water was leaking into her yard from the nearby 17th Street Canal levee. City workers dug up sidewalks and driveways in an attempt to remedy the problem, but neither LeBlanc's or her neighbor's yards ever dried out. The seepage kept the area a mud pit.

THE MICROCOSM OF US

LeBlanc's house sat literally in the levee's shadow, 100 yards south of the spot that six months later would crumble, drowning and destroying her block and helping to put 80 percent of New Orleans under water. Her entire neighborhood would temporarily disappear when the already leaking levees would become mortally weakened from the winds and storm surge from Hurricane Katrina, and begin to hemorrhage water.[1]

J. David Rogers, a forensic engineer from the University of Missouri, who specializes in levees and floodwalls, led the inspection that looked into what made the New Orleans levees fail. "The catastrophic nature of the floodwall failures indicate this was a systemic problem, something that had been building for some time," Rogers said of the 17th Street Canal. "It tells us that, in all probability, these levees and the soil under the floodwall were already saturated before Katrina came along. This report of saturated yards only adds weight to that."[2]

The Army Corps of Engineers, whose work on the levees was widely blamed as the cause of the break in the storm's aftermath, had no record of being contacted about the Lakeview leaks. According to Jerry Colletti, operations manager in charge of completed projects at the ACE's New Orleans office, "If someone had told us there was lake water on the outside of that levee—or any levee—it would have been a red flag to us, and we would have been out there, without question."[3]

University of California-Berkeley engineering professor Bob Bea helped lead an investigation of the levee failures for the National Science Academy. He took calls from residents living along the 17th Street and London Avenue canals that would later collapse who, before the storm, had reported sand boils but had never heard back from any city agencies. Sand boils result from water moving sand from the foundation aquifer through the soil to the surface. They are particularly worrisome because they indicate an advanced stage of seepage and weakness. The closer to a levee a sand boil is seen, the worse the prognosis for the levee.[4]

While seepage and sand boils indicate serious existing conditions, other things actually weaken the understructure of levees by opening up spaces for water to enter the soil that runs under floodwalls and levees. Among the activities to avoid near levees is uprooting big trees and driving pilings for buildings; but a couple of months before Katrina hit, a neighbor of LeBlanc's, Gary Breedlove, noticed two old homes on his block being demolished, their large trees uprooted. "They pulled them right out of the ground, roots and all." He remembers work crews bringing in pile drivers, pounding what was to be foundation for the construction to replace the demolished homes. "They were pounding away and the ground really shook," he said. "I'm sure the levee shook too. It was right before Katrina. But I didn't really think about it then." The two lots were to be the exact site of the levee breach that quickly became a hole spanning 300 feet.[5]

The layers of bureaucracy that permeate the oversight and maintenance of the levee system in the city are convoluted and real and their inefficiency turned out to be deadly. "We had a diffusion of responsibilities, we had a confusion of those responsibilities and the system appeared benign when it was warning us it was ready to fail," said Bob Bea. "You often find things like this could only have happened because people were not looking for it."[6]

What happened before, during and after Hurricane Katrina made landfall showcases much of what is at the heart of environmental issues that face our nation and world. No single factor can explain why the city of New Orleans was so brutally damaged on August 29, 2005 nor account for the paralysis of the local, state and national governments who, because of their incompetent response, shoulder much of the blame for the 1300 deaths that occurred across the Gulf Coast as a result of the storm and its aftermath. In the years preceding the storm, eerily prophetic books and newspaper series—even a weeklong FEMA-based disaster scenario carried out a year before Katrina—spelled out in excruciating detail what the outcomes were likely to be, yet in spite of the generally held opinion that The Big One was inevitable, no plan was implemented that looked squarely in the face of the likely consequences of a storm hitting the city with such catastrophic power. The Big One *would* come to drown The Big Easy. The only question was when.

The people of New Orleans are not alone. They are the microcosm of us. We as a nation are not looking for what is staring us in the face either. If we can take just one lesson away from Hurricane Katrina, perhaps it is that Ben Franklin's little maxim was true: "a little neglect may breed great mischief. " Not listening to the messages Mother Earth is blaring out at us is a path to disaster and heartache. This kind of willful blindness—this cooperative group unconsciousness—is a manifestation of a broken first chakra connection with the earth and, sadly, what its consequences look like.

New Orleans residents now commonly refer to their lives there as PK (pre-Katrina) and AK (after Katrina). They are living the consequences that so many of us cannot understand beyond scientific data and sound bites and bits of video on the nightly news. The story of New Orleans before, during and after Katrina gives us a sad but compelling context for what global warming and climate change can mean when mixed with the very human capacity to deny what is in front of us—until the very landscape we live on becomes unrecognizable. The victims of the Ninth Ward we saw atop their roofs terrified, neglected and dying were not nameless faces from a wartorn country halfway around the world. They were our countrymen.

Each year the headlines are showing a clearer picture of the extent of the changes in our climate and the effects of the earth's warming every day. It shows up in the milder winters and hotter summers and in the prolonged and violent storms that are increasingly becoming the norm in so many parts of the world. The early, false springs that are now so common ultimately weaken the stock of the grasses and other flora that provide the oxygen that keeps our planet's air breathable and life giving to us. When trees, plants, and flowers bloom early and then freeze, they may bloom again in that season, but the trickery that the changing climate plays on them reduces their vigor and, over two or three years, it can make them too weak to survive. When many food crops pop up early and freeze, whole harvests perish. The only recourse is replanting or waiting a full growth cycle. Our interactions with the sky above and the earth below have consequences. Like us, the earth has an immune system and when our actions feed the earth poison, it must spend some of its energy detoxing from those effects.

When we talk about the effects of climate change and global warming, it's important to remember that they are systemic conditions that affect every aspect of our world and are caused by a number of factors, some immediately recognizable and others more subtle but no less disturbing. They include a range of conditions that are often consequences of and feed one another: stronger storms and increased flooding, drought and longer wildfire seasons, heat waves and crop loss, spread of disease and loss of natural resources. All of these in turn affect human life, the cost of food, fuel and commodities, our economic viability and quality of life—even, says the Pentagon, our ability to keep our nation secure.

It's not just that we burn too much gasoline in our inefficient cars. It's not just that we eat so much meat that we increase the amount of methane pumped into the atmosphere from animal waste. It's not just that we poison our streams and waterways and soil with the countless tons of chemicals we pour onto our fields to make them deliver bigger, faster harvests. It's also the unconsciousness of our intention and willfulness of our ignorance. Just as with New Orleans, the warnings have been out there for decades. The earth has been trying to tell us something while we have been living in a buffer of grace, not yet ready or willing to pay the piper, hoping he'll end up being the stuff of fairy tales.

NEW ORLEANS PK

New Orleans isn't just the site of our greatest natural disaster to date. It has long played a key role in America's destiny and mirrors some of the brightest and darkest aspects of our national character. A French Canadian nobleman named Sieur de Bienville founded the town in 1718, simultaneously bestowing on it its polycultural roots and defiant attitude, declining against all urging to move the town eighty miles upriver to the spot where Baton Rouge now stands. When a hurricane inundated the fledgling town in 1722 (one of many storms that visited that year), Bienville was unmoved.

From the beginning, a sense of adventure trumped common sense. Hurricanes or no hurricanes, New Orleans stayed in the spot it holds today, defiant against the winds and water that nature regularly threw its way. Bienville saw New Orleans's potential as a port and ignored the fact that it was entirely surrounded by water. In fact, New Orleans is flanked and bisected by water—Lake Pontchartrain on the north, swamps on the west, the Gulf of Mexico on the near east and south with the ribbon of the Mississippi rolling through it, creating the boomerang shape on its eastern side that gives it its nickname, the Crescent City. Baton Rouge might have been drier, but sailing upriver against the Mississippi's mighty current in the days preceding engine-driven transportation was problematic. Likewise, the shifting sandbars that appeared without warning and ran ships aground added a definite chill to the forward march of commerce.[7]

New Orleans did grow into a vital port. It was this fact that made Napoleon Bonaparte loathe to part with it, but by 1803 he needed an infusion of cash to support his bankrupt republic and a way to consolidate his power, recently challenged by his malaria-ridden army's failure to quell a slave revolt in the French territory of Haiti. He was able to do both by selling France's territorial possessions to the United States.

At a price of $15 million (less than three cents per acre), the Louisiana Purchase immediately doubled the size of the continental United States, greatly increasing its president's cache while securing New Orleans as its greatest southern port, freeing the entire length of the Mississippi to river traffic. What had once been its western frontier became the country's circulation system and the heart of its water commerce. Within a year Thomas Jefferson would call on his assistant Meriwether Lewis to explore this mammoth addition of more than 820,000 square miles, which spanned an area from the Gulf of Mexico near New Orleans in the south to what now exceeds the northernmost border of North Dakota, and from the Mississippi River in the east to the Rocky Mountains in the west.

The Gulf Coast has had a long history of being in the bullseye of storms. One of New Orleans' coastal island neighbors, Galveston, Texas, which sat less than nine feet above sea level, suffered the deadliest natural disaster in U.S. history in September of 1900 when a 15-foot storm surge from a Category 4 hurricane blew ashore, killing from 8,000 to 12,000 people—as much as one-fifth of its population—and destroying much of the defenseless city, including 3,600 homes. With its bridges washed out, its railroad link to inland Houston fifty miles to the north wrecked and telegraph wires down, no one could know the predicament of the besieged Galvestonians. As mainland facilities for handling the dead were quickly exhausted, funeral pyres set up on the debris-strewn beaches burned the dead for weeks. By 1904 the city had begun to build a 17-foot wall that eventually stretched along ten miles of Gulf beach, which has, in large measure, protected it from storms ever since.*

In the Labor Day hurricane of 1935, which hit the Florida Keys, hundreds of encamped World War I veterans, hired by the WPA to build U. S. Highway 1, were killed when 200 mph winds ripped through the area for hours, destroying everything in their path, including the Florida East Coast Railway, the only means of escape.[9] Until the 2005 hurricane season, it was regarded as the most vicious Atlantic hurricane ever recorded. In the 1948 film *Key Largo*, hotelkeeper James Temple (Lionel Barrymore) immortalized the 1935 hurricane's fierce impact in a tension-filled scene set against the sound of a gale blowing outside.

---

*A recent exception was Hurricane's Ike Category 2 winds which struck in September of 2008, defying even this protection when its winds sent water surging over the wall, inundating the town. Natural gas explosions set off fires, but buildings were left to burn because the water was too deep for fire trucks to reach them. From there, Ike moved on to Houston where, in scenes reminiscent of Katrina, residents clung to rooftops begging rescue. At one point, ninety-nine percent of the city's energy provider Centergy's 2.25 million area customers were without any type of power. The company had to bring in 10,000 linemen from across the country to handle debris and repair work. The giant storm ran northeasterly from Texas, up through the entire Ohio Valley. Flash floods and deaths were reported from Texas to Chicago, where the water damage was so sudden and extensive, the Illinois governor had to declare the state a disaster area. One of Ike's deadliest characteristics was its size and slow motion. The storm lasted two full weeks from its days as a baby depression in the central south Atlantic. As it made landfall rolling over Galveston, it stretched nearly 600 miles, covering up much of the northern Gulf of Mexico, before blowing inland, wreaking havoc in a band that included the northern tier of states, eventually exiting to the North Atlantic via Canada.[8]

The weather service did not start naming hurricanes until 1954. (Until 1971 they all had women's names.) Now the rotation is twenty-one names per year. If the number of storms exceeds twenty-one, the convention turns to using Greek letters. In 2005, the year Katrina hit, fifteen hurricanes and a dozen tropical storms exhausted the official list of names, requiring the addition of six Greek letters (from Alpha to Zeta) to finish the season. Five of the hurricanes became Category 4, tying a record, and a record four become Category 5, including Katrina (winds of 175 mph, 902 mbar*), the most destructive, and Wilma, the most powerful recorded with winds in the eye wall exceeding 200 miles per hour (882 mbar, the lowest ever recorded in the Atlantic).

HURRICANE CATEGORIES

Category	Wind speed (mph)
5	156 and >
4	131-155
3	111-130
2	96-110
1	74-95
Tropical Storm	39-73
Tropical Depression	0-38

Hurricanes are simply a fact of life in communities that border the Atlantic on the east coast and to anyone living in the Gulf, all the way south to the northern rim of South America. Just as Galveston had tragic warnings from the 1900 hurricane, reinforced by a second storm fifteen years later, New Orleans has had plenty of practice preparing for and coping with storms. Besides the baptismal hurricane of 1722, only four years after its founding, New Orleans endured a couple of other big storms in the days before accurate weather forecasting gave residents enough time to leave. On an August night in 1856, a Category 4 hurricane struck off the tip of Terrebonne parish. More than 200 people, many of them summer vacationers, were drowned or crushed in the darkness by wreckage flying around in winds that exceeded 130 mph. An 8-foot storm surge "raked the island and tore it in two." In 1909 a hurricane with 110 mph winds hit the Louisiana coast with a 10-foot wave, killing 350 people.[10]

*A *millibar* (mbar) is a meteorological way to metrically measure the air pressure of a storm. The lower the pressure, the higher the winds and stronger the storms. Air pressure in a hurricane decreases as the storm's power increases, so the lower the millibars, the worse the storm.

Until Hurricane Camille (Category 5) made landfall in 1969, Hurricane Betsy (1965) was the storm by which a generation measured their memories of severe weather. Betsy made landfall as a high Category 3 storm and was the first hurricane to wreak high dollar damage in recent history, earning it the nickname Billion Dollar Betsy. Camille crashed into Bay St. Louis just east of New Orleans and roared across the Mississippi delta, its winds so powerful they destroyed the wind-recording equipment (best estimates are 200 mph). It veered east just south of Missouri and chugged back toward the Atlantic, splitting the country, stalling when it reached the Appalachian mountains of Virginia, dumping 28 inches of rain in eight hours and killing 150.[11]

After Betsy, New Orleans replaced existing floodwalls and levees with the current system that zigzagged 350 miles through the city and boosted the height of the protective walls to 10-15 feet. The system was geared to withstand Category 3 storms, but nothing higher. What no one could know was that Camille wasn't an aberration, but rather a coming trend. Storms in the decades to follow Betsy would become much stronger, move more slowly and take longer to blow themselves out.

The current process of calibrating hurricane categories was derived from a formula created by consulting engineer Herbert Saffir and the former director of the U.S. National Hurricane Center, Robert Simpson. Prior to the 5-level scale, hurricanes had been described simply as major or minor. After Hurricane Camille's devastating ride along the Gulf Coast, the two men decided that there had to be a better way to gauge likely wind and storm damage so that cities could make realistic preparations for evacuations and aid to survivors.

When Hurricane George chugged toward New Orleans in 1998, it first roared over Puerto Rico and the island of Hispaniola, leaving 603 dead in its wake. By the time it reached New Orleans, the city had opened the Superdome, using it for the first time as a shelter for the poor who could not leave town. In 2004, Category 5 Hurricane Ivan caused $19 billion damage and killed 92. Although it was to miss New Orleans and make landfall near Gulf Shores Alabama, Louisiana's Governor Blanco ordered an evacuation of the city nonetheless. With all the traffic converging on the same single highway, many people were unable to leave town. Blanco implemented the contra-flow evacuation plan that turned all lanes of city highways into exit lanes, basically doubling the capacity of traffic able to leave the city. A year later, that evacuation plan enabled a fairly orderly mass exodus of those who could flee from Katrina, doubtless saving many lives. Testifying before a House committee in 2006, the governor said that Hurricane Katrina "would have been far worse if the initial evacuation had not been so efficient and safe."[12]

The warning signs had been there ever since its inception, but particularly in the hours preceding Katrina, it was clear to everyone who still had some sort of access to weather bulletins that this would be a decidedly deadly storm. The now famous—and very graphic—warning issued by the U.S. National Weather Service minced no words.[13]

```
WWUS74 KLIX 281550
NPWLIX


URGENT - WEATHER MESSAGE
NATIONAL WEATHER SERVICE NEW ORLEANS LA
1011 AM CDT SUN AUG 28 2005


...DEVASTATING DAMAGE EXPECTED...


.HURRICANE KATRINA...A MOST POWERFUL HURRICANE WITH UNPRECEDENTED
STRENGTH...RIVALING THE INTENSITY OF HURRICANE CAMILLE OF 1969.


MOST OF THE AREA WILL BE UNINHABITABLE FOR WEEKS...PERHAPS LONGER. AT LEAST ONE HALF
OF WELL CONSTRUCTED HOMES WILL HAVE ROOF AND WALL FAILURE. ALL GABLED ROOFS WILL
FAIL...LEAVING THOSE HOMES SEVERELY DAMAGED OR DESTROYED.


THE MAJORITY OF INDUSTRIAL BUILDINGS WILL BECOME NON FUNCTIONAL. PARTIAL TO COMPLET
WALL AND ROOF FAILURE IS EXPECTED. ALL WOOD FRAMED LOW RISING APARTMENT BUILDINGS
WILL BE DESTROYED. CONCRETE BLOCK LOW RISE APARTMENTS WILL SUSTAIN MAJOR
DAMAGE...INCLUDING SOME WALL AND ROOF FAILURE.


HIGH RISE OFFICE AND APARTMENT BUILDINGS WILL SWAY DANGEROUSLY...A FEW TO THE POINT
OF TOTAL COLLAPSE. ALL WINDOWS WILL BLOW OUT.


AIRBORNE DEBRIS WILL BE WIDESPREAD...AND MAY INCLUDE HEAVY ITEMS SUCH AS HOUSEHOLD
APPLIANCES AND EVEN LIGHT VEHICLES. SPORT UTILITY VEHICLES AND LIGHT TRUCKS WILL BE
MOVED. THE BLOWN DEBRIS WILL CREATE ADDITIONAL DESTRUCTION. PERSONS...PETS...AND
LIVESTOCK EXPOSED TO THE WINDS WILL FACE CERTAIN DEATH IF STRUCK.


POWER OUTAGES WILL LAST FOR WEEKS...AS MOST POWER POLES WILL BE DOWN AND
TRANSFORMERS DESTROYED. WATER SHORTAGES WILL MAKE HUMAN SUFFERING INCREDIBLE BY
MODERN STANDARDS.


THE VAST MAJORITY OF NATIVE TREES WILL BE SNAPPED OR UPROOTED. ONLY THE HEARTIEST
WILL REMAIN STANDING...BUT BE TOTALLY DEFOLIATED. FEW CROPS WILL REMAIN. LIVESTOCK
LEFT EXPOSED TO THE WINDS WILL BE KILLED.


AN INLAND HURRICANE WIND WARNING IS ISSUED WHEN SUSTAINED WINDS NEAR HURRICANE
FORCE...OR FREQUENT GUSTS AT OR ABOVE HURRICANE FORCE...ARE CERTAIN WITHIN THE NEXT
12 TO 24 HOURS.


ONCE TROPICAL STORM AND HURRICANE FORCE WINDS ONSET...DO NOT VENTURE OUTSIDE!
```

Credit: NOAA website: http://www.noaa.gov

The sad fact was that many of the people who could not get out had no idea of the bulletin or what was about to blow their way. But other warnings came before the storm, too. Before Katrina hit, several people reported feeling a dread about what was coming. By Monday night the storm had veered easterly and not hit the city head on, and it seemed that the Big Easy had escaped the worst. But even as the mayor was easing everyone's fears, announcing to news cameras that they had "dodged the bullet," a sense began to permeate those who had stayed in town and made it through the storm that something was very wrong. "Many of these non-evacuees felt vaguely ill that Monday evening. They sensed that something was horrifically wrong with their beloved city, something deeper than surface wounds."[14] Just blocks from downtown the levees were rupturing but, much like the Houstonians during the 1935 hurricane, the people who were no longer in danger had not yet gotten the news about the people who were.

This was a systemic problem, something that had been building for some time.

— Forensic engineer J. David Rogers,
head of the team inspecting the failure of New Orleans levee system

Despite decades of warnings, New Orleans remained, because of its geography and lack of wetlands protection, as exposed as a saucer floating in a bowl of water. It was, at the moment Katrina first formed in the Atlantic, defenseless to what was about to come ashore. Afterwards, in heartbreaking pockets of desperation and death, it would seem to have taken on the visage that adopted son and author James Lee Burke described: "an insane asylum built on a sponge."[15] The common refrain from people who watched the bedraggled survivors of Katrina begging for food and water on national television days after the storm had departed was: "How could this be happening in the United States of America?" What *wasn't* wrong with this picture?

THE WIDENING IMPACT OF GLOBAL WARMING

While the blame for any storm can't be placed on a single factor, scientists agree that global warming was certainly a reason in play. While offshore drilling for gas and oil didn't bring Katrina ashore, the constant weakening of the marshlands by pipelines and toxic dumping helped hasten its natural subsidence which in turn took away much of the only land buffer the inland cities counted on to bear the brunt of the storm and dissipate its strength.

Author Nassim Taleb calls an event such as Katrina a black swan, an occurrence so out of the realm of the expected that it shocks our senses—yet in hindsight was clearly inevitable. New Orleans is the great and tragic example that has much to teach us about inertia. Awareness is growing that environmental problems have reached a critical stage on the scale being described in reports like the one issued by the Intergovernmental Panel on Climate Change in 2007, which states, "Warming of the climate system is unequivocal, as is now evident from observations of increases in global average air and ocean temperatures, widespread melting of snow and ice and rising global average sea level."[16] More than 2,000 scientists from 154 countries participated in the writing of the report.[17]

The facts speak for themselves and those facts are beginning to sink into our national consciousness. In February 2007, even Fox News, never reluctant to populate its talking heads with global warming debunkers, began to shift its reporting, noting then that 82 percent of Americans said that (while they might not agree on what's causing it) they believe that global warming was real.[18]

Each of us has a fair idea of what the rising cost of gasoline has on our bank accounts and it has begun to show its secondary effects as the cost of heating oil, natural gas, pasture land, food and endless other items march in lockstep ever higher. But what is the cost to our spirits? We know something's going on. You can't use up a finite resource with infinite sources of accelerating need without sensing something is very wrong. As Chapter 4 describes, we are on an eating binge, devouring our very seed, the stores of air, water, earth, plant and animal species that future generations must rely on us to shepherd into the future rather than devour with our own rapacious appetites.

If we are to understand what we are facing as a nation, we have to consider how the effects of conditions like global warming all depend on and dance with each other, and how our reluctance to confront the part of our national character that tells us we can straddle two sides of a fence that separate very different territories is already enabling the worst possible consequences. The effects of global warming are potentially monumental to our lives, its causes beyond our easy comprehension. But already the trail of evidence is available for us to put together like a jigsaw puzzle of seemingly disparate and unrelated pieces.

If it were possible to pluck an average American housewife from a 1942-era victory garden and put a cell phone in her hands, a tool that would be a mundane truth for her grandchildren, it's entirely possible she would react like Ethiopian Me'en tribal members who, when shown a coloring book picture of an antelope, could detect nothing because they had no "cognitive antecedent."[19] She might well look but without a frame of reference, not see. Our conundrum is similar: we are being asked to understand the changes we are in the midst of and foresee solutions that can save us without having a frame of reference for either.

Katrina was not a stand-alone phenomenon but rather part of a tableau of interlocking effects. Likewise, the shifts in our climate and the warming of the globe are not just about the heat but the long-term and cascading relationships that make up the earth and the elements and how they relate to one another and affect our psyches. The truth and consequences of the warming of the globe revolve around the tripling of the world's population in the last half century, the vast exploitation of resources that accompanied it, and the current effects of having so many consumers now vying for the same finite resources to satisfy their needs and cravings, with more of the same on the horizon.

The real stresses to the globe include the drying up of the planet's water resources, crop destruction and the loss of food integrity and security, the melting of icecaps and glaciers, more torrid heat waves and prolonged droughts, longer wildfire seasons, depleted and arid topsoil, stronger storms and increased flooding and the economic downturns that follow in the wake of such tragedies.

Unlike the victims of hurricanes from previous centuries who could be drowned at night as they slept, we have the technological know-how to see the future—at least enough of it to decide what our choices are—using our climate change models and our digital everythings. We need not settle for or resign ourselves to victimhood. Nor do we need to take the word of people whose vested interests profit most from no more than surface examination of complicated global issues. We must listen to the alarms going off inside each of us that are trying to get our attention.

DRYING UP—OUR DWINDLING WATER RESOURCES

Just as a hurricane swirls into life when given the right ingredients of heat, surface water temperature and wind, the effects of the warming of the globe have their own independent and lethal stand-alone ingredients. During an interview with a *New York Times* reporter in the summer of 2007, Nobel laureate and director of the Lawrence Berkeley National Laboratory Steven Chu pondered the health of the fresh water supplies in the western United States, noting that the Sierra Nevada snowpack was at its lowest level in twenty years. Even the most optimistic climate models suggested a 30-70 percent loss of this water source by mid-century. "There's a two-thirds chance there will be a disaster," he said, "and that's in the best scenario."[20]

The fact is that it's not just the western U.S. that's drying up. The entire fresh water supply on earth is disappearing. In the 1960s, Lake Chad was Africa's third largest freshwater source, covering a surface area of 9,600 square miles. In the last forty years, the lake has all but disappeared, shrinking by ninety-six percent. Bordered by Chad, Cameroon, Niger and Nigeria, the lake basin has been drained not only by a decline in rainfall and an increasingly severe drought, but even more by the many irrigation projects undertaken by the countries that count on it as their main water source. Water diverted from the lake quadrupled between 1983 and 1994 alone.[21]

The lake used to support a diverse ecosystem of birds, fish, crocodiles and herds of grazing animals as well as a population of fishermen. But with most of the lake evaporated, steadily encroached on during the prolonged drought by the nearby Sahara desert, most of the people who used to depend on the lake for their livelihood have turned to farming and agriculture, which itself drains the lake of its contents. Communities which once ringed its shores can now find themselves dozens of miles away. While an ambitious project is planned to divert water from nearby rivers to revitalize the vast dried lake bed, experts doubt the plan can be funded and executed quickly enough to bring the lake back.[22]

Much the same fate is unfolding for Florida's Lake Okeechobee, second only to Lake Michigan as the largest freshwater lake in the U.S. In the first decade of this century, portions of the lake have become so dried out, their exposed organic matter caught fire in May of 2007. The drought that has dropped its water level and shrunken its shoreline was so severe that that same year state and wildlife workers took advantage of the exposed lakebed to clean it of the toxic mud. Over two million cubic feet of sludge were removed from the lake floor in an attempt to restore it to a cleaner, safer habitat for wildlife.

Among the thousands of items they found in this key central Florida fresh water resource, many were not surprising: boats, anchors, tires, motors, chains and miscellaneous trash. Other items delighted them, including enough Native American artifacts to give archeologists and historians a much clearer picture of native life that existed before the first known inhabitants, the Seminoles. (One unearthed arrowhead is estimated to be 8,000 years old.) Still other finds were not so welcome. As they began to excavate the mud on the lake floor, the South Florida Water Management District discovered that arsenic levels in the mud were four times the legal limit. The lake bottom was, in fact, so polluted from decades of fertilizer and pesticide use, it could not be disposed of on agricultural or commercial lands.[23]

In the spring of 2009, near the end of the yearly dry season, the water levels were so low that pumps were installed to keep water flowing to South Florida. The lake is the area's backup water supply.[24]

Other bodies of fresh water are also visibly declining, including the Colorado River that feeds the ever-growing water needs of Nevada, California, Arizona, New Mexico and Colorado. It now often ends in a trickle or even dries out before it can reach the northern edge of the Gulf of California. California's Owens Lake, which at the beginning of the 20th century spanned 200 square miles, lasted barely a decade after it was diverted as a water resource to Los Angeles in 1913. Mono Lake, also in California, has dropped 35 feet since 1941 when it too was diverted to water-hungry Los Angeles. (In an effort to decrease escalating water use, in 2009 the city of Los Angeles Department of Water and Power offered residential customers an incentive—$1 for each square foot of turf that was replaced with drought-resistant plants, mulch or "water permeable hardscapes.")[25]

In October of 2007, the Southeastern United States reached the most severe category of drought it had known in 100 years, a condition so perilous that the city of Atlanta was only four months away from running out of water for its four million people. The drought, made worse by

Atlanta's soaring population and nearly eighteen months of mostly rainless weather had broken every one of the state's dry weather records.[26] The state of Georgia then tried to use the Army Corps of Engineers to siphon off more than their previous share of the water from Georgia's Lake Sidney Lanier to help alleviate their low supplies. The lake, which supplies much of northern Georgia's water, also supplies water and hydroelectric power needs to Alabama and Florida. An appeals court ruling in February 2008 voided the Georgia plan.[27]

Elsewhere in the world, Egypt's Nile, Pakistan's Indus and India's Ganges now regularly recede to a trickle or stop altogether in the dry season. Many of their tributaries are completely gone. China's Yellow River which once ran 4,000 kilometers before reaching the Yellow Sea began running dry in 1972 and since 1985 regularly fails to reach the sea. Of the 1,052 lakes that were once in Hebei province, which surrounds Beijing, only eighty-three remain.[28] Mighty Anguli Lake, once 187 square kilometers in size, has shrunk to dry lakebed in ten years. The temperatures in Hebei province have risen from 1.0 to 2.04 degrees Celsius (1.8 to 3.7 degrees F) in the last 50 years. The annual average temperature of the region of Anguli Lake has risen 2.1 degrees Celsius (3.8 degrees F) over that same time period while average annual rainfall has dropped by 62.1 mm.[29] As these once mighty water sources dry up, the ecosystems and agricultural communities they supported for millennia are disappearing.

These water source declines are exacerbated by widespread poor water management and lack of insight and they are setting the stage for an inevitable tragedy as the reasons for the declines collide with the far-reaching consequences for ignoring them.

There are basically two types of fresh water available on the earth: surface water—lakes, rivers, and tributaries—and underground water. Water from underground aquifers can be shallow or deep. Shallow aquifers are mostly rechargeable and can be pumped until their levels no longer accommodate further pressure; then you must simply wait for them to recharge before pumping them again. Deep aquifers, also called fossil aquifers are, like oil, not replenishable. What is extracted from them is a one-time gift. Since the middle of the twentieth century, overpumping has become the norm, with countries like China, India, and the United States, the world's main grain producers, leading the way.

"The failure of governments to limit pumping to the sustainable yield of aquifers means that water tables are now falling in countries that contain more than half the world's people."[30] The long-term consequences are dire because this is not just about drinking water. It's about the declining ability of countries to feed themselves and their people. The fact is that it takes an enormous amount of water to feed people. On average, each of us on the earth consumes about a gallon (four liters) of water in some form each day. Without considering what we use daily for showers, watering our yards and cleaning our clothes, consider that the food we consume each day requires another 528 gallons (2,000 liters) of water per day. Seventy percent of the world's water today is used to irrigate fields to produce food crops. The remaining thirty percent is divided between industrial and residential use.

The economies of growing food are unforgiving: it takes 1,000 tons of water to grow a ton of wheat. As gallons of water are measured in dollars needed to irrigate the land to be able to grow the ever-increasing tons of wheat needed worldwide, it becomes abundantly clear that as water tables decline while populations in countries like India and China continue to climb, each country's ability to feed its population is going to be strained to the breaking point. Even with wheat fetching record prices, as water becomes harder to reach and, therefore, a more precious commodity, countries are going to have to import more and more grain to cover their own growing domestic grain deficits. In fact, that is becoming the norm rather than the exception. Countries that don't have enough water to spare to grow their own food are "using grain to balance their water books. Similarly, treading in grain futures is in a sense trading in water futures."[31]

Grain imports march in lockstep with water shortages. It is conceivable, some say inevitable, that the substance deemed most precious in this and succeeding centuries won't be oil but water. Water deficits are already translating into grain deficits. The countries best suited to handle these changes are clearly the ones with the healthiest fiscal anatomies. The vast North China Plain, that country's breadbasket, producing more than half its wheat and a full third of its corn crops, is a case in point. As its water table levels continue to drop from overpumping, the country's grain production is becoming less and less sustainable. In 1998 grain production peaked at 392 million tons. By 2005, it had dropped to 358 million tons, while the country's population had increased by nearly sixty million.[32] China was able to avoid importing grain until it had used up its vast stores in 2004 when its grain imports reached seven million tons.

Its wheat crop alone has continued to dwindle from a peak of 123 million tons in 1997 to a total of 105 million tons in 2007, a fifteen percent drop in a decade that saw its population increase by eighty-five million. (By mid-2009 the USDA reported China's 2009 crop was likely to be 113.5 million tons.)[33]

China is already looking at losing more and more land to arid plains as hotter temperatures dry up surface water and turn once arable land into desert. In north central and western provinces enormous deserts are shifting and merging to form even bigger deserts. "Highways running through the shrinking region between them are regularly inundated by sand dunes."[34] Dust storms are not unusual in northwestern China. On April 5, 2001, a huge dust storm that originated there and in Mongolia began a trip across the Pacific, blanketing the entire western half of the U.S. from Arizona to Canada two weeks later. Swirling in that choking dust was a precious commodity: millions of tons of topsoil. A year later in Seoul, South Korea, a Chinese dust storm encased the city, closing down schools and filling clinics with people unable to catch their breath. Ten or so such dust storms now occur annually in China, providing "visual evidence of the ecological catastrophe unfolding in northern and western China." These occurrences have become commonplace enough in Korea to be known as the dread "fifth season." The principal cause: overgrazing.[35]

Desertification, the loss of once arable areas, is a process of land degradation that is often the result of a combination of factors including overgrazing, overuse and mismanagement of resources and longer, drier summers. It's a serious problem affecting many countries including India, the Mekong delta in southeast Asia, the Nile valley in Egypt, the Middle East, Mexico, Spain, South Korea and several nations in Africa. Africa is particularly vulnerable, losing from two to three billion tons of soil annually. That loss of soil represents a loss of agricultural heritage and a critical part of that continent's capacity to feed its present population and future generations. In far west Africa's Mauritania, the wind erosion is so severe, the number of dust storms has increased from two annually in the 1960s to eighty per year today.[36]

Even the U.S., which once suffered a devastating loss of topsoil during the Dust Bowl era of the 1930s, is not impervious to desertification. While only one-fifth of U.S. grain harvest depends on irrigated land (in India, it's three-fifths and in China a whopping four-fifths), and while the U.S. water supplies are much healthier than they are in many countries, three of our main grain producing states, Texas, Nebraska and Kansas, share a single fossil aquifer, the Ogallala, from which they glean seventy to ninety percent of their irrigation water. In the U.S. a little more than a third (thirty-seven percent) of all irrigation water comes from underground sources, while the remaining nearly two-thirds comes from surface water—lakes, rivers, tributaries. Underground sources are popular because they can often be drilled at the site they are needed, maximizing water economy and limiting waste. Ground sources have the added attraction of being available even during droughts when surface water often evaporates or is too far away from crop sites.

If there can be a bright side to surface waters disappearing, it is that they are at least visible. You know when their shore lines recede and water levels drop. With aquifers you do not know the water is gone until nothing comes up. There is no ten-year warning. The pumps simply stop bringing up water.

One of the drawbacks to widespread dependence on fossil aquifers to support grain production is a lack of food security. In the northernmost of China's three river basins, the Hai River basin has a population of 100 million people, and includes two of China's largest cities, Beijing (15 million) and Tianjin (11 million). As populations migrate from the country into the city where there is indoor plumbing, water consumption typically rises by as much as fourfold.

A study done by the World Bank notes that wells drilled around Beijing have to go down half a mile to capture fresh water now, making the sheer acquisition of water prohibitively expensive. Chinese wheat farmers who are having to drill a thousand feet for irrigation water are being driven out of business by the costs to hydrate their crops. As the water shortfall in the Hai basin reaches nearly 40 billion tons per year, once the aquifers are depleted, the loss to the country's grain harvest will be enormous, down by 40 million tons, enough to feed 120 million Chinese.[37] That would be the equivalent of the U.S. being unable to provide grain to more than a third of our people. But with much of our own grain growth dependent on the water from a single—though vast—fossil aquifer, it at least begs the question, "How do we grow enough food now and in the future without destroying an essential one-time source of water?" It doesn't take a rocket scientist to figure out that just as irrigation has helped triple grain harvests in the second half of the twentieth century, that kind of growth will be reversed when the water supplies needed for irrigation no longer show up at the other end of the pump handle.

THE HEAT IS ON

While 2005 holds the record for the hottest year on record, the European heat wave of 2003 also marked the hottest summer in 500 years of European history. Originally reported as totaling 35,000 fatalities, the number soared to more than 52,000 deaths (beginning in June and ending during the sweltering first two weeks of August) as updated reports trickled in over the next two years.[38] In France alone, 14,802 people died, most of them elderly. Because summers are mostly moderate, especially in the Auxerre section of France where temperatures hit 104 degrees, most residents do not have air conditioning, so respite from the heat's effects were minimal. Complicating the dogged heat during the day was the fact that the evenings did not cool off and provide needed relief from the day's soaring temperatures.

Even more shocking were the 18,257 deaths (vastly higher than the original estimate of 4,000) reported in Italy, when August temperatures

WHAT'S HOT*

The first decade of this millennium was the hottest since record keeping began in 1880.

1. 2005 was the hottest year ever recorded
2. 2002, 2003, 2006, 2007 and 2009 tied for second place

*Source: NASA Goddard Institute for Space Studies web site: http://www.giss.nasa.gov/

soared as much as 16 degrees Fahrenheit warmer than the previous August. Other countries also logged record-breaking temperatures and deaths from heat: Germany: 7,000 deaths (105.4 degrees, hottest since recordkeeping began in 1901), 4,130 in Spain, 2,139 in England and Wales, 2,099 in Portugal, 1,250 in Belgium and 975 in Switzerland, which recorded its highest temperatures since 1540. In London, where triple digit temperatures were recorded for the first time on August 10, 900 people died.

In total, the original estimates of the 2003 heat wave were fully 33 percent lower than the July 2006 totals. While deaths from heat waves don't usually get much press coverage, "they claim more lives each year than floods, tornadoes and hurricanes combined."[39] Eight years earlier during a hot mid-July week in 1995, more than 700 people died during a fierce heat wave that blanketed Chicago. In the U.S., heat waves don't just kill people, they also put an enormous strain on the country's antiquated power grid, much of which hasn't been significantly updated since the grid began getting pieced together in the late 1800s. The same August that Europe was baking in record temperatures, the U.S. experienced the giant rolling blackout of 2003 that affected 50 million people along the eastern U.S. and Canada, with an estimated $6 billion in damages resulting from the lost power. The U.S. power grid is a problem in its own right, causing a full one-third of the emissions that contribute to global warming in this country. It is simultaneously inefficient, undependable, and vulnerable. Much of what tripped the safety switches during the 2003 blackout could have easily been prevented by trees in some of the service areas being trimmed so they didn't come into contact with the power lines and trip overload switches.[40]

Hotter weather also dries up water supplies and kills crops, depleting grain harvests and endangering food security across the globe. It creates a vicious cycle. As increased and prolonged heat evaporates surface water faster, the soil grows drier. Without water to evaporate into the atmosphere, there isn't enough moisture to form rain clouds. The ground grows more arid, and when rain does come, the earth is too brittle to absorb the water and the runoff turns into floods. By the time autumn arrives, the warmer air heats up the moisture that does falls to earth, and more of it comes as rain and less as snow during the critical fall and winter seasons. It is these times that snow must build up to become the melt runoff that western farmers will count on for spring planting and our forests count on to keep from drying out.

It gets worse. According to *Science* magazine, "Snowpacks are now melting 1 to 4 weeks earlier than they did fifty years ago, and streamflows thus also peak earlier."[41] Snowpacks are essential to the western United States water security. In fact seventy-five percent of what shows up in our streams in the spring comes from snowpack. This in turn affects our high-elevation forests which used to be protected from wildfires by late snowpacks. Because of the earlier cycle of snow melt, these forests are becoming more vulnerable to fire.[42]

No one can predict the long-range effects of earlier springs and later snowmelts but every farmer knows how critical timing is to a growing season. During the lifecycle of a crop, the most critical phase is pollination. Of the world's three staple grains—rice, wheat and corn—corn is the most vulnerable to hotter temperatures during pollination. If the tassels burn up before they can open and drop pollen on the silk strands onto the corn cobs below or the silk itself burns before the endosperm can complete its job of traveling to each corn kernel, the corn cannot develop.

Rice is also vulnerable to high temperatures. In 2001, a paper presented by Pedro Sanchez, Director of the International Centre for Research in Agriforestry, showed that at 93 degrees rice can pollinate at almost 100 percent levels, but by the time it reaches 104 degrees Fahrenheit, its ability to pollinate is near zero.[43]

Higher heat in general will also lower crop yields. A study by the International Rice Research Institute found that each 1-degree Celsius rise (1.8 degrees Fahrenheit) in temperature above the norm lowers wheat, rice, and corn yields by 10 percent. In India where the population is expected to grow by another half billion people by midcentury, two scientists found that while a 1-degree Celsius increase in temperature did not meaningfully affect wheat yields, a 2-degree Celsius rise lowered yields at all test sites as much as 38 percent.[44]

These point to an additional corollary, possibly the one with potentially the most catastrophic side effect of the heating of the globe: the world's fast melting glaciers and icecaps. In September 2005, scientists reported a worrisome fact: the Arctic icecaps were melting much faster than originally predicted, in leaps and bounds in fact. The *New York Times* posted an animated graphic that shows the startling retreat from a single year—2006 to 2007—demonstrating how severely and quickly the planet is heating up.[45] In September of 2007, Arctic ice specialists were stunned to see the extent of the rapid decline as an area of ice twice the size of Great Britain melted away in a single week.[46] Two years later in September of 2009, after examining the results of 50 million laser readings from its satellites, NASA coined a new term for the alarming rate of disappearing ice in both the Greenland and Antarctic masses: runaway melt.

There are three main reasons why this is a fundamentally tragic planetary change. First, as the temperatures rise, they expose permafrost, some of which has been covered for millennia. Siberia is the country with the most potential CO_2 locked away in its permafrost. In 2007, the average temperature in Siberia rose five degrees centigrade. As melt happens, methane emerges, an emission that is 23 times more potent a greenhouse gas than CO_2.[47] Alaska and Canada also have vast amounts of melting permafrost. Besides the methane, no one can know what it would mean for melted permafrost to expose microbes to the atmosphere that had heretofore been locked in ice for untold thousands of years.

Second, glaciers and ice caps provide snow melt in the spring that feed the rivers, springs, lakes and tributaries that are the water sources for much of the earth. With more heat, there is less snow. With less snow there is less water available to irrigate the world's crops. "Every major river in Asia, where half the world's people live, originates in the Himalayas, including the Indus, the Ganges, The Mekong, the Yangtze, and the Yellow."[48] With glaciers melting in every highly populous part of the globe across Europe, Asia, Africa, North and South America, the outlook for fresh water is fundamentally grim.

In the United States, the southwestern states depend on the Colorado River which in turn depends on snowmelt from the Rockies to replenish it every spring. In California, the Central Valley counts heavily on snowmelt from the Sierra Nevada range as well as an ongoing supply from the overly stressed Colorado River. In addition when temperatures rise, rain is more likely to fall than snow. This in turn creates the conditions for flooding. Unless our national energy policy changes significantly and quickly, it's estimated that by mid-century, we will experience a 70 percent reduction in snow pack in the western states.

The connectivity issue is extremely important for people to understand. The Arctic is the early warning for the world. It is the health barometer for the world. We Inuit are in fact the mercury in that barometer.[51]
— Canadian Inuit Activist Sheila Watt-Cloutier,
Chair, Inuit Circumpolar Conference

The third reason that the melting of the glaciers and ice caps is bad news is the conditions that melting water will create on a large scale. While most of what is melting in the Arctic each summer does not add to sea levels because the weight of the water is already displaced by the existing ice, scientists estimate that the melting of the West Antarctic ice sheet or the Greenland ice sheet would raise sea levels worldwide anywhere from several inches to as much as twenty-three feet.[49]

"When you warm the ocean, you also increase it, because it expands thermally," says David Barber, Chairman of the Arctic System Science at University of Manitoba. What accompanies that is a quick and considerable rise in sea level. "If you live on a planet where most people live within a couple meters of the ocean level, the potential for problems [is] enormous. The poles of the planet are the early sentinels of global-scale climate change."[50]

A CO_2 PRIMER*

- Carbon dioxide is the greenhouse gas most responsible for making earth temperatures rise
- Carbon dioxide results from the emissions of burning fossil fuels (7.5 billion tons annually) and deforestation (1.5 billion tons annual)
- Atmospheric levels have risen substantially:
  - o 277 parts per million before the Industrial Revolution
  - o 387 parts per million in 2009
  - o NASA's head of the Goddard Institute for Space Studies says CO_2 levels should be reduced to 350 a.s.a.p. to begin to slow the melt of glaciers and Arctic ice
- Today levels are rising four times the rate they rose in the 1950s because of increased emissions
- No one can know the effect on ppm levels as warming temperatures melt permafrost in northern areas, exposing methane, a GHG which is more than 20 times worse than CO_2

* Source: Environmental Defense Fund website: www.edf.org

THE AGE OF WILDFIRES

In early June 2008, after the driest spring ever recorded had followed two years of low precipitation, Governor Arnold Schwarzenegger proclaimed a statewide drought in California. That same week farmers in some of the state's Central Valley, where $1.3 billion in cotton, tomatoes, garlic and onions is grown annually, were already dealing with an edict from the U.S. Bureau of Reclamation which had reduced the district's water share by 40 percent, forcing many farmers to perform a Sophie's choice on their upcoming season's harvests.[52]

Just two weeks later, on June 20, a dry lightning storm moved through central and northern California, peppering more than two dozen counties with 6,000 lightning strikes. The 2,096 fires that resulted burned throughout much of the summer and would eventually require the services of 25,000 firefighters from all over North America and from as far away as Australia and New Zealand to put them out.[53]

Drought causes tinderbox conditions that ironically are often ignited with the coming of rain or in the case of the California conflagration—collectively called The North California Lightning Series—dry lightning. The effects of wildfires, as with other natural disasters, aren't limited to the events they bring. Just as with floods and severe storms, crops, homes, businesses, natural resources and lives can be lost. The air quality can be contaminated and toxic. In the aftermath of Hurricane Katrina, a chemical plant near New Orleans exploded, sending benzene fumes into the air. Even from a helicopter exploring the scene 2,000 feet above the plume, people on board could not breathe.[54]

According to a report prepared in August 2004 by researchers with the U.S. Department of Agriculture, even a rise in summer temperatures of 2.8 degrees Fahrenheit could double the number of wildfires in eleven western states. Along with that goes the estimate that the annual wildfire season in the western states has already been extended by 78 days because of prolonged, warmer springs and summers.[55] Here again, the timing of the annual snowmelt is critical. In one 34-year study, the years that had an earlier snowmelt (setting up longer, drier summertimes) there were five times as many wildfires as in years when the snowmelt was late.[56]

Lightning is often the cause of wildfires because of dry conditions, exacerbated by longer, drier springs and summers. By the time the California fires were 100 percent contained, 511 structures had been destroyed and 15 people had died. An estimated 1.2 million acres were destroyed by the more than two thousand fires, most of them caused by lightning strikes.[57]

Like the California conflagration in 2008, the 1988 fire that consumed 1.2 million acres of Yellowstone National Park (36 percent of its total size) was started by dry lightning, lightning without rain. The fire blazed throughout the summer, requiring $120 million and the services of 25,000 firemen, with as many as 9,000 firefighters battling the blazes at a time. Seven of the hundreds of fires that burned that summer were responsible for 95 percent of the destruction, a statistic that typifies wildfire behavior: about 5 percent of the fires are responsible for about 95 percent of the damage. Despite nonstop effort, the fires continued unabated for three months, until the first snowfall began in September. The last fires were not fully extinguished until November.[58] Statistics show that since 1986, "longer, warmer summers have resulted in a fourfold increase of major wildfires and a sixfold increase in the area of forest burned" since the previous period of 1970 to 1986.[59]

Heat waves, drought and wildfires are all first cousins in the global warming family. They exacerbate and feed off of one another. Each is made worse by warming temperatures. Just as heat waves and drought threaten crop yields, wildfires threaten homes and businesses and vast natural resources, drying up stream and river beds, contaminating the air with smoke, causing respiratory difficulties downwind and altering the landscape of many of the parks and habitats we count as natural treasures.

The 2008 California wildfires may not be an isolated case. In a speech about global warming given on July 17, 2008 in the midst of the wildfire's onslaught, Al Gore stated that scientists at Tel Aviv University had determined that "for every one degree increase in temperature, lightning strikes will go up another 10 percent."[60] According to NASA Earth Observatory scientists, the Earth's average temperature over the past century rose at its fastest rate in a millennium—from 1.08°F to 1.62°F.[61] The year 2005 was not only the first year that saw four Category 5 hurricanes, it was also the warmest year recorded since recordkeeping began in the 1850s. The world's ten warmest years have all occurred since 1994 and five of those have been in the years 2002-2009.[62] With scientists predicting anywhere from a three- to ten-degree warming during this century, higher temperatures would clearly make wildfires an ever growing risk to the world's ecosystems.

STORMY WEATHER

Hurricane Katrina is the poster child for one of global warming's worst consequences, stronger storm systems. While there's no real indication that there are more hurricanes birthing in the Atlantic or Pacific each summer and fall, it is clear that the trend is toward stronger and more devastating systems. With stronger storms come increased flooding, infrastructure and economic devastation, higher storm death tolls and the countless personal tragedies that come with loss of life and home. A study done by researchers at the Massachusetts Institute of Technology in 2005 found that since the 1970s, hurricanes have doubled in intensity and duration, correlating that increase with higher sea surface temperatures. The frequency of Category 4 and 5 storms has also doubled during that same timeframe, a fact also attributed to the warming of the oceans.

While many businesses may not yet feel compelled to acknowledge the growing and continuing effects of global warming, one industry has faced it and launched its own frontal assault. During 2004 and 2005, insurance firms witnessed staggering losses as the amounts collected as premiums were overwhelmed by the massive outpouring of payouts in no less than ten major storms that devastated the Gulf and Atlantic coasts. In Florida alone, where 70 percent of the insured property sits on the coast, eight destructive hurricanes hit in a 15-month period during the 2004 and 2005 hurricane seasons. When Hurricane Andrew hit Florida in 1992, insurance losses topped $26 billion. A dozen insurance companies became insolvent while many others stopped writing policies altogether in the state. After Andrew, everything changed for the industry. "Andrew forced the industry to recognize the potential for multi-billion dollar mega-catastrophes of record-breaking proportions."[63]

Since the relatively hurricane-free 1970s, the industry has watched as coastal building has increased. A kind of collective amnesia set in. In adjacent coastal Mississippi, New Orleans' eastern neighbor, 90,000 people moved into three of its coastal and adjacent counties between 1995 and 2000. MIT Professor Kerry Emanuel observed, "Despite centuries of hurricane disasters, our society continues to disregard collective experience and invite future tragedy by building more and more structures in surge-prone coastal regions."[64]

In fact, the coastal population in the U.S. jumped 28 percent between 1980 and 2003. In Florida alone, the increase was a staggering 75 percent.[65] Indeed, by 2004, properties along the U.S. Gulf and Atlantic coasts were valued at $7 trillion. Looking the other way became the norm in Louisiana early on. As Tulane University historian Douglas Brinkley wrote in *The Great Deluge*, "Once Louisiana became part of the U.S. in 1803, entrepreneurial delusion became a mind-set in the region."[66]

Before the record losses became the new norm, insurance companies had a pretty good way of gauging risk. Based on decades of weather patterns, they could use actuarial tables to calculate what was likely to happen in the future. But as the planet warms and scientists warn that storms are likely to become more severe, the old rules no longer work. The result: the insurance industry believes global warming is real and getting worse and is responding accordingly by getting out of the high risk business of insuring coastal areas in times that seem increasingly unpredictable. The United Nations projects that climate change will cost the world's financial centers upwards of $150 billion annually for the foreseeable future.

"Allstate, one of the nation's largest insurance providers, has cut off coverage for 40,000 coastal homeowners in New York, and is no longer writing any new policies in Florida."[67] (In February 2010, State Farm Florida announced it would begin cancelling policies for 125,000 of its customers in August, the mid-point of the hurricane season because state regulators denied their request to raise premiums by 47 percent. Most of the customers being cancelled reside in coastal areas.[68]) The downstream effects aren't promising. As homeowners and business owners contemplate rebuilding, they face skyrocketing insurance premiums if they can find insurers at all. "Without adequate insurance, businesses can't borrow money to keep their doors open and those on fixed incomes can't afford to stay in the homes in which they planned to retire."[69]

In 2005, Lloyds of London, AIG and The Association of British Insurers all issued policy statements or reports that warn of the growing effects of global warming and climate change. The Association of British Insurer's report looked at what would happen if, as scientists predict, the CO_2 levels double, increasing wind speeds in the Atlantic by 6 percent. This differential in wind speed would make a Category 4 hurricane a Category 5, bringing with it possible losses on the U.S. mainland of $100-$150 billion *each year.*[70]

As losses become the new normal rather than the dread occasional aberration, the history of economic development along the Gulf Coast is being written on the wind. "Hurricanes and tropical storms represent the largest weather-related threat to economic stability along the U.S. coast."[71]

THE COMING OF THE WHIRLWIND

Hurricanes like warm water. That's why the hurricane calendar falls in the warmest months of the year. In late August 2005, nearing the end of the hottest summer ever recorded, the waters that would soon host three Category 5 hurricanes in the Gulf of Mexico had reached a very balmy 87 degrees, a full five degrees warmer than normal. Tropical Depression 12 began over the Bahamas on August 24, 2005. When it first dealt southern Florida a glancing blow a day later, it was as a Category 1 Hurricane Katrina. A million homes lost power and eleven people died before it moved off the Florida coast and spun into the Gulf of Mexico where it met the friendly loop current that runs deep and clockwise through the Gulf's warm water eddies. The heat in the water basically acted like "hurricane intensity engines,"[73] enabling the storm to feed off the warmth as it swirled in the Gulf for three days, maturing, picking up moisture, wind speed and slow-moving intensity, revving itself up before turning and journeying northeast. Loop currents like the ones Katrina rode are warm subtropical waters that flow from the Caribbean Sea at the tip of Florida southwesterly through the Yucatan Straits back into the Gulf of Mexico. They are the alchemists that created the perfect recipe for Katrina's transformation into the monster storm that would span 460 miles, an area equal to the distance between Boston and Washington, D.C.

GONE WITH THE WIND—
REALITY CATCHES UP WITH A POST-KATRINA WORLD

Will a post-Katrina insurance industry in shock change the idea of where we can live? Will living by the sea become a distant memory? For many it will at least become an exercise in living without a safety net. In coastal states, premiums between 2001 and 2006 skyrocketed:

- Alabama: Raised as much as tenfold
- Florida: Average premiums up 77%, by 500% or more in Miami Beach areas.
- Louisiana: Home insurance premiums rose 65.2%
- Mississippi: Homeowner premiums up by 63%
- South Carolina: Homeowner premiums up an average of 56.4%
- Virginia: Premiums up an average of 67.2%
- Texas: Premiums up an average of 50%[72]

By Saturday, August 27, Katrina was a Category 3; on Sunday morning, when the city's first-ever mandatory evacuation was ordered, it began the day as a Category 4 and ended the day as a Category 5. Winds were clocked at more than 175 mph. By dawn on Monday as it made landfall, it had dropped to a high Category 4, with winds at 155 mph (Category 5 wind speeds start at 156 mph). Twelve hours after landfall, it was downgraded to a Category 1 again but the damage had been done. Over 90,000 square miles of coast line between Louisiana and Alabama had been damaged or decimated, an area equal to the size of Great Britain. In New Orleans, as four tears widened in three levees, the bowl that was the city effectively tipped. An estimated 80 percent of the city was submerged, some areas under a dozen feet of water or more.

"Any hurricane acts like a vacuum as it drives across the ocean, literally pulling water up into its grasp. When the hurricane hits land all that vacuumed-up water is let loose, in a great wave known as the storm surge."[74]

In places Katrina's storm surges would reach nearly thirty feet as it rolled ashore pounding everything in its path. At 8:00 a.m. on that Monday morning, Mayor Ray Nagin was interviewed on NBC's *Today Show*: "We will have significant flooding, it's just a matter of how much." Fourteen minutes later, the levee on the Industrial Canal began to collapse, inundating the Lower Ninth Ward. One minute after that, in nearby Waveland, Mississippi, the twenty-seven members of its police force fled their building and sought refuge in trees as the storm came ashore, water inside their office rising three feet in fifteen minutes. They endured and survived the slashing winds and debris of the storms, clinging to the treetops.   Much of their small beachfront town was destroyed. Meanwhile, as they hung on, in St. Bernard parish a few miles to the southwest, thirty-five helpless and bedridden patients at the St. Rita's Nursing Home, some of them tied to their beds, watched the water rise around them quickly. All drowned within the next half hour.[75]

By 3 a.m. Tuesday, the power had failed at Methodist Hospital. Even back-up generators weren't working since many hospitals had stored this equipment in basements which flooded first. Volunteers, some of them children, used hand pumps to keep patients on ventilators alive. They did this hour after hour for two full days. By the next day temperatures inside the hospital were a sweltering 106 degrees. But not everyone was affected just by heat. Many who clung to rooftops and tree branches, light poles and floating debris, got severe hypothermia from the high velocity wind and water. More than any other injury the doctors who treated survivors said they saw not only cuts and punctures but hands whose skin had been torn or shredded off, sometimes cut to the bone by debris and wind. "The result was that many people had hands swollen and raw like slabs of red meat."[76]

Without air conditioning, anesthetics or analgesics, wounds were sewn up quickly and without anything to ease the suffering. Because of the insufferable heat and humidity, doctors and nurses shed their clothes and worked in their underwear, washing it out and hanging it on makeshift clotheslines to stay as hygienic as they could.

Everywhere the storm "created weaponry consisting of millions of pounds of airborne debris, cleaved from beachside buildings and out of unlucky houses. From garbage can lids to Ford 150 truck doors to Maytag refrigerators to 120-foot yachts, Katrina made shrapnel of everything." In nearby Biloxi, Mississippi, all ten of its floating casinos were pulverized.[77]

On Sunday, the day before Katrina made landfall, 18,000 vehicles were leaving New Orleans each hour. By Thursday, three days after Katrina hit, Baton Rouge replaced New Orleans as the largest city in Louisiana. Within a week, 1.7 million residents of the Gulf Coast would be scattered across all fifty states.

The damage was unprecedented. In Louisiana alone, 200,000 homes were destroyed. Another 45,000 had been declared unliveable, and 15,000 apartments had been destroyed. The parishes of St. Bernard and Plaquemines were 90 percent destroyed. In tiny Buras, a fishing village sixty-three miles southeast of New Orleans where Katrina first made landfall as it tailed northeasterly, winds struck at a Category 5 velocity of 161 miles per hour. Although everyone in the community had evacuated, every house was destroyed. The estimates of damage to the entire Gulf Coast vacillate from tens to hundreds of billions of dollars.

By Thursday, 4,000 people were stranded on Interstate 10 without water, food or medical supplies. Tens of thousands more still awaited help in the city's convention center, Superdome and hospitals. It would be Friday or later before coordinated assistance began to arrive. In the interim the U.S. Coast Guard and the Louisiana National Guard performed heroically, flying countless missions to rescue the stranded. The Ninth Ward and St. Bernard Parish were hardest hit, with an estimated fifty-thousand people awaiting help and rescue. A small flotilla of flat-bottomed boats manned by members of the Louisiana Wildlife and Fisheries took to the waters and were joined by local residents who showed up in rowboats, motor boats, pirogue canoes, jet skis and even wading on foot to rescue their fellow New Orleanians.[78] Bodies were visible for days, some still being discovered in abandoned houses more than a year later.

As bodies began being removed, reporters were told to stay back the equivalent distance of three football fields or face consequences varying from arrest to denial of press access to future military operations.[79] Katrina's aftermath was very bad press. When forty-five dead patients were finally recovered a full week after an NBC cameraman had filmed them in stages of decomposition and reported his findings to officials, the removal process was grim and traumatic.[80] The drowned are a particularly gruesome population to confront, especially during very warm and humid weather, days or months after death. "What the mythic flood stories don't convey is the reality of decomposing flesh, a process that is accelerated when a body is waterlogged. The abdomen swells, the tongue protrudes and blood from the lungs comes flushing out of the mouth, nostrils, and eyes. A hideous, repugnant, rotten-egg stench, caused by the release of the methane-like gas, permeates the dead skin, making it especially awful for those who found the corpses after Katrina."[81]

But nothing could hide the truth. The American public was seeing it on every news channel. The storm's enormous size had rewritten all the laws of hurricane expectations. Clearly, the coast lines suffered the most. Bridges, beaches, wetlands, bayous and byways were destroyed and towns virtually erased from maps. In some places only satellite "before and after" maps could help people locate where they had once lived.

We hadn't been prepared and no one seemed willing to step up and take responsibility. Danger filled the city. The water it stagnated in was toxic in countless and unknown ways, not only from the swirl created by thousands of barrels of oil, sewage, and chemical pollutants, but from the poisonous brew that came from flooding the medicine cabinets, garages, and refrigerators of thousands of homes, as well as the contents of flooded restaurants, hospitals, pharmacies, grocery stores, and other businesses.

The death toll in New Orleans alone would eventually rise to 1,200 but a complete total will never be known. There is no accurate count for those who perished from diabetic coma, untreated high blood pressure and other medical conditions, or the heart attacks and strokes caused by the shock or hardship that registered on survivors later.

Before Katrina, New Orleans had a population of 453,000. More than half that number waited out Katrina whether they wanted to or not. After the storm, 378,000 would be displaced either temporarily or permanently. Three full years later, 65,000 blighted lots in the city remained and the population was estimated at 272,000, or 60 percent of the pre-Katrina totals. In March 2009, population estimates hit 300,000 for the first time since the storm hit.[82]

PROPHETS WITHOUT HONOR

Given the mythic and historical precedents available on Gulf Coast hurricanes, the personal experiences with past storms of city dwellers and city officials, as well as the warnings given to government bureaucracies on the likelihood of Katrina delivering a five-star disaster, how could this particular storm have taken everyone by such surprise?

"If experts had prophesied a terrorist attack with that kind of accuracy, they would be under suspicion for treason," wrote Amanda Ripley in a *Time Magazine* piece the weekend after the storm struck. "If Hurricane Katrina turns out to be the biggest disaster in U.S. history to date, it will also be the least surprising."[83]

The signals had been everywhere, if anyone had been willing to look. But in a post-9/11 U.S., terrorism was getting the budget attention and the shuffling of agencies (FEMA was subsumed into Homeland Security and its funding cut) and hiring of personnel without adequate emergency training like FEMA head Michael Brown didn't help. The year before Katrina, FEMA conducted an elaborate simulation scenario called Hurricane Pam which had uncanny similarities with Katrina, predicting much of what happened. But as accurate as it ended up being, nobody wanted to listen.

Brian Wohson, a professor of engineering at Louisiana State University served as a consultant on the exercise. "I'll be honest with you. I'm the researcher. I'm doing all the models, and sometimes I could say to myself, 'Am I Chicken Little? Could this really happen?' Even I was in denial, and I was the one running all the numbers."[84] One of the goals of the simulation was to determine how to deal with the 100,000 or so poor and infirm that would need help fleeing the city. At disaster planning meetings following the simulation, he said, "the answer was often silence."[85] Hurricane Pam might have impressed its participants, but the scenario didn't stick with them. Recommendations were still being assessed when Katrina hit.

While Hurricane Pam dealt with probable outcomes from rain and wind, it did nothing to alleviate another troubling and long-standing problem with coastal Louisiana: the loss of the state's protective wetlands in the Gulf of Mexico. An environmental disaster all on its own, proponents of its restoration see it as one of the most preventable components of the weakness that made New Orleans so vulnerable. Louisiana has nearly three million acres of wetlands spanning 80 miles inland and running nearly 200 miles along the Gulf Coast. Some of what has happened to the wetlands is a natural result of the shifting of the 200-mile wide Delta plain of the Mississippi River, which is actually what created the barrier reefs and islands that comprise the wetlands.[86] Because hurricanes tend to gain strength over water and lose strength once they reach landfall, these reefs and islands created a buffer for inland areas, protecting them from a storm's harshest winds.

Their growing disappearance is no small issue. According to King Milling, an America's Wetlands spokesperson, for every 2.7 miles of wetlands lost, you can count on a one foot increase in storm surge. "Storm surges that used to be in the neighborhood of ten to twelve feet could suddenly be eighteen to twenty feet."[87] Katrina would create surges of thirty feet or more.

Between 1930 and 2005 when Katrina struck, southern Louisiana lost more than one million acres of wetlands across twenty parishes—an area equal to the size of the state of Delaware—both to coastal erosion and manmade interference. By 2005, that was a loss equal to one football field every 38 minutes. Park Moore, Assistant Secretary of the Louisiana Department of Wildlife and Fisheries believes this is critical. "The impact of losing their wetlands was overwhelming. All the habitat for animals and invertebrates was disappearing along with a vital natural filter, which prevents pollution in the Gulf from toxic agents from oil and gas. Dredging killed the wetlands which, in time, would leave Louisianans more vulnerable to hurricanes."[88]

This was a real problem for the half of the state's four million people who at that time lived in coastal parishes and for the 70 percent of birds that migrated through the Mississippi Flyway and used the area's coastal habitat as a stopover.

The manmade reasons for the destruction of the wetlands were easy to see in the offshore platforms that began to dot the Gulf in the 1950s when the wetlands began to pay off, delivering millions of barrels of oil and trillions of cubic feet of natural gas to energy companies. Louisiana is a big part of the U.S. energy scene, providing a full 25 percent of the nation's oil and natural gas. (Between them, Hurricanes Katrina and Rita destroyed 113 offshore platforms, in addition to damaging many offshore pipelines and processing facilities.[89])

Preceding the Hurricane Pam scenario run by FEMA, a number of magazines and newspapers took on the task of crafting possible scenarios of the aftereffects of a catastrophic hurricane that would make New Orleans the center of a bullseye. In 2005, John Barry's 1998 epic about the 1927 Mississippi River flood, *Rising Tide,* was "almost mandatory reading for the college-educated class in the Crescent City."[90] A five-part series written in the summer of 2002 by *Times Picayune* writers John McQuaid and Mark Schleifstein, "Washing Away," marched lockstep through the reasons New Orleans was vulnerable and why preparations and changes to the current hurricane protection system were drastically—and quickly—needed. *Drowning New Orleans,*[91] a prophetic article published by *Scientific American* a full four years before Katrina warned of such a storm's probable consequences. It examines the effects of 1965's Hurricane Betsy and 1998's Hurricane George in particular as the two which should have turned the tide on New Orleans' future.

When Betsy inundated parts of the city under eight feet of water, the city moved to upgrade the 350 miles of levees to withstand a Category 3 hurricane, with winds as high as 130 mph. Good but no cigar, said the Army Corps of Engineers. It had long recommended that the city's hurricane battlements be able to withstand a Category 5, warning that stronger storms were inevitable. "The Corps has been pushing for years for Category 5 protection," said retired Lieut. General Robert Flowers, former head of the Corps. "Decisions have been made to accept more risk."[92]

The issue, they said, wasn't just bigger levees, but rather restoring the coastal wetlands which had taken a beating the last five decades and which were disappearing at the rate of 25-30 miles per year. It is the loss and deterioration of marshland that they viewed as the greatest issue around defending the Gulf Coast against strengthening storms. Storms gain their strength from the heated waters in warm months, generally weakening as they make landfall. It is the marshlands that absorb the initial force of a storm by being that first extension of landfall that begins to slow the storm down.

But change comes slowly even in the face of theoretical disaster. When Category 5 Andrew missed the city by 100 miles, the town heaved a sigh of relief. (Originally determined to be a Category 4 in 1992, the National Oceanic and Atmospheric Administration (NOAA), considering new research in 2002, upgraded it and now officially lists it as a Category 5.) When Hurricane George came even closer, waiting until the last moment to head east, the truth became clearer even to the most ardent naysayers. George was a near terror. "Its fiercely circulating winds built a wall of water 17-feet high topped with driven waves, which threatened to surge into Lake Pontchartrain and wash into New Orleans," the exact scenario that would occur seven years later when Katrina topped the levees with 20- and 30-foot surges. But, again, catastrophe was avoided when George slowed and made a city-saving 2-degree turn east before reaching land.[93]

That was enough for the state, local and federal officials to sit down together and map out a serious plan to address the issue of their city's hurricane defense. Within months they had devised a bold plan called Coast 2050. Its goal: to restore the wetlands of coastal Louisiana by its target year. The two-step solution would have involved first rebuilding the marshland by creating river diversions at key junctures along the Mississippi, then building control gates to allow freshwater and sediment to wash through marshes down to the Gulf. The second step would involve bringing in half a billion cubic yards of sand from Ship Shoal in Terrebonne parish, just west of New Orleans. The cost for the 50-year program was calculated at $14 billion. The estimated cost of Katrina by 2008 dollars was $200 billion.

In an editorial written less than a week after Katrina sank his city, writer Richard Ford wrote about how words could not really express what it felt to be a New Orleans native post-Katrina. "It's like Hiroshima, a public official said. But no. It's not like anything. It's what it is. That's the hard part. He, with all of us, lacked the words."[94]

THE WAY WE WERE

During the time leading up to the actual signing of the papers finalizing the sale between France and the United States in March of 1804, Meriwether Lewis busied himself learning botany, zoology, celestial navigation, and the rudiments of medicine from the nation's leading doctors, not to mention signing on his Army friend Captain William Clark to lead the expedition with him. With their boats built, the trip fully provisioned and crew hired, the journey that would see the first Americans set foot in what was about to become the western U.S. was ready to commence. The initial funding hit to the American taxpayer: $2,500. (The eventual cost

REUNION: HOW WE HEAL OUR BROKEN CONNECTION TO THE EARTH

GLOBAL WARMING BY THE NUMBERS[95]

1. The world's 10 warmest years have all occurred since 1994, in a temperature record dating back a century and a half. The year 2005 was THE warmest on record for the US. Over the past 30 years, the earth has warmed by about 1.08°F.

2. Since 1990 the U.S. has increased its carbon dioxide emissions from fossil fuel burning by 20 percent.

3. NASA scientist James Hansen has warned that "the safe upper limit for atmospheric CO_2 is no more than 350 parts per million (ppm)." As of December 2009, the level was 387 ppm and rising as much as 2 ppm each year[96] (pre-industrial revolution levels were at roughly 275 ppm; in the 1970s the levels were at 325).

4. The IPCC and NASA state that Americans would need to reduce their global warming pollution by 80 percent by 2050 to prevent the worst consequences of global warming. The critical first part of that plan would require a 20 percent reduction of CO_2 by 2020.

5. The needed changes must be met as milestones. The magical year is 2012. According to IPCC scientists, if there is no significant action taken by then to curb toxic emissions, we cannot realistically catch up and make any meaningful difference in what will happen on the planet.[97]

6. Since the 1970s, hurricanes and tropical storms have increased in intensity and duration by 75 percent, as a result of the warming of

would be $38,000.) The expedition's assignment was twofold: to see what there was to see but also, and even more dramatically, to fulfill a quest that had haunted explorers who had preceded Columbus when he sailed from Portugal 300 years before: to find the Northwest passage, the mythical intercontinental water route to the Pacific Ocean that would enable unfettered access to the markets of the Orient.

The Corps of Discovery, as it was called, saw things no American had ever seen before and much that we can no longer see. Everywheretheir water route west took them, they witnessed endless repetition of wonder after wonder. There was a saying around the time of Lewis and Clark's the waters surrounding landmasses that are vulnerable to hurricanes. Warmer waters mean more frequent and powerful storms.

7. According to the EDF, since the 1980s, the U.S. fire season has increased by 78 days, another phenomenon tied to increased temperatures and earlier snowmelt. Some say it's basically a 12-month fire season.

8. Among the believed health effects that will be traceable to global warming in the future is an increase in the number of people suffering from kidney stones. Stones are formed from excess minerals in the urine, which hydration helps keep at bay. Since hotter temperatures require more water to keep people hydrated, being underhydrated can lead to increased instances of kidney stones, This is a common occurrence already in warmer areas of the U.S. and has been seen to be true with troops returning from deployment in Iraq.

9. Between the 1970s and the first decade of this century, the number of hurricanes classed as a Category 4 or 5 has jumped 60 percent.[98] Two (Katrina and Rita, both Category 5s) hit the Gulf coast within three weeks of one another between August 29 and September 24, 2005. Another (Wilma) followed a month later with 200 mph winds that made it the strongest hurricane ever recorded in 150 years. The 2005 hurricane season clocked a total of four Category 5 storms, a new record.

10. Warmer temperatures can also increase algae blooms that are toxic to fish and ease the spread of illnesses like Lyme disease and Rocky Mountain spotted fever which are carried by ticks.

journey that the eastern half of the United States was so heavily forested that a squirrel could start at the shore of the Atlantic Ocean and jump from tree branch to tree branch without ever touching the ground until it reached the Mississippi River, but that once it got to the Great Plains, it would have to start walking. The mostly treeless Great Plains took them weeks to cross, a calm and dazzling display of fertile grasslands that presented a stark contrast to the Rocky Mountain passages that would challenge them almost to death near their trip's end.

Near what is now Bismarck, South Dakota, they discovered populations of Native Americans that dwarfed the populations then living in St. Louis and Washington, D.C. At one point as they maneuvered down a river, they had to pause to allow a herd of buffalo to ford across in front of them. They waited for an hour, awestruck by the size and power of the massive herd. In the Pacific Northwest, they saw what one crew member estimated as ten thousand pounds of salmon setting out to dry on the river's edge. All along the way they saved species of animals and plants no American had ever seen before, shipping them back to a delighted Thomas Jefferson.[99]

Across the ocean, the English poet William Wordsworth was observing the wholesale march into full-scale materialism, lamenting how the human eye was drawn increasingly to mechanical processes and economic progress and less and less to the quiet redolent work of nature. He wrote:

> *The world is too much with us; late and soon,*
> *Getting and spending, we lay waste our powers:*
> *Little we see in Nature that is ours;*
> *We have given our hearts away, a sordid boon.*

Writing at the dawn of an industrial revolution that would span his century and the next, he could not foresee the details but he recognized the symptoms of people disengaging from their spiritual link to nature. As we were getting and spending, we were also losing and forgetting something whose simple sweetness would be a dim species memory two centuries later.

As long as there have been civilizations on earth, humans have strived for more—to create, conquer, quest for, achieve, master and invent, to continually reach beyond the limits of what we know and are able to do and even dream. Along the way epochs came and went, civilizations were born and disappeared. Progress is nothing new and it was not unique to the Industrial Revolution whose chronological beginnings are at best arbitrary. But what was different at the beginning of the 19th century was how quickly we stopped exploring horizontally across the face of the earth and began instead a massive shift to exploring vertically. It was when we pierced the earth's surface to mine its riches that we really began to affect life on the planet as man never had before in a spiral of effect and consequence that has shadowed us ever since.

In the span of what astrophysicist and storyteller Carl Sagan used to call the cosmic clock (he described man's time on the planet as the last minute of the last hour of the cosmic day, 11:59 and then some), this two centuries is barely a blink, but its effects have sent our mother planet reeling in ways that can no longer be denied. The advantage we have over our ancestors who had yet to envision what a Pacific beach could possibly look like is just that. We have that capacity to see. While the families of the crew who set out from St. Louis in 1804 could only sit and wait for two and a half years to find out if their kin were even alive, much less what had become of them, we know instantly. We can even see them in real time via invisible signals sent through the little transmitters of energy we call cell phones. No matter where they are, we can feel their breathing through the receiver, hear their lives in our own ears.

Today, two centuries after Lewis and Clark wrote the first story of our country's western expansion, none of these conditions still exist save one. We have not lost our hunger for exploration; it's just that we spend most of it digging for oil, gas, and coal—the discoveries that most interest us as 21st century beings. And we have been wildly successful, creating a society that is mobile and connected in ways Lewis and Clark could never have envisioned. But while the Corps of Discovery spent their time heading into the unknown and learning as they went, naming what had never been seen by Americans, we have treated nature primarily as a thing to be used up. We have long since forgotten the gentle practice of naming what surrounds us to honor it and value its preciousness.

As Chapter 1 points out, when we break the bond that exists between us and the earth that nurtures us, when we stop valuing what we can no longer name, the results are obvious. Just as Lewis and Clark thought they were going to find an all-water intercontinental route that would take them to the markets of the Far East and found instead the destiny of the United States, we are the new explorers who must dare to head into an unknown we can feel but not yet see. We are being lured by our right brains as our left brains move in step behind us and try to figure out a path that can work.

New Orleans, the port that made the Louisiana Purchase such a bright and shining possibility, has long had a reputation as a magical place. Its outrageous traditions, from its jazz funerals and above ground cemeteries to its Mardi Gras celebrations, voodoo darkness and polycultural historical roots make it unlike any other American city. Like a pulse, the mantra of the city calls out to celebrate life.

Once the Louisiana Purchase was complete, the Mississippi River officially became the country's tree of life, the artery that fed our other national parts, the body of water that thirty-one of our states feed directly into. Like the first chakra of our bodies, located at the tip of our tailbones, the Mississippi Delta is effectively our country's root chakra, the bottom tip of the spiritual spine that runs right up our middle. The wetlands are the lungs that filtered and cleared and allowed clean water to enter and exit the tributaries that feed off of it, that kept out the salt, the toxicity and storms; they were there to balance nature's elements.

When New Orleans was hit by Hurricane Katrina, scattering its children to every state in the union, our nation's first chakra was shattered. Watching events unfold in excruciating slow motion, we no longer knew what we were capable of ignoring. Looking at this from an energetic and spiritual perspective, consider what it means to lose a precious commodity like the diversity of an entire city. When New Orleans was drowned, it effectively dispersed some of the sweetness of our diverse history. How do we repair what has been so displaced, regather what is energetically ours from a sacred contract made by one of our country's forefathers?

We start by looking at what happened during Katrina as a fable, a tale of great meaning, a portent of things to come if we content ourselves to watch what is happening and let others do the heavy lifting rather than venturing out into waters that frighten us. One of the greatest ironies of this tale is still unfolding. Far away in the Arctic north, there is indeed an ending to the quest that the Corps of Discovery set out for. Because of global warming, for the first time in unknown eons, the ice pack that has kept the far north frozen solid has melted enough to create the elusive and until now nonexistent Northwest Passage that Lewis and Clark sought. At this writing, that passage is being carved out by ice-breakers from Russia. Their goal: the considerable store of minerals and fuel resources that lay locked beneath the North Pole, which is now, incredibly, fair game for oil exploration.

Once again, as Inuit tribes and wildlife are being threatened with extinction, diversity and wholeness are threatened for the sake of what's expedient. The paradox is inescapable. It is the heating of the globe, much of it from the burning of fossil fuels that has endangered our life on this planet so completely. Yet the first response to that alarm is to respond to the addiction with a full-scale assault to get more, like a heroin addict digging through a dumpster of used syringes in hopes of finding enough still left in one, diseased or not, for a final fix, anything to ease the inevitable pain of life without it.

In addition to the first chakra being the seat of our connection to the earth, as Caroline Myss wrote in *Anatomy of the Spirit*, it also represents the seat of justice, the idea of "what goes around comes around" and tribal consciousness. Tribes, say Myss, are rarely accountable for actions. As the country witnessed during the finger pointing post-Katrina, it wasn't possible to find a single person or cause to hold fully accountable. The first chakra also maps to the first Sefirot in the tree of life in the Kaballah as well as to the Christian sacrament of baptism.[100] Katrina, which comes from the Greek *pure*, offers us a new start, a clean slate, baptizing us into a new way of seeing, helping us to simultaneously bid farewell to our innocence and willful blindness and welcome the birth of new awareness.

Endnotes

1. "Residents Say Levee Leaked Months Before Katrina," *Morning Edition*, National Public Radio, November 22, 2005.
2. Bob Marshall, "Levee leaks reported to S&WB a year ago," *New Orleans Times-Picayune*, November 18, 2005.
3. *Ibid.*
4. Alan Dooley, *Sandboils 101*: *Corps has experience dealing with common flood danger, http://www.hq.usace.army.mil/cepa/pubs/jun06/story8.htm*
5. Michael Dyson, *Come Hell or High Water: Hurricane Katrina and the color of disaster* (New York: Basic Civitas Books, 2006).
6. "Levee leaks reported to S&WB a year ago."
7. Douglas Brinkley, *The Great Deluge* (New York: Harper, 2005).
8. Daniel Yovich, "Ike's remnants blamed for Midwest deaths, blackouts," Associated Press, September 15, 2008.
9. http://www.aoml.noaa.gov/
10. John McQuaid and Mark Schleifstein, "In Harm's Way," part of the 5-part series, "Washing Away," *New Orleans Times-Picayune*, June 23-27, 2002.
11. http://pubs.usgs.gov/of/1999/ofr-99-0518/ofr-99-0518.html
12. "Response to U.S. Senate Committee on Homeland Security and Governmental Affairs Document and Information Request Dated October 7, 2005, and to the House Of Representatives Select Committee to Investigate the Preparation for the response to Hurricane Katrina," December 2, 2005. http://www.blancogovernor. com/ index.cfm?md=newsroom&tmp=detail&articleID=1523&

13. http://www.noaanews.noaa.gov/stories2006/s2656.htm
14. *The Great Deluge*, xiv-xv.
15. "Anatomy of a Disaster," *U.S. News & World Report*, September 26, 2005.
16. Report from the Intergovernmental Panel on Climate Change, November 2007, available as a .pdf at http://www.ipcc.ch/
17. As dire as its warnings are, evidence suggests that even these statements were watered down and edited versions of what the scientists' findings reported. The Copenhagen Climate Conference held in December 2009 was historic in that it brought together dignitaries from 193 nations for the first time to discuss the severity of the issues surrounding climate change and global warming but generated little more than political, nonbinding statements at its conclusion. John M. Broder, "Many Goals Remain Unmet in 5 Nations' Climate Deal," *New York Times*, December 18, 2009.
18. http://www.foxnews.com/story/0,2933,250571,00.html
19. *Blessed Unrest*, p. 15.
20. Jon Gertner, "The Future is Drying Up," *New York Times Magazine*, October 21, 2007.
21. Lynn Chandler, "Africa's Lake Chad Shrinks by 20 Times Due to Irrigation Demands, Climate Change," GSFC press release (Greenbelt, Maryland: NASA, Goddard Space Flight Center, February 27, 2001).
22. C.T. Pope, "Vanishing Lake Chad—A Water Crisis in Central Africa," http://www.circleofblue.org/waternews/world/vanishing-lake-chad-a-water-crisis-in-central-africa/
23. Carol J. Williams, "Drought yields lake's treasures and trash," *The Nation*, July 19, 2007.
24. Andy Reed, "Lake Okeechobee level drops; pumps will keep water flowing," *Sun-Sentinel*, May 8, 2009.
25. Alexandra Zavis, "DWP offers cash incentives for water-saving landscapes," *Los Angeles Times*, June 2, 2009.
26. Brenda Goodman, "Drought-Stricken South Facing Tough Choices," *The New York Times*, October 16, 2007.
27. Brenda Goodman, "Georgia Loses Federal Case in a Dispute About Water," *The New York Times*, February 6, 2008.
28. *Plan B 2.0*, 52.
29. Report on Research on the Reasons for Anguli Lake's Shrinkage and Drying Up Using Satellite Remote Sensing, from the International Archives of the Photogrammetry, Remote Sensing and Spatial Information Sciences. Volume XXXVII. Part B7. Beijing 2008. www.isprs.org/congresses/beijing2008/proceedings/7_pdf/11.../02.pdf
30. *Plan B 2.0*, 42.
31. *Ibid*, 55.

32. China Statistical Yearbook; National Bureau of Statistics web site: http://www.stats.gov.cn/english/
33. http://www.chinability.com/Population.htm and http://indexmundi.com/china/population.html
34. *Plan B 3.0*, 97.
35. *Ibid*, 96.
36. *Ibid*, 92.
37. *Ibid,*, 70-71.
38. The revised 2006 number is significantly higher than originally reported in 2003. Lester R. Brown, Earth Policy Institute, *Plan B 2.0* (New York: Norton, 2005), 251, and www.earthpolicy.org/Updates/2006/Update56.htm
39. Environmental Policy Institute bulletin, available at http://www.earthpolicy.org/Updates/Update29.htm
40. Patrick Mazza, "Adventures in the Smart Grid, No. 1: Why the SmartGrid is important." Grist, June 10, 2007, available at http://gristmill.grist.org/story/2007/6/8/144854/0193
41. Steven W. Running, "Is Global Warming Causing More, Larger Wildfires?" *Science* Magazine, 18 August, 2006.
42. *Ibid*.
43. Pedro Sanchez, "The Climate Change-Soil Fertility-Nexus," presented September 4-6, 2001 at Sustainable Food Security for all by 2020. Available at: http://www.ifpri.org/2020conference/PDF/summary_sanchez.pdf
44. *Plan B*, 3.0, 53.
45. http://www.nytimes.com/interactive/2007/10/01/science/20071002_ARCTIC_GRAPHIC.html#
46. David Adams, "Ice-free Arctic Could Be Here in 23 Years," *The Guardian*, September 5, 2007, updated January 14, 2008.
47. www.climateprogress.org
48. *Plan B 2.0*, 67.
49. David Barber interview in *New York Times* online video, "The Big Melt: The Arctic Ice Cap." Available at http://video.on.nytimes.com/?fr_story=aa9ac8c8b71dbc3e2c455b7e6d51020c29c0cd8e.
50. *Ibid*.
51. *Ibid*.
52. Kelly Zito, Matthew Yi, "Governor declares drought in California," *San Francisco Chronicle*, June 5, 2008
53. CALFIRE website, http://www.fire.ca.gov/index_incidents_overview.php
54. *The Great Deluge*, 575-576.
55. http://www.edf.org/documents/8465_OMB_comments_TSDs.pdf
56. "Is Global Warming Causing More, Larger Wildfires?"
57. CALFIRE website

58. National Park Service website available at http://www.nps.gov/yell/naturescience/wildlandfire.htm

59. "Is Global Warming Causing More, Larger Wildfires?"

60. Text of Al Gore's speech at http://www.npr.org/templates/story/story. php?storyId=92638501 or at http://blog.algore.com/2008/07/a_generational_challenge_to_re.html

61. "Global Warming Update," by Holli Riebeek, May 11, 2007, NASA Earth Observatory website: http://earthobservatory.nasa.gov/ Library/GlobalWarmingUpdate/

62. United Nations Weather Agency at http://www.un.org

63. *Blown Away, How Global Warming is Eroding the Availability of Insurance Coverage in America's Coastal States*, Environmental Defense Fund, 2007 report, p. 1. Available at http://www.edf.org/documents/7301_ BlownAway_insurancereport.pdf

64. *The Great Deluge*, 84.

65. Jeffrey Kluger, "Global Warming: The Culprit?" *Time,* September 24, 2005.

66. *The Great Deluge*, 7.

67. *Blown Away.*

68. "State Farm cancels thousands in Fla.," MSNBC and NBC News, February 3, 2010. Available at: http://www.msnbc.msn.com/id/35220269/ns/business-personal_finance

69. *Ibid.*

70. "Financial Risks of Climate Change," Summary Report, Association of British Insurers, June 2005.

71. *Blown Away.*

72. Environmental Defense Fund website: http:/www.edf.org

73. "Gulf Warm-Water Eddies Intensify Hurricane Changes," press release. Statement from Nick Shay, a University of Miami Rosenstiel School of Marine and Atmospheric Science (RSMAS) meteorologist and physical oceanographer, National Science Foundation website**,** http://www.nsf.gov/news/news_summ.jsp?cntn_id=104483

74. *The Great Deluge*, 76.

75. *Ibid,* 629.

76. *Ibid,* 169.

77. *Ibid,* 157.

78. *Ibid,* 261.

79. Cecilia M. Vega, "As Bodies Recovered, Reporters told, 'No Photos, No Stories,'" *San Francisco Chronicle*, September 13, 2005.

80. Brett Martel, "45 Bodies Found at New Orleans Hospital," Associated Press, September 12, 2005 and *The Great Deluge*, 605-610.

81. *The Great Deluge*, 261.

82. Information on vacant lots and displaced population during Katrina from Rick Jervis, "New Orleans Population May Have Hit Plateau," *USA Today*, August 4, 2008. New Orleans population figures pre- and post-Katrina are from U.S. Census data. The 2009 total is based on information from http://www.nola.com/news/index.ssf/ 2009/03/no_tops_300000_in_census_estim.html.

83. Amanda Ripley, "How Did This Happen?" *Time Magazine*, September 4, 2005.

84. *Ibid.*

85. Scott Shane and Eric Lipton, "Federal Response: Government Saw Flood Risk but Not Levee Failure," *New York Times*, September 2, 2005.

86. U.S. Geological Survey website: http://pubs.usgs.gov/fs/la-wetlands/

87. *The Great Deluge*, 13.

88. *Ibid*, 9.

89. U.S. Department of Energy website: http://www.eia.doe.gov/pub/ oil_gas/natural_gas/data_publications/crude_oil_natural_gas_reserves/ historical/2005/pdf/ch2.pdf

90. *Ibid*, 15.

91. Mark Fischetti, "Drowning New Orleans," *Scientific American*, October 2001.

92. "How Did This Happen?"

93. "Drowning New Orleans."

94. Richard Ford, "A City Beyond the Reach of Empathy," *New York Times*, September 4, 2005.

95. Credit: UN Weather Agency, National Oceanic and Atmospheric Administration and NASA, Environmental Defense Fund, and IPCC paper of November 2007. Kidney stones reference: Jeremy Manier, "Global warming to spark rise in kidney stone cases, study says," *Chicago Tribune*, July 14, 2008, based on story in journal *Proceedings of the National Academy of Sciences*.

96. In June of 2008, the numbers were 388.02. Source: http://www.carbonify.com/carbon-dioxide-levels.htm

97. http://www.ipcc.ch/ for .pdf on 2007 conference.

98. www.climateprogress.org and www.edf.org

99. PBS, *The Journey of the Corps of Discovery*, directed by Ken Burns, 1997.

100. *Anatomy of the Spirit*, Chapter 2.

PART TWO

Waking Up

*It is said that when the Buddha arose from under the Bodhi tree, his state of
enlightenment gave him a luminosity. An approaching monk asked him reverently,
"Holy One, are you a God?"
"No, not a God," the Buddha replied.
"Then you must be a Deva," exclaimed the monk.
"No, not a Deva," said the Buddha.
"Then you must be Brahma himself!" proclaimed the monk.
"No," replied the Buddha.
"Then, tell me please, what are you?" asked the monk.
"I am," said the Buddha, "awake."***

**Adapted from *The Book of Awakening,* by Mark Nepo

Chapter 3

Oil is One

*We're borrowing money from China to buy oil from the Persian Gulf
to burn it in ways that destroy the planet.
Every bit of that has to change.*
—*Vice President Al Gore*

A DOZEN YEARS AFTER THE first Gulf War, what many still remembered most clearly were the fires.

In the early hours of January 17, 1991, the U.S., as part of a U.N.-led coalition, began a bombing campaign in Iraq against the regime of Saddam Hussein. The air campaign, which lasted for five weeks, was followed by a 4-day ground campaign that routed the Iraqi Army from Kuwait.

Shortly after the bombing began, 400 million gallons of crude oil dumped into the Persian Gulf, giving the world its worst oil spill ever. The oil seeped out into the stretches of the Gulf, washing up on beaches, contaminating everything it touched, killing untold numbers of marine and wildlife, among them an estimated 25,000 birds. More than 400 miles of the fragile Saudi coastline was drenched in oil. Because the circulation pattern of the Persian Gulf is slow and sluggish, scientists estimate the pollution done to waters could take a century to cleanse itself.

The U.S. accused Iraq of dumping the oil to create a barrier to a potential Marine landing. Iraq accused the U.S. of intentionally bombing oil tankers in Gulf ports. No matter. The effect was the same.

Before the U.S. could declare victory and order a cease fire on February 28, engineers from the Iraqi armed forces set fire to an estimated 789 of Kuwait's 1,000 oil wells, creating what experts gauge as the world's worst environmental disaster. Firefighters faced extreme obstacles, not only because most of the fires were far from water but because the U.S. air assault had left thousands of unexploded cluster bombs hidden in the sand where they fell.

Many of the wells were in Kuwait's Burgan field, second largest oilfield in the world. Only the Saudi Ghawar field is bigger. The wells would burn Kuwait's particular brand of light sweet crude for nine months, turning the area to smoke-choked permanent night. It would take 10,000 workers from 27 countries to extinguish the blazes. As many as six million barrels of oil gushed into the air each day. The final estimated tally of oil let loose into the Kuwaiti desert: one billion barrels.

A few million barrels were recovered. Much of what didn't burn pooled in more than 300 lakes. In southern Kuwait one such lake stretched for half a mile and reached depths of 25 feet. The Kuwaiti oil ministry estimated that the lakes contained 25 to 50 million barrels of oil but over time much of that sank into the sand, possibly with the bombs dropped to kill its despoilers.

What didn't end up in lakes went into the atmosphere and eventually into people's lungs, including the tons of soot that covered the desert for months after the fires were extinguished. This sand and oil mixture turned patches of what was once tillable land into a substance called *tarcrete*. The combination of contaminants of the oil—soot, sulfur and acid rain—covered agricultural lands as much as 1,200 miles in every direction. Eventually the damage made the soil so unfit, only weeds grew there. Once again we humans were destroying the epidermis of the earth.

The smoke from the fires was so dense, it was clearly and quickly visible to NASA space satellites stretching as it did from Baghdad to Iran. The noxious cloying black rain of oil and smoke blew as far away as Turkey, Syria and Afghanistan.

As a second Gulf War was about to get underway in 2003, the memories of what Hussein had been willing to do to ruin a victor's spoils haunted people still reeling from the effects of the first war. When he was interviewed in January of 2003 by CNN, Dr. Meshal Al-Mesham, head of the Kuwait Environment Protection Agency said, "Right now in Kuwait we are noticing an increasing number of cases of cancer. We think it's related to what happened in '91 when we had the oil fires. A lot of people breathe very bad air."

Jonathan Lash, president of the World Resources Institute, a

Washington-based think tank that focuses on environmental issues, seemed to concur when he wrote, "What many recall as a short-lived conflict resulting in the liberation of Kuwait was an environmental disaster—one from which the region and its people have yet to recover. The oil that did not burn in the fires," he added, "traveled on the wind in the form of nearly invisible droplets resulting in an oil mist or fog that poisoned trees and grazing sheep, contaminated fresh water supplies, and found refuge in the lungs of people and animals throughout the Gulf."[1]

Paul Hohnen of Greenpeace International summed up a lesson we may be learning throughout this century. "History may show that just as Chernobyl illustrated the horrors and dangers of nuclear power, the Gulf war underlined the real costs of the oil economy in terms of its impacts on the environment, human suffering and ultimately war."[2]

At the end of his definitive history of the pursuit of oil, *The Prize,* author Daniel Yergin says that while "our civilization has been transformed by the modern and mesmerizing alchemy of petroleum...its power comes with a price."[3] In our attempt to acquire and master it, it has acquired and mastered us. As we have pricked our planet's surface in a million places like countless mosquitoes feeding on the blood of the earth, we have found ourselves not just feeding but tethered to the consequences of our own gorging, nakedly guilty, sick at heart from its effects, but still hungry for more.

"When we decided to separate humanity from all of the rest of creation," says Thom Hartmann, "we created a schism that was deep and profound. When we decided that the world was here for us, separate from us, and it was our holy duty to control and dominate it, we lost touch with the very power and spirit which gave birth to us."[4]

If the universe had set out to teach us earthlings a lesson about our own willful blindness and neglect, our own creativity and brilliance, perhaps it could not have crafted a more purposeful journey for us nor a more compelling story for us to learn about ourselves. At the center of that story sits the break that needs to be repaired, our ruptured connection with the earth, our first chakra spiritual birthright. It is in that repairing that hope and healing wait.

In a very real sense it is the story of darkness and light, of best intentions and worst motives. It's about finally waking to a possible future where our great-grandchildren await us with a single question: "What were you all thinking?"

THE OPPOSITE OF NATURE

Landing at LAX in one of the 700,000 planes that come and go there each year, taking a shuttle to a rental car, then driving up La Cienega toward Hollywood in one of the twelve million vehicles that travel the L.A. freeways each day, you can begin to get a sense of how oil enables every mile of movement in the United States. As you quickly head through Baldwin Hills and look up to your right, you see the paradox that is America's energy appetite. Puncturing the rolling hills that flank the 319-acre Kenneth Hahn State Recreation area, sometimes called the Central Park of L.A., is a sea of pumping jacks bobbing up and down, pulling up the oil that has helped keep California's economy running smoothly, making it the eighth largest in the world. It's an example of our national energy schizophrenia: a lovely, pastoral slice of earth dedicated to nature while surrounded by the symbols of what might be called the opposite of nature, the wresting from the earth of toxic gold.

No American city personifies the idea of America on the move better than Los Angeles. It is a city literally built on oil and crisscrossed with hundreds of miles of asphalt arteries that depend on a hydrocarbon diet to keep its mighty and diverse commercial heart beating. Without oil, like most of America, the city would come to a standstill.

California is also the most populous state in the country and its thirty-six million residents and three million businesses pump enough noxious fumes into the atmosphere to give it a designation it would rather not have and is trying hard to change: the 12th largest emitter of greenhouse gases in the world.

Normally when you think of oil in this country, you might think Texas, Alaska, or Oklahoma. But California? Actually, yes. According to the Bureau of Land Management, in 2008 the state was the third largest onshore producer of oil and gas from federal lands. In fact, offshore drilling began in the U.S. in 1895 off the coast near Santa Barbara. The LaBrea tar pits in Los Angeles, a gift from the last Ice Age to the city's urban heart, were once a gathering place for settlers who collected oil from the pit's seeps to distill it for their lamps, lubricate their wagon wheels or seal their roofs.[5]

When the price for a barrel of oil peaked at nearly $150 a barrel in July 2008, it was accompanied by a sinking feeling that there may not be quite as much of this stuff left as we once believed. Better get it while we can. It also meant that a lot of those pumping jacks that had formerly been stilled were once again going at the oil for all they were worth. And during that summer, they were worth a lot. For all its bad raps, oil is still being pulled up out of the ground in record amounts everywhere anyone can find it and it's still very big business. In 2008, the year of the great oil price runups, both Shell Oil and Exxon Mobil profits jumped to record highs of $31.4 billion and $45 billion respectively, even though profits dropped drastically after the July price peak. While the rest of the economy was sinking, the oil industry was doing just fine.

The pumping jacks you see all over the state resemble little mechanical dinosaurs, their heads bobbing up and down, pecking up the waste of their ancestors. It is that waste that transports, feeds and moves the world. And we are still the mega users. Even in the midst of their era of rocketing GDP growth, China and India can't touch us for oil consumption. While they each use two barrels of oil per person per year, in 2009 each man, woman and child in America used 26 barrels per year (that's nothing; in 1978 we guzzled 32 barrels per capita).

The oil coursing through our national veins not only makes possible our transportation in all its mechanical forms, it also provides thousands of derivative products to provide us with everything from asphalt to nanosynthetics, part of a list that has spread like smoke into every nook and cranny of our lives. And its easy, cheap access has given us a silent entitlement, an esteem that is so deep in our national character, we'd rather be locked in bumper-to-bumper freeway traffic than surrender our beloved gas-powered steeds to something as banal as a car pool.

When asked by a *Wall Street Journal* reporter in late 2008 what it was like trying to wean Americans off their addiction to oil in the late 1970s, Jimmy Carter responded dryly, "It was like gnawing on a rock."[6]

No fun, that weaning. It's Mother's milk most of us are unwilling to contemplate a life without. We Americans stubbornly love our oil and the vehicles that guzzle them. It's part of why we burn 21 million barrels of it every day of the year. Its many forms of fuel—diesel, marine oil, jet fuel, heavy oil and the light sweet crude that makes up our gasoline— make possible more than 80 percent of our transportation and much of the urban and suburban life that is uniquely American. Today fossil fuels (much of it converted to electricity from coal-powered plants) heat our homes and businesses, run our factories, power our transport, light our cities and towns, and keep us connected via the phone and internet. "Virtually every aspect of modern existence is made from, powered with, or affected by fossil fuels."[7] Without it the American lifestyle would nosedive in a freefall.

We couldn't eat either. Oil is not only the lifeblood of our transportation and industrial base; it's also the engine of modern agribusiness, inextricably involved in our food chain. Counting the amount of oil it takes to plant, fertilize, spray pesticide, harvest and process its food, the typical steer that spends an average of 21 weeks in a CAFO (concentrated animal feeding operation), eating enough corn to reach about 1,200 pounds before he is slaughtered, ingests the equivalent of nearly a full barrel of oil in his short, stuffed life. And that's just the carnivorous part of our diet.[8] (Nor is the easy solution for the world's omnivores to just stop eating meat. Nearly one-fourth of the world's population relies on livestock for some form of livelihood. If meat eating suddenly stopped, the world's unemployment figures would skyrocket.)

Most of the animal and vegetable material we eat travels an average of 1500 miles before it reaches our plates. While the average family of four in the developed world consumes about 1,070 gallons of gasoline per year to keep their cars running, it takes another 930 gallons just to feed them.[9]

Oil runs the machinery that plants, harvests, processes, stores, distributes and prepares our food. It provides the raw materials for the chemicals and pesticides that are sprayed on the crops that feed both us and the animals we eat. Its byproducts fill every aspect of our lives. And every day it's getting and spending becomes more problematic. "Its volatile price erodes prosperity; its vulnerabilities undermine security; its emissions destabilize climate. Moreover the quest to attain oil creates dangerous new rivalries and tarnishes America's moral standing. All these costs are rising."[10]

The other two substances that make up the trio of hydrocarbons that form the backbone of our energy system—natural gas and coal—are also critical players in our national infrastructure. And each is failing us on significant levels which not only endanger our economy, our way of life and our national security, but also—through the air we breathe, food we eat and water we drink—our health and the very future of life on this planet. Our century-long dependence on them is at the core of our first chakra disconnection and the way they became woven into a single central, controlling story is unique.

Spindletop: the mother of all salt domes

It could be said that the 20th century was birthed in oil, christened by a fount of green, then black, muck that shot out of a coastal Texas salt dome on a January morning in 1901. The roar that accompanied its route from the ancient depths could be heard in Beaumont, two miles away. Townspeople thought something had exploded and, looking toward the sound's source, saw the 200-foot plume that announced the arrival of Spindletop, the world's first viable gusher and the true beginning of the age of oil. In one moment the entire daily output of U.S. oil tripled. It would take nine days to cap the monster well "with a firmly-anchored valve," while nearly a million barrels of oil spewed across the hillock.[11]

If the 20th century was really the American century, then historians will doubtless point to the breadth and depth of the natural resources that grace this country's landscape from ocean to ocean. But it's the drive to see what's on the other side of the horizon, to explore and test ourselves that is also an American characteristic. When Thomas Jefferson sent Lewis and Clark on that first land voyage to see what they could see, he perhaps set in motion a tendency to quest that became part of our national DNA.

In 1978 author William Least Heat Moon set out to recover from a divorce and found himself in a long meditation that carried him in his humble van across the so-called blue highways that cross the American landscape from coast to coast. "As a nation there are few things that draw us more strongly than a piece of roadway heading to we know not where," he said later. "This is the way we grow up. This is the way that we enter our history—get in a car and find the country."[12]

Our history became entwined not only with the car and the rite of passage it enabled but the hydrocarbons that ran it and our industries. Together, oil, coal and natural gas became our energy spine. The American lifestyle is what rising nations want—and are increasingly getting. That freedom and access to the material things that make up the western good life are driving the growth of China and India who today compete with the same resources we have long taken for granted as cheap and instantly available. The truth is that if the rest of the world used the world's resources at the rate that the U.S. does, it would require three planets to accommodate them. Today U.S citizens and industries use six times as much of what is out there as the next most developed nation. But it's a party that won't accommodate another round of such ecological hedonism.

One of the big drawbacks to our strategy of putting all of our energy eggs in a big oily basket is that this substance that keeps Western civilization up and running is disappearing. "Our lifestyle, our entire world-wide modern civilization is possible only because we're rapidly using up a 300-million year old nonrenewable resource: ancient sunlight, principally in the form of oil, but also coal and gas."[13]

OIL AND THE OPEN ROAD

Today Americans drive more than 240 million cars. When Ram Dass chose the title *Be Here Now*, he might have been describing the state of being that accompanies the American driver alone, behind the wheel of a car on a road never before traveled. It is at once a skill in action, an adventure, and a leap of faith. We are gifted as no other country with a travelscape more than 3,000 miles wide, that is crisscrossed with more than three million miles of roads from coast to coast. The American open road is an adventure waiting to happen, an expanse that cannot be crossed by car in less than several days. It awaits our exploration as the unspoken birthright of every citizen. In our little (and not so little) metal tubes shooting down a superslab highway at speeds that might have given our pioneer ancestors the bends, we can enter its larger or lesser paths, zone out and disappear—at least for a time.

Like Lewis and Clark before us, we quest, striking out for what Thomas Jefferson called the *terra incognita* of our own lives, finding our inner selves the way no one else quite can. It is our national meditation, the response to an endless curiosity about what's out there. In *Song of the Open Road*, Walt Whitman said the lure of the road is about testing yourself on your own, tasting freedom, experiencing first hand how seeing outside of you changes what's inside of you. It is a kind of curiosity that he called "the profound lesson of reception." Listening, it turns out, is also an activity of the eyes.

Two years after Spindletop came in, exactly 100 years after Lewis and Clark began what could be called the first American road trip, a 31-year-old retired physician named Horatio Nelson Jackson made a similarly critical imprint on our national DNA. Over drinks at the posh San Francisco University Club, he bet a friend $50 that he would be the first person to drive from San Francisco to New York and he would do it within ninety days. It was not a task to take lightly. At that time the only real coast-to-coast conveyances other than shoe leather and horseback were the exceedingly slow stagecoach which could take three months, or the transcontinental railroad, which could do the job nicely within a week or less. But these were passive tours, and Jackson and the others who followed him were the first to set out on the road simply because the automobile offered them the freedom to do just that.

It was a perilous journey, one in which Jackson's car, a slightly used cherry red Winton with neither windscreen nor roof, broke down with great regularity, forcing the erstwhile adventurer to wait days at a time for parts to arrive by the more reliable alternatives, the train and stagecoach. But Jackson's original 90-day estimate provided more than enough time. He arrived in lower Manhattan, along with his chauffeur/ mechanic Sewall Crocker and bulldog companion Bud, in the wee hours of July 26, 1903, a mere 65 days after he set out.

In short order others set out to break his record. The open road became an American fever, despite the fact that finding gasoline was a daily hunt, camping out and cooking were the most likely amenities, mechanics were nowhere to be found (blacksmiths made most car repairs) and there were virtually no navigable roads or maps to follow. Getting lost was part of the package.

Of the 2.3 million miles of roadway that existed in the first decade of the 20th century, a paltry 150 miles were actually paved and those all lay within city limits. Another 190,000 miles were surfaced with stone, gravel, shells, clay, bricks or bituminous. The rest were really rural dirt paths, often full of rocks and ruts, used most often by horses, wagons, and livestock traffic. To get across ravines, lakes and bridges, early automobile travelers followed stagecoach routes and railroad tracks and used bridges and trestles built by the railroads.

That started to change as automobile manufacturers and suppliers began to see the wisdom of creating a highway system that could accommodate their products and fix them firmly into the American mainstream. In Indianapolis, on Memorial Day in 1911, an automotive entrepreneur and racing enthusiast named Carl Fisher was celebrating the opening day of his new motor speedway. More than 80,000 residents had paid $1 each to watch the new phenomenon, a 500-mile car race around a 2.3-mile oval surfaced with more than three million paving bricks. This was the debut production of what would become a fixture on the American scene that announced the beginning of summer. It is now known as the Indianapolis 500.

Fisher had a passion for both automobiles and speed and he was a born promoter. As both a headlamp manufacturer and a car dealership owner, he saw the necessity of an infrastructure that would enable the new automobile industry to continue to grow. In 1913 he began to promote the building of what would become the country's first transcontinental "rock highway," the Lincoln Highway, stretching from Times Square in New York to Lincoln Park in San Francisco. He began raising the estimated ten million dollars required for its construction from private donations, including highly publicized checks from Theodore Roosevelt, Thomas Edison, and then President Woodrow Wilson.

Perhaps Fisher's greatest promotion sealed the future for the American automobile when he convinced the U.S. Army to follow the Lincoln Highway (at that time primarily composed of still unimproved paths) on its first transcontinental motor convoy in 1919.

The convoy had originally been dreamed up as a multi-purpose exercise. More than 50,000 American servicemen had died during the single year that America had been in the war and half a million more Americans had succumbed to the ravages of an influenza pandemic. The trip was meant to get people's minds off their worry and grief and show off the new Army's modern look. Given that three million soldiers were being mustered back into the population, it was also meant to encourage recruitment. Lastly, it was part war game. After seeing what it took to haul men and materials across Europe, the U.S. Army wanted to see how well our own military could do if we had to fight a foreign aggressor in our own land, using existing roads and bridges, sustaining itself as it went. It also wanted to see how the Army's new vehicles would function in "wartime" conditions.

Historically, this road trip was of particular importance because of one of its staff observers. Having missed action in the recent war and feeling trapped and bored in what he feared would be a post-war letdown, Lt. Colonel Dwight Eisenhower volunteered to join as one of more than a dozen War Department observers who would submit a report on the convoy.

As it set off from Washington, D.C. on July 7, 1919, it was an instant success and a curiosity. Nobody had ever seen anything quite like the entourage. Spread out along a two-mile procession were 81 vehicles, including two trucks that carried spare parts, another that served as a blacksmith shop, two tankers carrying 750 gallons of gasoline apiece, a third carrying the same amount of water, motorcycles, staff cars for officers, five ambulances and kitchen trailers, a tractor, a 3-million candlepower searchlight, a pontoon for floating large vehicles across rivers, and a monster vehicle with a wench on it called the Militor which pulled men and machinery out of every conceivable mishap and many no one had imagined.

In each spot on the map that the convoy stopped for the night, newspapers trumpeted the convoy's arrival and wrote glowing stories after its departure. Thousands of townspeople showed up to cheer its entrance and bid it farewell when it moved along its way. It was a slow trip. The roads were evenly awful, only slightly improved since Horatio Jackson's days. There were no road signs, no means of direction, no way to know where you were or even if you were headed toward the town you imagined (and hoped) was ahead.

There were plenty of object lessons. Most of the mechanics were not only green recruits, they had never worked on engines before and had to learn as they went. The worn and narrow bridges often could not accommodate the heavy tanks and collapsed. The Army reengineered them and moved on, a boon for the fledging highway project. Heat and cold, rain and sandstorms plagued the trip, reinforcing the idea that these sorts of trips were hard enough in warm weather but would prove much more hazardous in colder conditions with fewer hours of daylight.

The single printed guide that served as the convoy's reference was written by previous adventurers who had driven the paths in their automobiles. The scout who led the convoy was one of this small stalwart group. Nobody else in the country knew the way. The convoy averaged five miles per hour during its two month sojourn. When at last it reached its destination, San Francisco, on the morning of September 6, 1919, the entourage that accompanied it had grown so large, it took over half an hour for it to pass any single spot on its parade route. The town bubbled over with joy and pride as the Pacific fleet, docked for the occasion, saluted the adventurers. The trip and its extreme challenges left a lasting impression on Eisenhower. The country required a highway infrastructure.

The Lincoln Highway that provided the beginnings of a thoroughfare from east to west early in the century was just the beginning. Twenty-five years later as commander of Allied forces in Europe, General Eisenhower was directing troop movements down the autobahn in Germany after D-Day and understood how Germany's modern highway system had enabled the Third Reich not only to successfully move troops and artillery throughout the country quickly, but even made possible (some would say impossible) a two-front war. This in turn convinced him that a robust highway system was essential for the U.S. The "ribbon of highways" he envisioned would connect city and countryside as never before, enabling faster, more interconnected commerce while providing seemingly endless growth opportunities.[14]

A dozen years later, as President, he would sign just such an all-encompassing law into effect, calling for a 41,000-mile network of superhighways that would take the next four decades to complete. And along the way it would seal America's post-war identity as a car-driving and oil-consuming nation.

Even now, we still feel the need to use the road trip to both demonstrate and celebrate the latest developments in road travel. In August 2008, the "Hydrogen Road Tour '08" set out from Portland, Maine on an 18-state coast-to-coast trip to advertise the virtues of hydrogen as a clean fuel alternative and to build enthusiasm for expanding the number of hydrogen stations in the U.S. As if to underscore the nascent movement's own shortcomings, the cars, represented by nine of the world's largest automobile manufacturers, at times had to be transported on flatbed trucks—running on traditional hydrocarbons—because of the lack of hydrogen stations. (Only two of the sixty such fueling stations in the U.S. are accessible to the public.) The longest dry stretch was from central Missouri to Albuquerque, a distance of 900 miles or nearly one-third of the 3,000 mile long trip. Like Horatio Jackson, the father of the American road trip, the transportation pioneers had to rely on the technology they hoped to replace to help them complete their journey.[15] All roads no longer lead to Rome, just to the next fueling spot along the way.

THE MERCHANTS OF LIGHT
Decades before Lewis and Clark set out on their road trip, Pennsylvania's Seneca Indians were showing settlers how to use the black gunk that seeped out of the ground in numerous spots to weatherproof their boots and canoes and even apply it to burned flesh, inflamed gums and saddle sores. The settlers dubbed it Seneca oil, which eventually evolved into the *snake oil* sold as a cure-all in the 1800s. Although the manufacturing rigors associated with the industrial revolution required more and more of the stuff to lubricate its machinery (lard had been dismissed as too

Road trips come to television

In the fall of 1960 an hour-long television drama, *Route 66,* premiered on CBS. Its two protagonists were young men in their twenties who wandered the country looking for adventure in a sharp new Corvette convertible. The route the show was named for was rarely mentioned and the characters often traveled far afield from it but the show's title spun off the hip song of the same name whose lyrics ticked off the cities from Santa Monica to Chicago that the road connected. It popularized the idea of the road trip taken for the sake of adventure and self discovery, opening the lens on what America looked like as a new social and political era got under way. While its storylines explored topics never discussed on television before (abortion, rape, and drug addiction among them), its constant change of scenery and rootless main characters presaged a decade of tempestuous change and started a national love affair with fast, sleek, cool cars. While it gave us a snapshot of who we were, it also celebrated the freedom and uniqueness of the American pioneer spirit, animated by the open road available to everyone with a car.

What the characters in *Route 66* gave voice to is as old as our history: our love affair with what lies out there, just down the road, over the horizon, in whatever shape it comes.

heat and friction intolerant), there was no other real widespread use for the sticky stuff, until a bright scientist figured out how to distill kerosene from it.

For a country that had to make do with the feeble light afforded by candle tallow after the sun went down, having the ability to light up a room with a single bright lamp catapulted kerosene, "the light of the age," to prominence not just as an illuminant but as a potential commodity market. The challenge to entrepreneurs was this: how would a clever speculator find enough of this stuff to satisfy the public's growing demand, then get it out of the ground and transport it to market?

Such was the thinking of the first known American oil speculator, George Bissell, a dissatisfied school superintendent, self-taught lawyer and linguist. While traveling through western Pennsylvania on a train he saw people harvesting oil from seeps and oil ponds. He knew that kerosene was distilled from oil and that salt miners often found oil before they found salt. It followed that if you intentionally drilled with the same kind of drill used for salt, especially in this part of Pennsylvania, the odds were good that you would find oil. He quickly pitched his idea to some East Coast partners and convinced them that they could corner the kerosene market and get rich if they moved quickly.

One of Bissell's partners had struck up a conversation with a down-on-his-luck ex-railroad conductor named Edward Drake in the hotel they shared and the partner liked Drake's can-do attitude and recommended him for the job. Not only was Drake willing and available, as an ex-railroad employee, he could ride back and forth from Pennsylvania to New Haven, Connecticut for free. Drake accepted the job and prepared to venture to western Pennsylvania to secure the necessary land, find a spot and begin drilling. Bissell attached the title of Colonel to the front of Drake's name on the letters of introduction that went with him, in the hope that this bit of fakery would convey a measure of gravity and authority.

Shortly after he arrived in the spring of 1858, Colonel Edward Drake acquired a property with a known oil spring two miles from Titusville, Pennsylvania from which three to six barrels of oil were gathered daily by traditional methods: skimming the surface of the pool or laying out rags to soak up the oil, then wringing them out into buckets. Drake was at something of a loss because no one had ever drilled for oil before. But he followed Bissell's idea and set to work building a derrick and fashioning a steam engine to both pound the surface with a pole and pump the oil up.

After a year of Drake's failures, Bissell and his partners were growing impatient, then discouraged. In August of 1859, in despair and disgust, the Seneca Oil Company dispatched a final money order to the erstwhile Colonel, telling him to pay off his remaining bills and shut the enterprise down. But before the message and final funding arrived, Drake and his tiny crew hit paydirt, at 69.5 feet. The crude that ebbed to the top kept on coming, coaxed up by a simple water pump. At first Drake and his driller found buckets to decant the oil into, but it was coming up at the rate of twenty barrels per day, forcing the pair to scour the nearby town for whiskey barrels to store the oil. When those ran out, they built wooden vats.

Drake was experiencing a fact of life that went with success in the oil patch. Once you've got the oil coming up, you have to be prepared to store, market and transport it. In those days, this was a new dilemma. In no time, whiskey barrels cost twice as much as the oil they held. Within fifteen months of Drake's discovery, seventy-five oil leases dotted the hillsides around Titusville with derricks. By the end of the Civil War six years later, Pittsburgh would claim fifty-eight oil refineries, Cleveland thirty. Besides Pennsylvania, oil was being discovered in West Virginia, New York, Ohio, Colorado and California. The first oil boom was on.

In the four decades before Spindletop, the focal point of the oil industry was acquiring and transporting oil for the purpose of distilling kerosene. The country's first "oil patch" was not only perfectly suited for kerosene production because of the kind of oil it produced, it was also confined largely to the eastern part of the United States. John D. Rockefeller, the founder of Standard Oil, controlled every phase of the business, from production at the well head to delivering and marketing the final product to the customer. In beginning of the 1870s, Standard controlled 10 percent of all refining capacity in US. By the beginning of the 1880s it controlled 90 percent.

Rockefeller's giant refineries produced one-fourth of the world's kerosene, all of which his company transported in their proprietary barrels via their own fleet of ships. His workforce was twice the size of the entire U.S. Army. Eventually his monopoly of the business would result in the antitrust suit that would break up the huge company, but Rockefeller was still the richest man in the U.S. thanks to "the light of the ages."[16] (In 1998, two of the companies split up by the Standard Oil antitrust suit would join again to become ExxonMobil, the world's largest private oil company.)

Superlatives seemed destined to follow this wild new industry. Fortunes were made and lost overnight. After Drake's find and the mad dash to create other oil leases followed, overproduction drove prices from $40 a barrel to ten cents a barrel. In Pithole, near Titusville, a 500-day boom ensued. Within that timespan the town went from an anonymous dot on the map to a growing urban concern with banks, telegraph offices, businesses and more than fifty hotels. As the oil fields were beset by swarms of locust-like oil crews, the oil quickly dried up and the boom turned to bust. A $2 million plot of land bought in 1865 sold for $4.37 a dozen years later.[17]

But the sheer scale of the 1901 Spindletop discovery dwarfed everything that preceded it. Unlike the daily output of the eastern oil wells that together brought in 2,500 barrels per day, Spindletop brought in from 75,000 to 100,000 barrels a day. When cynics told the two brothers who had been drilling the well that their find was a fluke, the story goes that they drilled three more and got the same output from them. Within three months, the town's population had tripled. Excursion trains brought the curious by the thousands on any given Sunday. By the end of the year, more than 200 wells were operating under the ownership of a hundred different oil companies.[18] From those oil fields arose the oil giants Gulf Oil and Texaco.

A string of big strikes followed In Texas, Louisiana and Oklahoma, where the massive Glenn pool was discovered near Tulsa in 1905, making that state the leader in oil production in the southwest for the next 27 years, when the vast East Texas oil fields, 45 miles long and as wide as ten miles in places, were discovered in the 1930s in a little town called Kilgore. Dwarfing Spindletop and rivaling the Saudi fields yet to be worked, the oil pumped from these fields daily topped half a million barrels. Derricks were built practically on top of one another. Oil seemed to be everywhere, even beneath the terrazzo floor of the Kilgore National Bank which in short order shuttered its doors and became another derrick site.[19]

What made these oil discoveries in the American southwest so significant was not just their size or number but the fact that while its oil—the characteristic light sweet crude—was not really fit for making kerosene, it was considered perfect for fuel oil. The discovery of its many veins came at an opportune juncture. This type of oil would be poised to quench the devouring thirst of a nascent automobile industry and it would enable the rise of the United States as a superpower. Its rise as a commodity would also parallel the demise of its parent industry, kerosene, as a new form of light arrived that would change human culture forever.

THE BIRTH OF THE ENERGY AGE

At the same time that kerosene speculators were making and losing fortunes and helping to transform little hamlets into boomtowns, another source of energy was being harnessed simultaneously by many gifted minds, most notably in America by an inventor in New Jersey who would eventually hold more than 1,000 patents, among them the phonograph, the stock ticker, the first commercial fluoroscope, an early motion picture camera and the carbon microphone which was used in Bell telephone receivers until the 1980s. The face of the country and eventually the world was about to be given the power to dispel the dark in an instant.

While kerosene was becoming widely accessible and created a much brighter light than candles could, by 1879 Thomas Alva Edison had perfected the incandescent bulb, combining a long-lasting carbon filament in a vacuum glass tube that would burn for hundreds of hours, making it not only a vast improvement over kerosene but a commercially viable venture for his own ambitions. Within three years he had formed the first publicly owned electric utility, the Edison Electric Illuminating Company. After supervising the implementation of the earliest U.S. utility infrastructure, Edison oversaw a dramatic demonstration that would whet the public's appetite for electricity as he lit up 59 homes in an area in lower Manhattan, near his Pearl Street generating station.

It was the beginning of the age of harnessed power and the end of the age of kerosene. Electricity was quickly recognized as a safer, more dependable form of illumination than kerosene which had claimed many lives from fires and suffocation. It surely dawned on some petroleum magnates that, although it would take decades to put the infrastructure for widespread electricity in place, if their lamp markets disappeared, petroleum might be consigned to merely providing lubrication for machinery.

But that was not to be. Through a synchronistic turn of events, the man who helped give the petroleum industry a new lease on life was in fact the chief engineer at Edison's own electric utility company who had helped enable that first dramatic demonstration that lit up a piece of the New York skyline for the first time. For if Edison seemed to put the future of petroleum on the skids by inventing a light that made kerosene redundant, the engineer, a visionary inventor named Henry Ford, was on fire with ideas that would transform the culture by putting the freedom to move distances at will within the reach of the working class. Although the early 20th century offered a dizzying number of automotive choices to a curious public, Ford probably did more than any single individual to help launch the era of the automobile and with it establish the markets for the fuel that ran it during the era of oil.

Steam-driven engines and vehicles had been seen as early as 1769, when Nicholas Joseph Cugnot's "Steam wagon" was invented as a transport vehicle for the French Army. The Stanley Steamer was in great demand briefly in the first decade of the 20th century and a Stanley model would set the speed record for a steam-driven car in 1906 (127 mph).

A few years before, in 1899, French inventor Camille Jenatzy reached speeds of 65 mph in his electric car, *Jamais Content.*

But the 20th century market belonged to the internal combustion engine and the automobiles it would power. Steam engines could take a half hour or more to heat up enough to generate the pressure needed to move their pistons (and passengers had to sit uncomfortably above the hot steam engines) and electric cars had a limited range. This made them perfect as taxis and trolley cars but less modern than the automobiles powered by the gasoline guzzling third option, the internal combustion engine.

When Daimler and Benz introduced their first automobile in 1895, fuel was hard to find and the machines themselves were louder, dirtier and more difficult to drive and maintain than either steam or electric cars. Nonetheless they appealed to the public's new demand for speed, mobility and access to the open spaces, no matter how often they broke down, or how poor and scant the available roadways were. The gasoline-powered automobile quickly became the dominant conveyance preferred by the public. In 1900 car registrations in the U.S. numbered 8,000. By 1912, there were 902,000. By 1920 they were over nine million.[20]

Henry Ford got the idea for the assembly line from an employee who had toured a Chicago slaughterhouse and noted how quickly and efficiently the animals were dispatched, then moved down a conveyor belt to be cleaned, divided and packaged for market. Although he initially offered Models N and S after opening his first plant in Detroit, it was the Model T and its successor, the Model A, that made Ford's fortune.

The Model T was the most popular car of its day. In October, 1913, the Ford plant in Highland Park, Michigan began implementing the moving assembly line. Before that change, it had taken more than twelve hours to assemble a car. With the new process, a car rolled off the line in one hour and thirty-three minutes. The assembly line was really a series of subassemblies of interchangeable parts, each created prior to everything being connected to the main chassis. The era of mass production was underway.

The shorter assembly time allowed Ford to cut costs and over time make its Model T affordable to a much wider market. By the time Ford retired it from production in 1927, more than 15 million had been sold. Little changed on the Model T during its heyday. The idea of different looks for each model year had not yet sunk in as a marketing device. However, as sales on the Model T began to sink, Ford shut down production for six months and replaced the Model T with the Model A, which was built in Michigan's Rouge plant from 1927-1931 and sold four million.

Starting in 1914, Ford shocked Wall Street and the rest of the auto industry by mandating a higher wage for his workers, enough so that they could afford to buy the product they helped to make. Ford not only paid his workers $5 a day (the going wage was less than half that) after six months, but by 1926 he had also shortened the work week to five eight-hour days. His reason: he wanted his workers to get in their cars and get out and enjoy the countryside.

The American middle class and the dream that accompanied had been born.

As America moved into the Depression-era 1930s, the automobile industry breathed life into a staggering economy. It was easy to see why automobile manufacturing was such a boon to industry. By 1930 there were 23.1 million cars in the United States and they used lots of resources and, in some cases, substantial amounts of entire sectors. One analyst pointed out that automobile manufacturing had "doubled iron consumption, tripled the use of plate glass, quadrupled the use of rubber."[21] The world had never seen its like. It was the personification of a growth market. As a sheer consumer of raw materials it had no equal in the modern world.

CHANGING THE FACE OF WAR

Oil was becoming more important in areas other than the automotive industry. It was clearly the form of energy drawing the eyes of international industry. In 1901 the Santa Fe Railroad which had run on coal—the previous century's golden child—had one oil-driven locomotive. By 1905, it had 227. Having ready access to it was also becoming a national security issue. In 1908, Great Britain, acting on the advice of Winston Churchill (who had been nervously observing the increasing military might of Germany), mandated that the Royal Navy convert from coal to oil and began the building the first of its five battleships that would run on oil.

Fearful of the growing strength of Germany's navy, Britain began to keep a presence in the Middle East to ensure ready access to oil, much like the American Navy Fifth fleet does today in the Persian Gulf.[22] The country started the Anglo Persian Oil Company (later called British Petroleum), in which it held a 51 percent interest, making it the first state-owned oil venture.

Two Swedish armaments manufacturers, Ludwig and Alfred Nobel came to the Russian port city of Baku in Azerbaijan and brought oil refinery equipment, quickly becoming the premier group in the Russian oil industry. In 1901, when Spindletop instantly tripled America's oil output, the oilfields in Baku were turning out more than 200,000 barrels of oil per day, more than 95 percent of the entire country's oil and half of the world's total oil. Four years later as the Russian Revolution came into full swing, oil field workers in Baku, hearing the speeches of Joseph Stalin, revolted, setting fire to the vast oil fields, marking the first time that political conflict had interrupted the flow of oil.[23]

World War I was the first war run on oil. Motorcycles, troop transports, mobile ambulances and tanks all became part of the war machinery. For the first time, airplanes made three-dimensional reconnaissance possible and introduced aerial bombing and combat. Early in the war, when the German offensive came close to Paris, the entire taxi fleet was pressed into service to usher French troops to the front and save the city.[24]

After the war, oil began moving to the center of industry, growing more important to the production of food as agriculture began relying on oil to speed up transportation to markets. Due in large measure to the output at Henry Ford's plants, by 1929 the U.S. was manufacturing 75 percent of the cars in the world. In America alone, there were nearly 23 million cars on the roads.

While Germany had made a push to capture the Baku oil fields in 1918 and failed, these vast quantities of crude were also a key component in Hitler's thinking as he mapped out his plans to conquer Europe less than two decades later. Oil loomed more and more important as a resource. The machinery of war now officially ran on its products. Germany had virtually no petroleum and consequently was forced to import most of what it needed from the Western hemisphere, but it had vast amounts of coal, still the source of 90 percent of its energy by the late 1930s.

It was with this in mind that Hitler blessed the project of scientists at I.G. Farben who in 1926 had bought the patent rights to a process that turned coal into a synthetic fuel. The Farben executives who met with Hitler in 1932 were looking for a patron for their process, which although promising, remained very expensive. The idea ignited Hitler's imagination. Here was a way for him to replace oil as fuel for his planned war machinery.

Japan also had no natural petroleum resources and before World War II actually got 80 percent of its oil from the US. In 1931 Japan invaded Manchuria on its way to commandeer the natural resources of Asia, including the oil-rich area then known as the Dutch East Indies (now Indonesia) whose vast reserves were already spoken for by Dutch, American and British petroleum interests (from which Shell Oil would eventually emerge).

In June 1941, six months before the Japanese struck Pearl Harbor, Germany invaded Russia to attempt once again to secure the Baku oil fields. Both Axis powers saw how critical a part oil would play in fueling their navies, air forces and ground forces. To their thinking, the earlier these fuel supplies were seized, the better.

The attack on Pearl Harbor was an essential first step in securing the oil Japan would need to fuel its war machinery. With the U.S. Navy out of the way, it would have unfettered access to the oil fields in the Dutch East Indies.

But America's response was as quick and overwhelming as our access to our own oil. On one island in the Pacific theater of operations, 120,000 barrels were delivered per day. The entire Japanese air force in all its military theaters used only about 20,000 barrels per day. "So on this one island alone, six times as much oil was being delivered by the Americans as the Japanese air force was consuming everywhere." Oil was so abundant in the Pacific theater of operations that it was sprayed on the island roads to hold down the choking dust.[25]

To accommodate this massive effort and the billions of barrels of oil it would require, a $95 million 1500-mile pipeline was built in a little over a year, stretching from the west Texas oilfields to the eastern seaboard where a steady supply of oil was loaded and sent overseas.

As the war progressed into its final stages, Germany's synthetic fuel needs grew larger. More plants were needed and eventually concentration camp workers were recruited to complete them. By the closing months of the war, these plants had become the focus of nearly 100 American bomber missions. Germany was getting 90 percent of its fuel from them and by the time the bombing campaign was over, the fuel supplies that the

German air force relied on had been reduced to less than one-fourth of one percent of what was needed. Before the end of the war, the Germans had managed to develop a small (three plane) jet air force, but before one took off, it had to be hauled by cows to the runway to save the fuel that would have been required to taxi.[26]

By the end of the war, the allies controlled 86 percent of the world's oil supply. The Japanese resorted to running their jeeps on charcoal and using pine root for airplane fuel. A single roundtrip mission required 100,000 roots. One effective solution was the kamikaze, the suicide pilot who only needed fuel for the first half of the mission. Deadly efficient, kamikazes managed to do with a single plane what might otherwise have required several fighters—and much more fuel—to achieve.

Oil even had a direct effect on the ends of the lives of the vanquished leaders. Rather than surrender, Tojo shot himself but botched the job. The American military who had come to arrest him called for an ambulance but none of the available vehicles had any gas. Eventually Tojo was taken to a hospital in time to save him from his wounds. After he recovered, he was executed. Inside his bunker at the Reich Chancellery, a defeated Adolf Hitler shot himself in the right temple. His personal SS bodyguards doused his body with gasoline and set it on fire.[27]

Gas rationing ended in the United States within 24 hours after the end of the war was declared. The good times rolled again in earnest. Plenty would enter the American diet: beef, pork, sugar, chocolate, flour, milk, and eggs were all available again. Slowly, so was steel. The American car industry, which had quickly retooled after Pearl Harbor to build war armaments, began to return to post-war production after a two-year hiatus.

FUELING THE POST-WAR BOOM

After the war, oil and the automobile changed the landscape of the country. By the 1950s, suburban America exploded, becoming the dream of the growing middle class. The world around American cities flattened out and spread in every direction, with roads covering the country like a million threads. And with it came a mobile support structure: drive-in movies, drive-in eateries, drive-in cleaners, even drive-in churches, as well as motels, truck stops, billboards, and a new full-fledged industry: tourism.

As the 1940s ended and the cold war began to heat up between the U.S. and the Soviet Union, the need to keep the oil flowing was increasingly an American security issue. In the 1950s Iran booted out British Petroleum and nationalized its oil, taking all of BP's assets, including the world's largest refinery. Fearing that the oil would eventually go to the USSR, the CIA and Britain's MI6 staged a coup, installing the Shah in 1954. Likewise, American fears that the USSR might take over the vast Saudi oil fields (for which engineers and U.S. oilmen had negotiated drilling rights) resulted in expanding influence there from Aramco and its original partners SoCal (today's Chevron), Texaco and others.

At the end of World War II, the industrial base of the U.S. was guzzling oil and life was good. New oil-based products began to fly out of the hundreds of new businesses that began to take form. Besides its uses for fuel and heating oil, a cornucopia of other products began to emerge: plastics, synthetic rubber and fiber, asphalt, fertilizers, pesticides, clothing, paint, detergent, medicine, food additives, makeup, dyes, candles, and thousands of subcategories within these. Oil was being woven into every fabric of the American lifestyle.

In 1945 U.S. oil consumption was at 6 MBPD (million barrels per day). By 1955, the number of passenger cars in the U.S. had reached 48 million and oil consumption rose to 8.45 MBPD.[28] By 1955 Americans were using fully one-third of all the energy produced in the world. Some of this was due to American consumption of gasoline but much of it was due to the post-war explosion of business and industry infrastructure.[29]

By 1960, we had so much excess oil, we were the Saudi Arabia of the oil world, producing one of every three barrels pumped worldwide and pumping out six barrels for every one barrel we used. At the same time we wanted to secure our relationships with other oil holders, so the US agreed to "offer military protection in exchange for drilling rights for US companies."[30]

That same year the Organization of the Petroleum Exporting Countries, called OPEC, met for the first time. In October 1973, as the Yom Kippur war began between Israel and Egypt, OPEC members were still arriving at Vienna's Intercontinental Hotel to begin negotiations about where to set the price of oil. As the tide of the war went against Israel, the U.S. sent in military aid, infuriating the OPEC members. When the group met again in Kuwait, they voted a substantial increase in price as well as a cut in production. The result in the west was chaos and panic. Not only did gas prices rise 40 percent almost overnight, but gas supplies quickly dried up. Lines at gas stations stretched for blocks. For the first time since World War II, controls were put on the amount of gas you could buy and sometimes the days you could buy it.

For Americans used to having easy access to all the cheap gas they wanted anytime they wanted it, this was a sobering moment. For the first time, America as a 20th century imperial power was being challenged by an outside force—and suddenly it was uncomfortably clear that the most basic elements of our culture, our lifestyles and prosperity had become dependent on the whims of others. What had once made us strong had become our greatest vulnerability.

In 1977, after just three months in office, Jimmy Carter became the first American president to raise the public awareness of how our dependency on oil was jeopardizing our security and our way of life. We were using more oil than we could produce and our energy fate was being increasingly handed over to the whims of other countries, most of which didn't particularly like us. We had, he told us, used twice as much oil in the 1950s as we did in the 1940s and twice as much in the 1960s as we did in the 1950s. In each of those decades more oil was consumed than in all of history combined.

But no one wanted to listen.

In Alaska, BP, Arco, and Exxon were rushing to develop the huge reserves discovered underneath the North Slope; in the North Atlantic, the large fields of the North Sea were up for grabs and a feeding frenzy ensued, with the U.K. and Norway eventually wresting control over most of the oil and gas reserves. OPEC continued trying to find the perfect price point that would keep prices, supply and demand in balance.

In 1988, the eight-year long Iraq-Iran war ended in a draw but it had been hugely costly for Saddam Hussein who tried to get Kuwait to forgive Iraq's war debts. Kuwait declined. Needing money to stem the tide of loss and debt, Hussein invaded Kuwait in the morning hours of August 2, 1990. Fearing that he would move into nearby Saudi Arabia (and some say, giving the U.S. an opportunity to establish a military base on Saudi soil), the U.S. led a coalition of forces into Kuwait in February 1991. In 100 hours the Iraq army had been routed and vanquished. In defeat, Hussein gave orders to set fire to the Kuwaiti oil fields.

But no one knows how far reverberations go or where consequences end. On a cool, crisp Tuesday morning in September 2001, eighteen young men, 15 of them Saudis, commandeered four commercial aircraft on the American east coast, crashing two into the World Trade Center towers in the financial district of New York City, a third into the Pentagon and the fourth into a field in Pennsylvania. Armed with cheap box cutters and knives, the young men were disciples of Osama bin Laden, an Arab prince who had vowed vengeance in response to U.S. presence on Saudi soil since the first Gulf war.

The quest for oil has come full circle. In just over fifty years, the U.S. went from being the world's oil well to being incapable of supplying itself with more than 30 percent of its own daily oil needs. In that same time period, as our domestic oil supplies shrank, our auto ownership soared from 48 million in 1955 to 240 million in 2009 or a 500 percent increase in autos as our domestic supplies available to run them shrank by 66 percent.

Although the U.S. is still third in world production behind Russia and the Middle East, in 2010 it depends on the Middle East, Central and South America and Canada for nearly 70 percent of the 21 million barrels of oil it uses each day—14 million of which go to keeping our cars, trucks, buses, boats, motorcycles and scooters running—to feed the fierce energy-consuming mouths of its population and industries.

EMERGING UNCOMFORTABLE TRENDS

As America was discovering its post-war embarrassment of riches and enjoying its greatest period of prosperity in the 1950s, some interesting conundrums began to rumble through the culture. A geologist for Shell Oil named M. King Hubbert predicted that the domestic oil we were awash in was in fact running out and would hit its peak (the halfway mark in its total consumption) by 1971. This was complicated by the fact that our growing population would be requiring increasingly more oil with increasingly depleting supplies to answer their needs.

Deriders pointed to our uncanny productivity and our firm alliances with other oil producing countries. The United States was basically the Saudi Arabia of the world. Our oil fields, though less robust, still supplied one out of every seven barrels produced worldwide. During the war we had contributed six of the seven billion barrels required to defeat the Axis powers. And we were building deep infrastructure and protection agreements in the Arab world to ensure we would have access to their oil as well, just in case.

But it wasn't just about supply and access to oil as a resource anymore. Other voices were being heard. Besides oil industry prophets like Hubbert, writers like Rachel Carson and Aldo Leopold were making an out-of-touch public aware of the toxic effects that the chemical compounds of industrialization were having on the planet. When we poison the earth, they said, we ultimately poison ourselves.

But as lines were drawn on different sides of these issues, the growing messages of dissent took decades to take hold. Meanwhile the Department of Energy yearly reports duly showed that, as Hubbert had predicted, U.S. oil production had indeed peaked in 1970 and has declined ever since.[31] The first oil crisis in 1973 did put panic into the national heart when we visualized for the first time what life without easy access to oil might be like. But still nothing happened.

By 1974 we were importing 35 percent of our energy needs.

Through the decade, a paradox began to emerge: the U.S. was becoming "an economic and military giant whose lifeblood was controlled in other parts of the world."[32]

During his single term in office, President Carter gave five energy speeches, trying to enlist the aid and interest of the public as part of a first-tier response to changing our hydrocarbon-laden way of life. Wearing a cardigan sweater during the first of these televised speeches, he assured us that we still had time, but there was no time to waste. We needed to begin now to reverse our usage habits, start searching for fuel alternatives and start practicing more energy conservation. Turn down the thermostats in the winter, he said, and up in the summer.

He modeled what he was talking about. He had solar hot water panels installed on the White House roof, ordered thermostats with controlled minimum and maximum temperatures installed in government buildings and had a wood stove added in his living quarters. He created a cabinet level Department of Energy and began to fund the fledgling solar and wind alternative energy industries. Between 1977 and 1982, U.S. dependency on foreign oil imports fell by 50 percent. This in turn helped swamp the world with oil by the mid-1980s and resulted in not only a weakened OPEC but facilitated the fall of the Soviet Union, which had overextended itself with more ramped up infrastructure investment than it could then manage. "As a result," said Yegor Gaidar, director of the Institute for Economies in Transition in Moscow, "the Soviet Union lost approximately $20 billion per year, money without which the country simply could not survive."[33]

Calling the effort to conserve "the moral equivalent of war" Carter set the tone for his administration by implementing the first CAFÉ

(Corporate Average Fuel Economy) standards for automobiles, which mandated an established fuel efficiency minimum (measured in miles per gallon in city and highway driving) that manufacturers had to meet for new cars and trucks. That in turn sparked a surge of interest in saving energy and the commercial world fell into step. As mpg information began to show up on the windows of new cars, energy efficiency estimates began to show up on consumer goods. Everything from automobile and toy batteries to washers, dryers and building insulation became more efficient. We also learned an important lesson: that heightened efficiency gave us more service without a loss of performance, and as an added bonus, often saved us money. Between 1978 and 1985 CAFÉ standards for cars went from 18 mpg to 27.5 mpg where they stayed until 2007 when President Bush signed a new law designed to raise car and truck standards to 35 mpg by 2020. (Fuel standards for light trucks went from 17.5 mpg in 1979 to 22.2 mpg in 2007.) In May of 2009, President Obama raised the standards again to a combined 35.5 mpg by 2016 (42 mpg for cars, 26 mpg for trucks).

Carter had reason to be concerned. Storm clouds had begun to appear on the horizon. By 1977, the year of that first speech and only six years after the U.S. hit peak oil, 98 percent of our imported oil came from OPEC or Persian Gulf suppliers. For the next eight years, although our rate of consumption continued to climb, our imports from OPEC and the Persian Gulf decreased steadily as we found other suppliers and conservation and higher energy efficiency in cars, appliances, heating and cooling systems and building materials became more commonplace. In 1986 the percentage began to rise again. In 2009, the amount of our total imports was close to 70 percent (although U.S. consumption in general had begun to slow slightly). We count on other countries, many of which don't like us very much, for more than 14 of the 21 MBPD we use to keep our country and its population running.

Of his five energy speeches, perhaps the most famous was nicknamed the "malaise" speech in which he set the stage for what would actually ensue after his only term ended. When morning dawned in America under the Reagan administration in 1981, U.S. demand for foreign oil began to rise again. Conservation was regarded as weakness and with the help of a Democratic Congress, he was able to slash the budgets of the fledgling alternative energy projects and let the tax incentives for solar and wind start-up companies lapse (putting a serious damper on that financing for such ventures for years to come). Instead of America leading the way, Japanese and European firms enjoyed the fallout of this. When repairs to the White House roof made it necessary to remove the solar panels Carter had installed over the West Wing, the decision was made not to replace them.[34] Instead they were sent to Unity College in Maine where they heated hot water until they were retired in 2004.

In a speech made at the London Institute of Petroleum in 1999, then Halliburton Chairman Dick Cheney lamented the Sisyphean task that oil companies had faced for a century, that "Producing oil is obviously a self-depleting activity. Every year you've got to find and develop reserves equal to your output just to stand still, just to stay even. For the world as a whole, oil companies are expected to keep finding and developing enough oil to offset our seventy-one million plus barrel a day of oil depletion [in 2009 it was over 85 MBPD], but also to meet new demand. By some estimates there will be an average of two percent annual growth in global oil demand over the years ahead along with conservatively a three percent natural decline in production from existing reserves. That means by 2010 we will need on the order of an additional fifty million barrels a day."

And this was in the days before the growing resource appetites of China and India had begun to make headlines. Less than two years later, in April of 2001, Vice President Dick Cheney delivered a speech that did an about-face from that perception, setting the tone for the Bush Administration while mocking the attempts of previous administrations. "Conservation may be a sign of personal virtue, but it is not a sufficient basis for a sound, comprehensive energy policy," Cheney opined, when in fact it had been.[35]

It took less than twenty years to put an end to the high flying days when we were producing six times what we consumed. What Jimmy Carter—and Halliburton CEO Dick Cheney—had warned us about is now the situation in which we are mired. Our culture and lifestyles revolve around oil. It not only runs the machines which transport us on the land, sea and air, it's woven into every fabric of our society from pharmaceuticals, fertilizers and pesticides to the thousands of synthetic formulations on which we depend in every corner of industry and manufacturing.

WHAT WE USE

Today the pervasiveness of hydrocarbons in our culture is staggering. Each year every American uses:[36]

- 8,000 pounds of oil
- 4,700 pounds of natural gas
- 5,150 pounds of coal
- 1/10 pound of uranium (for nuclear power)

From 1977 to 1985, the economy grew 27%, oil use fell 17%, oil imports fell 50%, oil imports from the Persian Gulf fell 87% and it would have been gone if we'd kept that up one more year. That was with very old technologies and delivery methods. We could run that play a lot better now and yet we proved we have more market power than OPEC. Ours is on the demand side. We are the Saudi Arabia of megabarrels. We can use less oil faster than they can conveniently sell less oil.

—Amory Lovins, co-founder, Rocky Mountain Institute, from a February 2005 speech, *"We must win the oil endgame."*

THE PLOT THICKENS: GLOBAL PEAKING

Increasingly, the problem we are in is a global one. "In 1900 the world produced 150 million barrels of oil. In 2000 it produced 28 billion barrels, an increase of more than 180 fold."[37] Production figures are only half the story. What they don't tell you is how much we're using. One of the growing problems with oil is that since 1981 the nations of the earth are using a lot more than oil companies worldwide have been able to find. Globally three times as much oil is being used as there is new oil being discovered and experts agree that modern technology, including high resolution deep water scanning confirms there are no more major finds out there waiting to be found. In fact there have been no major oil field finds since 1962. (Oil discoveries like BP's 2009 Tiber find in the Gulf of Mexico would seem to disprove this but it is not yet commercially guaranteed. The oil—estimated at 3-4 billion barrels—is beneath 4100 feet of water and estimated dates for recovery are still speculative.[38])

In 2008 oil companies worldwide pumped 81.8 million barrels of oil out of the earth each day while the world consumed 84.45 million barrels per day. That means that consumption overran production by 967 million barrels—and that was during a year when high gas prices caused U.S. consumption to actually drop 475 million barrels for the year.[39]

So how is that deficit covered? By pulling from the total reserves in all the world's remaining oil fields. This is where the oil drama gets a little fuzzy because no one knows (or will admit) how much oil any one country really does or does not have. Persistent rumors abound that the Middle East is way overblown in its reports of the amount of oil it has. In general, most petroleum experts believe the globe's original total supply of oil was about two trillion barrels. What remains is roughly anywhere from 850 billion to about a trillion barrels, although some oil analysts insist the lower end of the range is actually much lower than that (some forecasts predict the real numbers are as much as 80 percent lower than reported statistics).

And that's if oil consumption remains stagnant which no one predicts it will. Increasingly, China is the elephant in the room nobody wants to talk about. Because of China's increase in demand since 2004, there are no longer any "shock absorbers" to allay sudden peaks in demand. These used to exist in the form of spare crude oil capacity, refining capacity, or discretionary oil product inventories. "These three reserves were the safety margins that the world oil market counted on. And year after year, as oil demand continued to increase at about 1 percent a year, these shock absorbers would absorb that gradual increase and ensure that prices went up only gradually—until 2004."[40]

That's when things really changed for the stability of the global oil supply. "At the start of 2004, the International Energy Agency predicted that global demand for crude oil would grow by 1.5 million barrels per day, that year. Instead," said Larry Goldstein, an oil industry expert from the Energy Policy Research Foundation, "it grew by three million barrels per day, and [demand in] China alone grew by over one million barrels a day," he said. [41]

At three million barrels a day, that's more than a billion additional barrels to add to what's already becoming a huge oil deficit. And that's the best case scenario *only if demand stagnates*. With the GNPs of China and India growing at their present rates, no oil futurist expects that scenario to go anywhere but south.

Another problem is that those first trillion barrels were what the industry calls the *easy oil*, from deep, vast wells that were easy to extract from. The rest, much of which exists in parts of the world where the

West is not well liked, including the Middle East and Russia, will not be so easy to get at. It's spread out in spots all over the globe, some deep under the sea, some well under ice masses in the Arctic. Even if the oil can be extracted there, which will be difficult enough, there are as yet no accessible storage facilities or close ports.

Energy industries point to the huge tar sand fields in Alberta, Canada and the giant oil shale reserves in the American west. The estimates of supplies for both of these are vast but problematic. They are not only grossly expensive to extract, they are something of an environmental nightmare. Producing tar sands, for example, requires not only massive amounts of water but large quantities of natural gas to separate out the oil and refine it. As an industry, tar sands create three times as much CO_2 as oil in its extraction and refining. Its burning produces a third more CO_2 than coal. It also takes two tons of tar sands to yield one barrel of oil. Broken down into a barrels-to-barrels ratio, this means it takes two barrels of equivalent fossil fuel energy from tar sands to create one barrel of oil. The mining and processing of tar sands also release sulfur dioxide, hydrogen sulfate, sulfuric acid mist and nitrogen oxide into the environment, at a minimum contaminating water, air and nearby wildlife.

Despite its inefficiency and environmental drawbacks, Canada's tar sands are becoming a significant part of the U.S. oil supply. Canada's proximity and reliability as an oil source is an easy sell compared to Saudi Arabia. In 2009 Canada provided 19 percent of America's total oil imports. Massive deposits of oil shale—estimates go as high as five times the proven oil reserves of Saudi Arabia—can be found mostly on federal lands in Utah (also home to deep reserves of tar sands), Colorado and Wyoming. Once thought too expensive to convert, as foreign oil sources become less accessible and more costly, harvesting this substance—also an environmental nightmare—is warranting heavy investments by the petroleum industry as a rich fallback resource.[42]

Because of its deeply ingrained place in our lifestyle, oil in America has long been the darling of our people and even when it wasn't, its defenders have stepped in and done what was necessary to keep it in its place at the top of the pedestal of the American lifestyle. During the Bush Administration, the oil and automobile industries had a tireless champion, helping to stave off moves toward cleaner, more efficient engines, which would have hit both industries hard. If mandated, such increased efficiencies would have meant costly manufacturing changes to the automobile manufacturers and begun, however slightly, to slow the driving public's per capita oil requirements.

But to the oil industry which saw its profits go up and down over the last uncertain decades before eventually hitting the stratosphere in 2008, conservation has long been a four-letter word. While the automobile industry was crashing in debt and moribund sales, it too, has historically been less than anxious to retool and change, especially since it had been enjoying a binge of profit from the SUVs and trucks it had been selling in record numbers from the 1990s until the middle of the first decade of the new century when rising prices at the pump began to change the public's car buying habits. The image of the CEOs from America's top three automakers testifying before Congress, in a direct appeal for funds as recession deepened into depression in the fall of 2008, was a jarring one.

CRACKS IN THE VENEER

Clearly, as hydrocarbon resources become scarcer and demand worldwide increases, bringing inevitably higher prices, something has to give. But that hasn't kept vested interests from fighting the coming trend or individual states from embracing the inevitable. While the state has long been teased for being "Lala land", its head in the clouds contemplating New Age truths, California has long been America's environmental canary in the coal mine, and as an early adapter of everything from organic farming to solar power to electric cars, it repeatedly shows the next possible future to the rest of the country. In 2007, Governor Arnold Schwarzenegger's goal to cut California's emissions to 1990 levels by 2010 was dealt a severe blow when he was told that he could not dictate a change in energy policy at the state level that involved tightening the laws on tailpipe emissions, which would have forced auto manufacturers to make more fuel-efficient cars.

Two days after Barack Obama became President, Schwarzenegger asked the new president to intercede in having the EPA reverse the decision made by the Bush administration which stated that only the federal government has the authority to do what California was trying to do itself: impose greenhouse gas standards for new cars, pickup trucks and sport utility vehicles. (The EPA did reverse the decision in June, 2009.[43]) This came under the purview, the administration claimed, of regulating fuel-efficiency standards, which is not a power granted to the states.

It was a first. In the forty years since California had been granted the right to obtain such waivers from Congress, the EPA had never before denied the state a waiver under the Clean Air Act.[44] Under that act, California is allowed to set stricter anti-pollution rules than the federal government, but it must get EPA approval to do so.

Oil is one.

COMING TO AN INHALATION NEAR YOU

Along with those 26 barrels of oil each of us use per year are some sobering statistics about what all those threads of meaning spell out at the other end of the tailpipe (petroleum) as well as the smokestack (coal). The bottom line is that between all of our uses of hydrocarbon to heat, transport and feed us, each American adds 6.6 tons of greenhouse gases (GHGs) into the atmosphere annually, part of the 6.2 billion tons that become a part of the underside of our atmospheric umbrella each year. Since the earth can absorb only about three billion tons a year, it's easy to see how all that extra CO_2 keeps making the future of our habitation on the planet harder and harder.[45]

Of the fossil fuel trio—oil, natural gas and coal—coal is by far the dirtiest and most toxic. While oil runs our cars and shows up in every phase of our food supply, natural gas figures in the widespread manufacture of fertilizer as well as heating and cooking. Coal fills in the considerable space that's left. It is the main source of electricity in our country, supplying more than half of our energy needs. It also is responsible for nearly a third of our country's GHG emissions. Burning coal not only emits CO_2 but a host of other toxins—mercury, sulphur dioxide, nitrogen oxide and particulate matter—all of which have been traced to creating and exacerbating respiratory ailments and heart disease as well as raising the risk of heart attacks and strokes. Not only do these contaminants pollute our air, they eventually settle back down on the earth, sinking into our water resources and contaminating our food supplies.[46]

Then there's also the coal ash by-product held in containment ponds near or around coal plants, which have a separate set of risks, especially when they fail. This is the reality that the citizens of Harriman, Tennessee awoke to on December 22, 2008, when a wall of the 40-acre containment pond that surrounded the Kingston Fossil Plant gave way, dumping a billion gallons of coal ash into the surrounding area. That flood not only buried parts of the town in lakes of toxic sludge but poured into the tributaries of the Tennessee River, the water supply for millions of people downstream in Tennessee, Alabama and Kentucky. In sheer volume, the Kingston spill is nearly 100 times greater than the amount of contaminant involved in 1989 when the Exxon Valdez ran aground and dumped eleven million gallons of oil into the fishing waters of Port William Sound in Alaska, polluting 1,200 miles of shoreline. No one can guess yet the literal and figurative downstream effects.

Overall, coal is looking less and less like a viable and intelligent energy source to trust into the future. Increasingly, it is being marginalized in an age that is growing tired of the environmental costs of our hydrocarbon-based energy system.

As John Passacantando, former executive director of the U.S. arm of Greenpeace said, "We don't really need companies grinding up mountains in West Virginia to get the coal out. It's not the way we want to create energy in the 21st century."[47]

While the figures are enough to make anyone's eyes cross, they cannot be ignored because they affect the other essential fuel that sustains us: the very air we pull into our lungs hundreds of times each hour. Increasingly, this oxygen is no longer life giving. In China alone, hundreds of thousands die each year from respiratory failure as a direct result of the toxins in the air. "In Beijing alone, 70 to 80 percent of all deadly cancer cases are related to the environment. Lung cancer has emerged as the No. 1 cause of death."[48] This is no mystery, considering that most of China's power is generated via highly inefficient and cheaply built coal plants. "Dirty" coal provides China with 70 percent of its energy and two new coal plants come online each week to keep up with demand.

Coal is cheap and plentiful in China and not likely to be replaced any time soon with a different energy form. But what happens in China doesn't just stay in China. According to the U.S. Environmental Protection Agency, on certain days 25 percent of the pollution in the skies over Los Angeles can be blamed on the air that migrates eastward across the ocean.[49] Like the air blowing east from China, other contaminants collect in other invisible but highly potent ways.

RAINFORESTS, OIL AND THE AIR WE BREATHE

Rainforests have been called the lungs of the earth. If that's so, then our global lungs are getting smaller and weaker. The way Mother Nature set it up, trees everywhere, but especially those in lush widespread rainforest, serve a critical purpose. They are our carbon sinks, their branches and leaves enabling the absorption of billions of tons of CO_2 that find their way into the atmosphere from manmade and natural sources. "Forests, especially in the lush tropics, suck and store carbon, which is released when trees are cut down or burnt."

To put it simply, when they inhale, they take in CO_2. What they exhale is our oxygen, minus the energy they have removed and used. More and more these carbon sinks are disappearing, mostly for economic reasons. In the Amazon and the forests of Indonesia (which together represent the regions that contain 81 percent of the world's rainforests), rushing to clear cut the valuable mahogany trees (also called "blood wood")

THE TOXINS AMONG US

In *Plan B 3.0*, Lester Brown, environmentalist and president of the Earth Policy Institute, describes the extent of much of this toxicity. He points to a July 2005 report by the Environmental Working Group and Commonweal on an analysis of umbilical cord blood from U.S. newborns. The test revealed a total of 287 chemicals in the blood of ten randomly selected newborns. "Of the 287 chemicals we detected...we know that 180 cause cancer in humans or animals, 217 are toxic to the brain and nervous system, and 208 cause birth defects or abnormal development in animal tests."[56]

Brown also reports that according to the WHO, airborne pollutants kill three million people worldwide annually, 70,000 of them in the United States, triple the number of Americans who die in automobile accidents.[57] Air and water pollution together damage the health of people all over the world. "A joint study by the University of California and the Boston Medical Center shows that some 200 human diseases, ranging from cerebral palsy to testicular atrophy, are linked to pollutants. Other diseases that can be caused by pollutants include an astounding 37 forms of cancer, plus heart disease, kidney disease, high blood pressure, diabetes, dermatitis, bronchitis, hyperactivity, deafness, sperm damage, and Alzheimer's and Parkinson's diseases."[58]

As Rachel Carson, Aldo Leopold, and countless others since them have pointed out, what we put into the air and onto our soil affects everyone and what everyone else does affects us. A report by a research team in the United Kingdom noted a rise not only in Alzheimer's and Parkinson's diseases but in motor neuron disease in general in six European countries as well as the U.S., Japan, Canada, and Australia.

From the late 1970s to the late 1990s, the number of annual deaths for profit is matched only by the mania to clear the way for agricultural land to grow biomass for oil alternatives, from corn to grass.

But tearing down forests to create oil alternatives is ludicrous. "The cruel irony is that deforestation will result in more GHGs being released into the atmosphere than the use of biofuels will eliminate."[50] That's because deforestation doesn't just involve cutting. It involves burning up what's left after the trees have been hauled away. That burning of the rainforests alone accounts for 20 percent of all the GHGs dumped into the atmosphere annually.

It gets worse. Losing the trees also means being subjected to what they have long kept to themselves. "The amount of carbon stored in tropical forests is staggering — Brazil alone has nearly 50 billion tons — and its loss would ensure dramatic climate change. Scientists estimate that without a change in business as usual, more than half of the Amazon

attributable to these brain diseases rose from 3,000 to 10,000. The death rates from these diseases, many of them from Alzheimer's, "more than tripled for men and nearly doubled for women. This increase in dementia is likely linked to a rise in the concentration of pesticides, industrial effluents, car exhaust, and other pollutants in the environment."

In addition, a 2006 study done by the Harvard School of Public Health reported that "long-term low-level exposure to pesticides raised the risk of developing Parkinson's disease by 70 percent."

The deadly neurotoxin mercury shows up now in virtually all countries which have coal-burning power plants and many who have gold mines. "For example, gold miners release an estimated 290,000 pounds of mercury into the Amazon ecosystem each year, and coal-burning power plants release nearly 100,000 pounds of mercury into the air in the United States." The mercury from power plants in the U.S., according to the EPA, "settles over waterways, polluting rivers and lakes, and contaminating fish."[59]

This contamination is so serious that in 2006 only Alaska and Wyoming did not issue any of the "3,080 fish advisories warning against eating fish from local lakes and streams because of their mercury content. EPA research indicates that one out of every six women of childbearing age in the United States has enough mercury in her blood to harm a developing fetus. This means that 630,000 of the 4 million babies born in the country each year may face neurological damage from mercury exposure before birth."[60]

forest would be logged by 2030, releasing 20.5 billion tons of CO_2 into the atmosphere."[51] Not only do we lose their cleansing effects and life-giving oxygen, we gain more pollution.

Clear cutting destroys the land for a short-term profit; it sets it up to erode and go fallow. With the trees gone, there is not only nothing to catch the CO_2 and convert it back to oxygen, there is nothing to absorb the water during the rainy season, so water tables decline. Because of the relationship between weather patterns, rainfall and forests, when forests decline, the rainy season brings less rain. Destroying vast stretches of rain forest also destroys the diversity of plant and animal life, causing their mysteries and benefits to be lost forever.

Once destroyed these old growth forests cannot be easily restored. Despite any reassurances from clear cutting advocates, replanting takes decades to begin to do the work of the mature trees. The shallow root systems of saplings cannot capture enough water to help balance the rainfall needs of a forest, nor are they capable of holding soil in place to prevent erosion.

Because of this full-scale clear cutting, Conservation International estimates that one species is going extinct every 20 minutes, over 1,000 times faster than the norm throughout most of earth's history.[52] In that same 20 minutes, 1,200 acres of rain forest will disappear. "We have no idea how many natural cures, how many industrial materials, how many biological insights, how much sheer natural beauty, and how many parts and pieces of a complex web of life we barely understand are being lost."[53]

The cost to our ecosystems is steep; so is the loss of all that biodiversity. According to John Holdren, a Harvard and Woods Hole environmental scientist, "The biodiversity of the planet is a unique and uniquely valuable library that we have been steadily burning down—one wing at a time—before we have even catalogued all the books, let alone read them all."[54]

Strands are being obliterated as the species web breaks and fails in spots. Like the burning of the library in Alexandria, we are being cut off from knowledge before we get to know what we are missing.

"Destroying a tropical rain forest and other species-rich ecosystems for profit," says entomologist Edward O. Wilson, "is like burning all the paintings of the Louvre to cook dinner."

There was a time when we knew better than to behave like this. We have forgotten. As Thom Hartmann says, "Older [indigenous]

Cultures, with few exceptions, hold as their most foundational concept the belief that we are not different from, separate from, in charge of, superior to, or inferior to the natural world. We are part of it. Whatever we do to nature, we do to ourselves. Whatever we do to ourselves, we do to the world. For most, there is no concept of a separate 'nature': it's all us and we're all it."[55]

Unborn U.S. babies are soaking in a stew of chemicals, including mercury, gasoline byproducts and pesticides… The report by the Environmental Working Group is based on tests of 10 samples of umbilical cord blood taken by the American Red Cross. They found an average of 287 contaminants in the blood, including mercury, fire retardants, pesticides and the Teflon chemical PFOA. "These 10 newborn babies … were born polluted," said New York Rep. Louise Slaughter, who planned to publicize the findings at a news conference Thursday. "If ever we had proof that our nation's pollution laws aren't working, it's reading the list of industrial chemicals in the bodies of babies who have not yet lived outside the womb."
—Maggie Fox, "Unborn Babies Soaked in Chemicals, Survey Finds," Reuters, 14 Jul 2005

EXTERNALITIES: THE REAL COST OF THINGS

In the fall of 2008 Americans saw in dramatic detail the cost of denial as the markets that are the foundation of our system began to fray and collapse. Our banks, investment institutions, the real estate market, and automobile industry all seemed to be coming apart at the seams. In a real way we were reeling from the effects of a very long party where no one wanted to look at the real costs of lowering federal income while wildly inflating government spending and pairing that with stratospheric borrowing, much of it to enable what was by then a five-year war begun to secure oil fields in the Middle East. As trillions of dollars were flying everywhere and Americans watched their retirement accounts, jobs and the very homes they owned begin to disappear before their eyes, it begged the question: how did we not see this?

Much the same condition exists with our environment and the way the market has refused to acknowledge the real costs, the so-called externalities, that surround our willful denial of the state of our planet's resources. Nicholas Stern, once the chief economist at the World Bank, warned in late 2006 that the accounting for this would be expensive, in the trillions of dollars. Lester Brown points out that the market's refusal to acknowledge externalities shows that it "does not value nature's services properly. And it does not respect the sustainable yield thresholds of natural systems. It also favors the near term over the long term, showing little concern for future generations."[61]

As a key example, he points to the probably real cost of gasoline at the pump. The current price of gas, he says, reflects what it costs to get the oil from the ground, refined and delivered to the service station. What it doesn't include is the costs of climate change, government subsidies, military costs to keep our supply free and secure or the health care costs from all the respiratory illnesses we cope with as a result of the polluted air we breathe. When you add those up, he says, the real price for gas is closer to $15 per gallon.[62]

Nor are these externalities common only to the U.S. In 2008, China overtook the U.S. as the world's leading emitter of CO_2. It also leaves us in the dust when it comes to the amount of meat eaten (twice as much as the U.S.), the amount of grain (a third more than the U.S.) and steel used (three times as much).[63]

Environmental externalities have their own term: *green debt.* Pan Yue, Vice-minister of China's State Environmental Protection Administration, wrote of China's green debt in 2006, pointing out that if all the environmental damage it has done in the last three decades were calculated, all of its GDP gains of that entire timespan would be neutralized. China had, he said, seen its Marxist philosophy only through the lens of class struggle. "We believed that economic development would solve all our problems." This in turn, "morphed into an unrestrained pursuit of material gain devoid of morality. Traditional Chinese culture, with its emphasis on harmony between human beings and nature, was thrown aside."[64]

Vice-Minister Yue's concerns are well founded. In an earlier interview with *Der Spiegel,* he spoke plainly about the pollution dangers his country faces: China's problems are frightening. The miracle that is Chinese progress, he said, will end soon, "because the environment can no longer keep pace. Acid rain is falling on one third of the Chinese territory, half of the water in our seven largest rivers is completely useless, while one fourth of our citizens do not have access to clean drinking water. One third of the urban population is breathing polluted air." According to the World Bank, sixteen of the world's twenty most polluted cities are in China. Their population of 1.3 billion is twice the size it was just fifty years ago. During the same timespan that its population doubled, the amount of land available for habitation and cultivation has been cut in half.[65]

Any single thing that China does, because of its scale, packs a huge wallop. Just providing enough disposable chopsticks for its massive population requires 25 million trees per year. With its forests disappearing at an alarming rate and in an effort to discourage the use of the traditional mainstay—introduced by the vegetarian philosopher Confucius 5,000 years ago—and promote a greener alternative, the government passed a tax on their use. Nor is that the only way trees are endangered. If China's size and ravenous appetite continue on its current trajectory, by 2030 China will need twice as much paper as the entire world produces today. If by then, it is at par with America in automobile ownership (three cars for every four citizens), it will need the equivalent of 98 MBPD per day or about 13 MBPD more than the entire world uses today.[66]

It's all a set of unseen truths and consequences, thing that happen whose cascading effects we cannot see or envision. That's because the earth is not composed of separate parts but is a harmonious synchronized body of interrelated pieces which not only fit but are symbiotic. We have stuck our finger into the center of all that and twirled to our heart's delight.

Slowly, the world is awakening to the reality that finite fuel resources by their very nature have no future in a world that is growing and constantly craving more. These fuels are not a sustainable option. So also is not caring. As the journalist and economist Dame Barbara Ward said, "To say we do not care is to say in the most literal sense that 'we choose death.' "[6]

These sprays, dusts, and aerosols are now applied almost universally to farms, gardens, forests, and homes—nonselective chemicals that have the power to kill every insect, the "good" and the "bad," to still the song of birds and the leaping of fish in the streams, to coat the leaves with a deadly film, and to linger on in soil—all this though the intended target may be only a few weeds or insects. Can anyone believe it is possible to lay down such a barrage of poisons on the surface of the earth without making it unfit for all life? They should not be called "insecticides," but "biocides."
—Rachel Carson, *Silent Spring*, 1962

COAL'S KILLING FOG

Before oil was helping lubricate the machinery that made possible the industrialization of the 20th century, there was coal in the 19th century that made Great Britain into a giant of the industrial revolution's first century and powered the beginnings of U.S. industry. Coal has a brilliant, warm, reliable heat but it has a nasty side effect. It chokes people to death.

The killing coal fog that encompassed London in 1952 effectively ended the age of coal in England. On the cold morning of December 5, 1952, smog (fog combined with coal smoke) encased the city, filling the air with particulate matter that contained sulphur dioxide, nitrogen oxides and soot. The unusually cold air had encouraged Londoners to burn more coal in their fireplaces. The additional smoke, accompanied by the cold temperatures created the foggy shroud.

Unable to see a foot in front of them, people abandoned their cars where they stopped. Children got lost on the way to school. An opera performance had to be called off because the air inside of the theater became intolerable. Bodies began to stack up in the morgue and undertakers ran out of coffins. The Ministry of Health started taking a daily tally to determine how many more deaths were occurring than usual. Most of the deaths were attributed to either the onset of respiratory illness or people who had chronic asthma or bronchitis succumbing to their conditions. The count reached more than 4,000, the daily totals rising from 250 on day one to 900 by the fourth day. The smog got everywhere, into homes and churches, through any crack. An unexpected vulnerable target ended up being a number of prize cattle ready to be shown at the Smithfield Show at Earl's Court. The animals started to have trouble breathing, and then dropped dead, their lungs destroyed by the acid in the smoke.[68]

The World Health Organization has guidelines that stipulate 50 milligrams per cubic meter as the limit of acceptable air quality for short term exposure. The numbers during the Great Smog were 1,600 milligrams per cubic meter.

Londoners had long been used to the inconvenience of the coal-induced fog but this was different. "This was accompanied by an apparent disbelief that nothing could really be done to attenuate the pollution problem, especially given the public's awareness of the growing availability of alternative fuels to coal; all this in the waning, but still present post-war spirit of a fresh start and the opportunity to rebuild collectively."[69]

The City of London passed Clean Air Acts in 1956 and 1968 that required the conversion to smokeless fuels. Coal use as a domestic fuel was banned in urban areas.

THE OIL WE EAT: THE UNITED STATES OF CORN

In October of 2008, food culturist Michael Pollan wrote about how the well-being of the nation's food supply was interwoven with the three main campaign issues of the coming election: energy independence, health care, and climate change. You cannot deal effectively with any one of these, he said, without understanding how intimately all three are connected.

What did Pollan mean? One, the U.S. now relies on other countries to supply 70 percent of our petroleum needs; two, our ability to maintain our daily food supply relies on dependable access to more than four million barrels of oil per day (out of a total 21 MBPD needed);[70] three, our food cycle—the way we farm, grow livestock, transport, market, package, prepare, and consume it all—produces 37 percent of all the greenhouse gas that escapes into the atmosphere each day[71] and four, the health of our citizenry is declining as a direct result of not only our oil usage but of the failure of our overstimulated, overworked, toxin-filled soil to produce food to nourish and sustain us.

We are, said Pollan, "eating oil and spewing greenhouse gases."[72] We cannot, he explains, expect that people will continue to eat cheap food grown with cheap oil that has little nutritional value and not see the results show up in our bodies. As the nutrition levels of our food go down (see Chapter 4), our levels of heart disease, stroke, Type II diabetes, and cancer continue to go up, in some cases precipitously. The Center for Disease Control now reports that one out of every three children born in America in 2000 will contract Type II diabetes.

"Cheap food," he says, "is dishonestly priced—it is in fact unconsciously expensive."[73]

Part of what is behind what he is saying is the preponderance of one grain in our diets: corn. No, not just the bushel or so of corn you might eat in a year that goes into your corn muffins or the tortilla for your taco or even the corn starch you add to thicken your beef stew. Much of the other ton of *Zea may* Americans consume per capita each year comes in the form of hidden ingredients, from the meat of our cattle, hogs and chickens grown in the great industrial CAFOs that dot our former pasture lands to the ubiquitous high fructose corn syrup that is in so much of the processed food on our grocery store shelves and handed across the counters of American fast food franchises.

As we eat these creatures of the corn, we're eating what they eat too. Corn feeds the steer that feeds us. It also feeds the chicken and pigs, turkeys and lamb, as well as the farmed catfish, tilapia and even the carnivorous salmon. So in a real sense, even our eggs are made of corn, as are our dairy products—milk, cheese and yogurt—because, for the most part, these products which once came from grass-grazing pasture animals, come from Holsteins tethered to machines, eating corn.

The quaint pastoral little farms of our mythic past have given way to giant agricultural enterprises tended by farmers who are now corporate partners and whose primary connection with the land is from the cab of a high-dollar piece of planting or harvesting equipment. The rising tide of cheap corn made possible the evolution of the modern agrimegaplex and eventually the disappearance of the farmyard and the interdependency of the land, the farmer and the animals who all lived in concert on a healthier landscape.

"Eating puts us in touch with all that we share with the other animals, and all that sets us apart," says Michael Pollan. "It defines us."[74] As each of us in America consumes a full ton of corn annually, much of it completely out of our awareness, we are increasingly becoming defined by corn. We are, he says, "corn walking."

In the 2007 documentary *King Corn*, Steve Macko, an environmental scientist at the University of Virginia performs an isotope analysis on hair strands of Ian Cheney and Curt Ellis and tells the two young filmmakers that the carbon in their bodies comes from corn. "I'm not talking about the corn you eat off of the cob. I'm talking about the corn that's being used as a material that's going into the foods ubiquitously," from the canned fruit drinks to the corn-based additives in packaged food to the meat of the animals we eat, who have fed off of corn—in other words, the industrial #2 corn that is mostly what's grown on the farms in the United States.[75]

After World War II, the U. S. had a vast amount of unused war materials, among them tons of ammonium nitrate—which had been central to the building of bombs—and DDT, which was used to prevent the spread of disease. Ammonium nitrate is also a key source of nitrogen, the substance that plants normally get from photosynthesis. DDT, the Army noticed, was very effective in getting rid of the lice that made the serviceman's life a nightmare. Once this dynamic duo—a synthetic version of nitrogen and a way to kill plant pests—was introduced into American agriculture, the largely organic way of growing food via natural photosynthesis gave way to growing it with fossil fuels. That meant faster and vastly larger yields but it cost us our consciousness about where our food comes from and how it's grown. With the ability to fix nitrogen, farmers could now call the shots on the growth cycle of their crops.

"Fixing nitrogen allowed the food chain to turn from the logic of biology and embrace the logic of industry. Instead of eating exclusively from the sun, humanity now began to sip petroleum."[76]

Of all the crops that took to this new kind of fast farming, corn was ideally suited. Since the 1970s, it has become the central link in the food chain and oil has enabled corn's dominance. In 1970 American farmers produced four billion bushels of corn. By 2009, the total was 13.2.[77] Every acre of corn requires 1.2 barrels of oil.

To accommodate this massive exercise requires turning away from the diversity nature practices automatically toward the efficiency and quantity and uniformity of the corn monoculture. By simplifying our food chain, we are complicating our own health.

Among these corn products are the dozens of ingredients that show up as food additives in packaged and processed food. If you see words like ascorbic acid, lecithin, dextrose, lactic acid, caramel color, lysine, maltose, and xanthan gum, it's all the same thing: corn. Among these is the king of corn subproducts, high fructose corn syrup (HFCS).

Annually, each of us consumes 83 pounds of HFCS in innumerable places in our diet. It has been blamed for everything from ADHD to diabetes. In late 2008 the Corn Refiners Association launched a multi-million dollar PR campaign designed to put the shine back on the product's name. No wonder. Corn is the largest crop in the U.S. Its additives, including the ubiquitous HFCS, permeate a fourth of the 45,000 items in an average American supermarket. (Chapter 4 covers other problematic aspects of HFCS.)

Like a series of Faberge eggs, corn has become nested into our economy. Growing corn requires half of the synthetic nitrogen made in the U.S. The process that achieves the critical fixing of nitrogen that makes it an effective fertilizer requires both electricity and fossil fuels. The pharmaceuticals fed to the animals tethered to machines during their lives of confinement comprise more than 50 percent of that industry's sales per year.

Corn makes many parts of the industrial economy possible. It also makes our food supply vulnerable, not only because it requires our unwavering access to increasingly larger supplies of fossil fuels that are growing harder to reach and more expensive to buy, but because the massive concentrations of fertilizer and nitrogen that make its pervasiveness possible have depleted the ability of our soils to nourish us.

Today most of the food we eat comes from vast industrial farms, our meat from sprawling animal cities and much of it is built around the same crop: corn. About 80 percent of all the grain we produce goes to feed livestock, much of which was never engineered to digest it. More than ¾ of all our beef comes from CAFOs where the animals eat corn and wheat. At birth they are dosed with antibiotics to prevent or deal with the diseases this kind of confinement is bound to engender.

With cows and their unique four-stomach digestive systems geared to handling ruminant, the antibiotics help deal with the bloat that would otherwise kill them since the grain they are eating is not what they were designed to ingest. Our chickens and hogs suffer the same fate. Chickens often have their beaks shorn off so they can't fight or defend themselves, just gobble grain until their short fat lives are over. The effluvia from hog farms has been widely reported as a health hazard because of air quality near rural hog CAFOs and known high levels of E coli making its way into the surrounding waters through broken containments or leaks into local wells.[78]

On the surface, this way of producing food is efficient but in terms of externalities, the costs to animals, the environment and ourselves is incalculable. And along the way one of the barnyard animals' greatest gifts of fertility—its manure—is treated as a nuisance. Its nitrogen-rich product is wasted, hosed out of the containment areas or just abandoned to sink into the water table and wash off the tops of the land during rainstorms, settling into the rivers and streams that take it south into the Gulf of Mexico where in long stretches nothing grows but the oxygen eating algae that have now taken over much of the coastline between Texas and Alabama.

DIFFERENT KINDS OF EFFICIENCIES

John Locke, one of the father's of the 17th century age of reason may have helped set the tone for our hubris about nature when he said in his second of *Two Treatises of Government*, that "land that is left wholly to nature… is called, as indeed it is, waste." Nature, to this way of thinking, was to be used. It was there for us, under our dominion. And that pretty much represented the American mindset of the last half of the 20th century.

If your only goal is to save time and manpower and maximize yields, oil gives us efficiencies that would have made our ancestors' heads spin. They are so refined, that even though the practices of modern agribusiness are highly wasteful, it takes about 20 seconds worth of energy to create one person's food for the day. If done by hand, the tilling, seeding, watering, harvesting, refining and shipping for the same meals would take three weeks.[79]

Time is money. It's also the highly treasured currency of the American lifestyle. And to support that lifestyle where anything is available to us 365 days a year, we have spent ourselves into multiple forms of resource debt. Between surface water and underground aquifers, agriculture now uses a full 85 percent of our fresh water. Since World War II our use of pesticides has increased by 3000 percent. The highly toxic chemicals used to rid the soil of targeted pests have the nasty habit of decimating all the members of the soil infrastructure, good and harmful, and each year crop loss to pests has increased. As Chapter 4 details, as we put increasing pressure on our soils to produce, they grow weaker, their soil less able to nourish us, their yields less able to fulfill the nutritional requirements of our population.

The bottom line is in the pre-Green Revolution days of the 1950s, our ultra-efficient agricultural world used to produce 2.3 calories of energy for every calorie expended. We now get a paltry one calorie of energy for every *10* calories expended. In other words we've turned our productivity ratio upside down. Where we used to get more than twice the bang for our buck, we now get one-tenth. We've turned our backs on the free energy that was our planetary birthright and spent wildly with the ancient blood of our prehistory. Just as our automobiles waste 85 percent of the energy in every gallon of gas, the oil we spend to feed ourselves is just as surely wasted. About 20 percent of the 4 MBPD of oil used daily in agribusiness is used on the farm; the remaining 80 percent is spent transporting, processing, packaging, marketing and preparing the food in our kitchens.

Growing food organically does use about a third less fossil fuel because organic farmers do not use fertilizers and pesticides. But the costs to transport an organic lettuce spring mix from the San Fernando Valley to upstate New York amounts to about 3,000 food miles.

"The fossil fuel era freed human beings from the slower seasonal rhythms of an agricultural period and thus also from dependency on nature's constraints and divine intervention."[80] But it also broke our connection with our own intuitive sense of how we were born to operate in concert with the earth rather than trying to dominate it. Once that sacred contract was broken, we went on a resource spending spree that finds us now in the woozy, aching aftermath of a gluttonous bender.

Facing the end of a way of life—even as a gradual shift—without envisioning what will replace it is unnerving, with good reason. The task before us, building a new energy economy, will be an undertaking of staggering scale and repercussions. "We need to take all our current energy assets—our coal-fired power plants, our oil pipelines and refineries, our tanker ships, our trains and planes and automobiles—worth well over ten trillion dollars and replace them all with an equally colossal and interwoven system of technology processes, and network (many yet to be invented), which by 2050 must be efficiently producing enough energy for 9 billion people, their companies and their lifestyles, all while emitting half the carbon per capita that is currently the case."[81]

Here's where the math inevitably breaks down because, as Richard Hindberg and other resource analysts point out, much of what we are basing our calculations on today—fossil fuels, water, food, wood fuel—will likely not exist in the quantities they exist today because they will have been decimated by then. The feedback loops are unchangeable.

SEEING OURSELVES ANEW

With Galileo came the concept that we were not the center of our solar system after all, that we actually circled the sun rather than it circling us. This was so radical and infuriating a concept that it took the Catholic Church until 1992 to reverse the proclamation that had originally banned his theory in 1616, leaving him an outcast who died in seclusion. It left people in a psychological state not unlike the one we are facing now. Without our egocentric beliefs that we are the center of nature, then who exactly are we? Galileo didn't just show us the Earth wasn't the center of our solar system, he also set the stage for a bigger understanding—that the earth does not revolve around us. We need it. It doesn't need us. We're fellow travelers and residents, not its sovereign.

As we refashion our idea of 21st century stewardship, we can see this as a surrendering to cosmic law, not as giving up but in bowing in recognition to its mystery and our part of its whole. Spirit is in the theories of science as well as in the trees. When we move to see ways to outdo nature, to fool it and coax more out of a day, we are not doing it in cooperation and fellowship with nature. Rather, we are operating from a hierarchical space, dictating terms and using the precious resources that are there as though they were ours to waste, without any accountability or consciousness.

At the same time that Edison was putting on a light show in lower Manhattan, Albert Einstein was using his imagination to understand how light worked in a different form. He was enchanted less with its usefulness than its invisible properties and behaviors. He saw nature not just as the earth we can see but the laws which govern it. He saw beyond mere measuring and calculation to the elusive and harmonious randomness that is paradoxically a constant in our lives.

It is not easy to give up cherished ideas about who we are and how we work. But we are not only uniquely positioned to do just that, we are already doing it. In the 1980s while Steve Jobs and Bill Gates were trying to convince us that computers and software were going to become essential magic, we could not see at first why or how. Our minds could not comprehend them as tools yet.

But what at first became an interesting way to do word processing and crunch numbers in endless spreadsheet configurations soon morphed into something bigger: a little screen on the world that, via the Internet, gave us the ability to cross the once formidable barriers of time and space instantly. It was just as easy to email someone halfway around the world as the person in the next cubicle. Nobody foresaw Facebook or blogs or YouTube or instant and powerful social and political activism or being able to browse the Library of Congress in your pajamas at 3 a.m. because you couldn't sleep. Nor did they foresee a much compressed TV and keyboard turned into a telephone that fit nicely into your pocket and carried in its tiny membranes a thousand times the capability of those early clunkers.

It took a little time and considerable imagination and revelation. But when the interest and energy of hundreds of millions of people get involved, things change. Walking through the dawn of the computer age, we had no idea we would end up where we were or have yet to go.

"You are not going to see it coming," Bill Gates told *New York Times* columnist Thomas Friedman about where we find the solutions to our planet's energy crises. "The breakthrough will probably come out of somewhere you least expect, and we'll only know how it happened looking backward."[82]

If Gates is right, we won't really be able to identify the solutions until we see them in our rearview mirrors. They won't show up the way we might think because they will occur as an invisible cascading set of effects. Computers really matured when the Internet and the World Wide Web gave us the beginnings of our new communications grid—an invisible matrix that most Westerners under age 30 have no memory of being without. Perhaps the new energy grid we cannot yet see, the one that will power our transportation, heat and light up our homes and industries, will follow a similar path. By the time we replace the current grid with one that's invisible and clean and works in partnership rather than against nature, we will enjoy the sweet feeling of taking it for granted again. This is the invisible way we move into what's next, recognizing its shape only when we look back.

Becoming more conscious doesn't happen all at once. We become worthy vessels one insight at a time. Like the natives who could not see Columbus's ships when they first came ashore because they had no frame of reference for what they were looking at, we too cannot see the answers around us because we lack the template that helps us make sense of the information that surrounds us. Yet they are everywhere, not just inside our thinking but beyond it. Whatever form the solutions eventually take doesn't matter. What matters is starting to engage the process.

Eudora Welty said, "The events in our lives happen in a sequence in time, but in their significance to ourselves, they find their own order… the continuous thread of revelation."

It is time to reweave the tapestry that was our collective species memory and rediscover the revelations that lie within it. We can learn much from the wisdom mankind relied on for the millennia before coal and oil defined what we could coax out of the earth to bloat a short-term rise in GDP. While fossil fuels freed us from nature's slower rhythms, they also enslaved us to an ever-thinning tether and a future we never dared envision during the extreme highs of our fossil fuel party. As it fed us with steady and ever bigger transfusions of what Colombia's U'wa tribe calls the blood of Mother Earth, it also sucked dry the birthright of our topsoil and helped throw our planet's species diversity into chaos.

The path to healing our broken sense of where our center is lies in our willingness to be accountable for what and how we spend what the earth presents for all of us to share. Martin Luther King said, "The arc of the moral universe is long, but it bends towards justice." Increasingly, it also bends toward wanting to do the right thing.

    As Barbara Kingsolver said at the end of her one-year experiment of living off of the food she and her family grew themselves, "We so want to believe it is possible to come back from our saddest mistakes, and have another chance ... Something can happen for us, it seems, or *through* us, that will stop this earthly unraveling and start the clock over. Like every creature on earth, we want to make it too. We want more time."[83]

Endnotes

1.   NASA website: http://www.nasa.gov/centers/goddard/news/ topstory/2003/0321kuwaitfire.html; World Resources Institute 2003 report: *The Environment: Another casualty of war?*; *The Prize, the Epic Quest for Oil, Money and Power,* by Daniel Yergin. New York: Simon and Shuster, 1991 (revised 2008), 758-759; Gulflink, Office of the Special Assistant for Gulf War Illness website: http://www. gulflink.osd.mil/owf_ii/owf_ii_tabc.htm; "Kuwait Still Recovering from Gulf War Fires," by Ryan Chilcote, CNN, January 3, 2003.
2.   From an interview with author Thom Hartmann.
3.   *The Prize: The Epic Quest for Oil, Money & Power,* by Daniel Yergin. New York: Simon & Schuster, 1991 (references from updated 2009 version), 762.
4.   *The Last Hours of Ancient Sunlight: The Fate of the World and What We Can Do Before It's Too Late,* by Thom Hartmann. New York: Three Rivers Press, 2004, 271.
5.   *Oil and Gas Production History in California.* Available at: www.ca.gov
6.   "A Past President's Advice to Obama: Act with Haste," by Neil King, Jr. *Wall Street Journal,* Dec. 11, 2008.
7.   *The Hydrogen Economy,* by Jeremy Rifkin. New York: The Penguin Group, 2002, 64.
8.   *Omnivore's Dilemma,* 83-84.
9.   "All About Food and Fossil Fuels," by Rachel Oliver, March 17, 2008. Available at CNN online: http://edition.cnn.com/2008/WORLD/ asiapcf/03/16/eco.food.miles
10.   *Winning the Oil Endgame, Innovation for Profits, Jobs and Security,* by Amory B. Lovins, E. Kyle Datta, Odd-Even Bustnes, Jonathan B. Koomey, and Nathan J. Glasgow. Snowmass, Colorado: Rocky Mountain Institute, 2005, ix. Available for free download: http:// www.rmi.org/images/PDFs/WTOE/WTOE.pdf
11.   *Texas: A Guide to the Lone Star State, Compiled by Workers of the Writers Program of the Works Project Administration in the State of Texas.* New York: Hastings House, 1940, 196.

12. "Horatio's Drive," PBS. A Film by Ken Burns, from a book by Dayton Duncan, 2003.

13. *Last Hours of Ancient Sunlight*, 163.

14. *American Road: The Story of an Epic Transcontinental Journey at the Dawn of the Motor Age*, by Pete Davies. New York: Henry Holt, 2002.

15. "Hydrogen Road Tour '08." http://hydrogenroadtour08.dot.gov/

16. *The Prize*, 4-12.

17. *Ibid*, 15.

18. *Ibid*, 70.

19. Kilgore Chamber of Commerce website: http://www.kilgorechamber.com/community.htm

20. *The Prize*, 178.

21. *The Hydrogen Economy*, 72.

22. *The End of Oil*, by Paul Roberts. New York: Houghton Mifflin, 2004, 36.

23. *The Prize*, 149-168.

24. *Ibid.*

25. *The Prize*, 287-368.

26. *Ibid.*

27. *Ibid.*

28. Williamson and Andreano, *The American Petroleum Institute*, 2:805

29. *End of Oil*, 41.

30. *Ibid*, 40.

31. U.S. Department of Energy website: http://www.eia.doe.gov/emeu/aer/txt/ptb1105.html

32. *End of Oil*, 42.

33. *Hot Flat, and Crowded: Why We Need a Green Revolution—and How It Can Renew America,* by Thomas Friedman. New York: Farrar, Straus and Giroux, 2008, 109.

34. In the fall of 2002, the National Park Service installed three solar power systems on the White House grounds, on both a maintenance building to provide electricity and hot water for personnel and on the roof of the presidential cabana to heat water for the pool and spa.

35. *Hot Flat, and Crowded,* 16.

36. *The Hydrogen Economy*, 49.

37. *Plan B, 3.0*, 27.

38. "Giant oil find by BP reopens debate about oil supplies," by Terry Macalister, *The Guardian*, September 2, 2009 or at http://www.guardian.co.uk/business/2009/sep/02/bp-oil-find-gulf-of-mexico

39. British Petroleum website, Oil Consumption and Oil Production figures: www.bp.com

40. *Hot, Flat and Crowded,* 39

41. *Ibid.*
42. U.S. Department of the Interior Bureau of Land Management website: http://www.blm.gov/wo/st/en/prog/energy/oilshale_2.html
43. "Governor Schwarzenegger Applauds EPA Decision Granting California Authority to Reduce Greenhouse Gas Emissions," Office of the Governor Press Release, June 30, 2009.
44. "Schwarzenegger Asks Obama For More Auto Emissions Rules," by Samantha Young, Associated Press, January 22, 2009.
45. These are cumulative figures; 82% of GHGs come from burning fossil fuels used to generate electricity and power our cars, buses, trucks and commercial airplanes. As yet, there are no reliable figures that include calculations that include the additional 40-50 million tons of methane GHG being added the atmosphere daily because of the rising loss of permafrost in places like Siberia, due to global warming.
46. National Resources Defense Council: "Dirty Coal is Hazardous to Your Health." To download .pdf, go to http://www.nrdc.org/health/effects/coal/index.asp
47. "This too shall Passacantando," by Kate Griffith, *Grist*, Dec. 29, 2008.
48. "The Chinese Miracle Will End Soon," interview with Pan Yue, from China's ministry of the environment. *Der Spiegel*, March 7, 2005.
49. "China Hit by Rising Air Pollution," BBC News, August 3, 2006. Available at: http://news.bbc.co.uk/2/hi/asia-pacific/5241844.stm
50. *Hot, Flat and Crowded*, 149.
51. "The Secret Life of Trees," by Bryan Walsh/NUSA DUA, *Time*, December 14, 2007.
52. *Hot Flat and Crowded*, 141.
53. *Ibid*, 142.
54. *Ibid.*
55. *The Last Hours of Ancient Sunlight*, 190.
56. *Plan B 3.0*, 113.
57. *Ibid.*
58. *Ibid*, 112. Sourced from Lester Brown: Sarah Janssen, Gina Solomon, and Ted Schettler, *Chemical Contaminants and Human Disease: A Summary of Evidence* (Boston: Alliance for a Healthy Tomorrow, 2004); Geoffrey Lean, "US Study Links More than 200 Diseases to Pollution," *Independent News* (London), 14 November 2004.
59. *Plan B 3.0*, 113-114.
60. *Plan B 3.0*, 114.
61. *Plan B 3.0*, 6.
62. *Ibid.*
63. *Plan B 3.0*, 13.
64. "China's Green Debt," by Pan Yue, *Daily Times* (Pakistan), December 1, 2006.

65. "The Chinese Miracle Will End Soon."
66. *Plan B 3.0*, xii.
67. *Who Speaks for Earth?* Barbara Ward and others. (Originally a Distinguished Lecture Series given to the UN in 1972). New York: W.W. Norton & Company, 1973, 31.
68. *When Smoke Ran Like Water*, by Devra Lee Davis. New York: Basic Books. p. 43.
69. *Air, the Environment and Public Health*, by Anthony Kessel, New York: Cambridge University Press, 2006, p. 85.
70. This figure incorporates hydrocarbons in general: oil and diesel, plus the natural gas used to fix nitrogen fertilizer or refine oil sands and the coal used to operate power plants and generate electricity.
71. The GHGs come not only from gas-driven farm equipment but from transport as well as methane produced from livestock and the carbon dioxide released when land is tilled and soil is turned over.
72. "Farmer in Chief," by Michael Pollan. *New York Times*, October 9, 2008.
73. *Ibid.*
74. *Omnivore's Dilemma*, 10.
75. *King Corn*, a film by Aaron Wolf, written by Ian Cheney and Curt Ellis. Mosaic Films, Inc., 2007.
76. *Omnivore's Dilemma*, 45.
77. January 12, 2010 *Annual Crop Production* report of 2009 crop yields by USDA. Available at http://www.nass.usda.gov Newsroom/2010/01_12_2010.asp Average yield per acre in 2008 was 153 bushels; U.S. farmers planted 85.9 million acres in corn. Average yield per acre in 2009 was 165.2 bushels on a total of 86.5 million acres. Pollan quote from *Omnivore's Dilemma*, 62.
78. "Surrounded by factory farms: Indiana environment revisited," by Steven Higgs, *The Bloomington Alternative*, March 9, 2008.
79. *Eating Fossil Fuels: Oil, Food and the Coming Agriculture Crisis*, by David Allen Pfeiffer, Gabriola Island, BC: New Society Publishers. 2006 and http://survivingpeakoil.com
80. *The Hydrogen Economy*, 244.
81. *End of Oil*, 261.
82. *Hot Flat and Crowded*, 188.
83. *Animal, Vegetable, Miracle: a Year of Food Life*, by Barbara Kingsolver. New York: Harper Collins, 2007, 345-346.

CHAPTER 4

Seeds of discontent

A nation that destroys its soil destroys itself.
-- *Franklin Delano Roosevelt*

As petroleum gets more expensive and the age of the so-called 3,000-mile Caesar salad gives way to food that is more locally derived, the intrusion of oil into the circulatory system that currently nurtures most of our food will slow. But if oil has become the lifeblood of modern agriculture, then biotechnology is its heart. And it is on this stage of oil and biotechnology that key elements in a drama about the future of our food converge: the seed with which the earth sustains us, the farmers who have traditionally been the stewards of the earth's bounty, and the GMOs (genetically modified organisms) being grown in increasing numbers across our farmlands by agribusiness.

Even before the earliest introduction of GMOs in the late 1980s, American agribusiness played a big part in soil and water table contamination, in the disruption of historic ways of planting and sharing seeds, in the health and immune systems of our seed stores, in the potential health of both our population and global consumers, and in the disruptive and depressive effects on the farmers who serve as our sacred link to the food that comes from the earth.

The change in patent law successfully lobbied by the chemical and biotech corporations has altered the character and integrity of our national seed supplies and threatened the health, integrity and biodiversity of the most ancient seed archives on earth from North America and the Middle East to Asia. This in turn is having a profound physical, monetary, and spiritual effect on farmers worldwide. As the increasing demands of agribusiness widen the physical gap between the farmers' native ingenuity and the soil and seed they are trusted to nourish us with, this loss of the hand-to-heart link between farmers and the earth represents a rift that must be examined.

THE SEED SAVERS

Seed is a big deal. Its very meaning connotes totality, life producing life in a constant chain. It's the chicken *and* the egg, separated by a little calendar time. All living things from a fungus to a Super Bowl quarterback begin as some form of seed. When it comes to the seed that, through the grace of good soil, water, and a cooperative climate, becomes the food that sustains us, keeping it whole and safe must be instinctual, at least for the many scientists who spend their lives wondering at its miracles and saving it for future generations.

From 1941 to 1943, during the 900-day siege of Leningrad in World War II, while more than 600,000 of its citizens starved, a cadre of Soviet botanists blockaded themselves inside a makeshift seed vault at the Research Institute of Plant Industry. Founded by the visionary botanist, biologist and geneticist Nikolai Vavilov, the institute—under his leadership—gave the USSR the world's first seed bank, a repository for more than 200,000 types of seeds and plants.

While their countrymen fed themselves by devouring sawdust, grass, shoes, tree bark, their pets, the dead, and eventually nothing, these 31 people, flanked by bags of rice, corn, wheat, potatoes, peanuts and countless sacks of edible seed, waited out the siege. They burned every stick of furniture in the building to keep the fledgling plants and themselves from freezing to death.[1]

When at last the siege ended, the liberators found 14 of these brave botanists collapsed on the sacks of food, dead from starvation, preferring to martyr themselves than let Nazis—or their fellow starving countrymen—break into their seed stores and destroy their botanical heritage. The institute's rice specialist, Dr. Dmytry S. Ivanov, was found dead at his desk, with stacks of rice sacks beside him. Before he died, he reportedly said, "When all the world is in the flames of war, we will keep this collection for the future of all people."[2]

While they starved, their leader, Nikolai Vavilov, languished in prison. Having enraged Lenin with his new-fangled ideas about seed gathering and its humble but likely centers of genetic diversity (Lenin could not tolerate either Vavilov's or Linnaeus' theory of humanity having "a common genetic origin in the African savannah" [3]), Vavilov himself died of starvation in prison in 1943 before the siege ended.

After the war, with much of their seed intact, the Institute continued to thrive and today its collection has grown to 380,000 gene types representing 2,500 plant species. Vavilov was celebrated as a hero and even today his likeness is usually found in the various seed archives around the world. The seed bank he spent his life enriching now bears his name, the Vavilov Institute of Plant Industry.

During the 1920s and 1930s Vavilov and his researchers went on more than 100 seed-gathering missions in 64 countries, combing the earth for seed samples, taking their botanical treasures back to Russia, where he created what was at that time the greatest living seed archive in the world. The scientists who died saving his life's findings during that terrible siege never knew whether their country would survive the war. But they did know there could be no rebuilding of their homeland without viable seed being safe. Safe seed was ultimately more vital than who would win the war. Without it, there could be no future. Victors and vanquished alike would starve.

THE SEED SAFE

In a remote archipelago in Norway only 480 miles from the North Pole, the Svalbard International Seed Vault began its slow work late in February of 2008, when it received 100 million seeds from 100 different countries—varieties of eggplant, lettuce, cowpea, wheat, sorghum, potato, rice, and maize among them. Well on its way to becoming the latest—and eventually the earth's largest—high-tech repository dedicated to saving the world's seed heritage, the seed vault's goal is twofold: to serve as the archive of the current diversity of seeds available worldwide and to safeguard the future agricultural stability of every country on the planet.

Buried over 400 feet inside a mountain, deep enough below the permafrost to be impervious to the ravages of global warming, terrorist attacks, even nuclear explosions, the vault is reachable only through a stretch of tunnels punctuated by multiple heavy metal doorways. The latest high-tech surveillance and refrigeration gadgetry protect it from intruders and temperature deviations. Internal conditions are monitored and uploaded by satellite to the Nordic Gene Bank in Longyearbyen.

The choice of Longyearbyen isn't accidental. Serving as the capital of Svalbard, it is as about as far north as humans can live and among its claims to fame are its telling celebrations. The Svalbard Ski marathon is billed as "the worlds' northernmost cross country ski race." The Svalbard Museum is likewise the globe's northernmost museum. And during the second week of March, the local population celebrates Sunfest week, when the sun shines continuously for a whole week.[4]

The naturally (some might say *unnaturally*) cold surroundings will keep the seed safely stored at 0.4 degrees (F), ensuring it will remain dormant and not sprout. The remotely located vault was built so far underground that its creators estimate that seed will stay dry enough to allow wheat to endure for 1700 years and sorghum for a whopping 20,000 years. Even if the refrigeration fails and global warming becomes so severe that the polar icecaps melt, scientists say it would take 200 years for the temperature of the vault to rise above freezing.

By the time the vault has reached its seed storage goal, it will hold over 2 billion seeds, divided up into about 4.5 million varieties. (The precise number will depend on how many counties choose to participate.) Built by the Norwegian government as a service to the global community, the purpose of the Svalbard vault is to be the go-to site for any country in the world that is facing a crisis with its seed stocks because of drought, war, pestilence or severe weather anomalies. Should some form of disaster strike, countries can "borrow" duplicate seed samples from the vault to kickstart their agriculture,[5] not just for food and grain but for essential herbs and medicinals. The duplicates of these bits of "seed royalty" stored here never deplete the stock of originals. There is no charge to any country for the vault's storage services.

Today, scientists have it a little easier than the scientists who braved war, cold and lethal hunger to save their seeds, but bravery still comes in handy. Seed hunting can get hazardous as some of the scientists who are out gathering the seeds that will one day go to the vault can tell you. One wild variety of the chickpea grows only in southwest Turkey, very near the potentially dangerous locales of Iran and Iraq. Another variety grows in the former Soviet republic of Georgia, also a frequently inhospitable area. Other quests can take seed hunters on missions into desert or mountain terrain or even into unlikely seed stores.

Daniel Debouck, a Belgian scientist based in Cali, Colombia, is one of these intrepid hunters who seeks and finds rare seeds for the Svalbard Vault. He has had all these adventures and some less dangerous.

He has a particular affinity for bean types, having spent much of the last 30 years searching for varieties in North America. Once he happened on a rare bean from North America in a box of woody plants he was poking through in a Paris herbarium. "I realized that that plant was collected by a French explorer, exploring an area from Florida to the area that is today Quebec. It might even be a new bean species for the eastern U.S."[6] As Vavilov and his band of seed hunters discovered, the quest to find and save forms of life has a way of beckoning its seekers to ever new haunts.

In the United States, the seed archive at Fort Collins, Colorado, has been stockpiling seeds for food and plants (as well as animal germplasm) for nearly 50 years. It's sort of a lending library, used as a backup resource when crops fail or to help restore food production after wars or natural disasters. It helped rejuvenate agricultural life for war-torn Cambodia and Rwanda and Malaysia when their rice paddies were destroyed by a tsunami. In poor countries, a single bad season can be devastating . One failed harvest can not only spell disaster for the food stores this year but, because no new seeds are produced to save and germinate, it can mean poverty and starvation and cropless fields for years to come. In addition to sending seed out, the center takes in an estimated 40,000 new seeds annually.

Ongoing wars across the globe demonstrate the need to have this sort of archive available, far from the site of the conflict. On September 10, 2002, almost one year to the day after the events of 9/11, both of the stores of precious seed that represented the agricultural diversity of Afghanistan were looted and destroyed. Each store was hidden within a private home, one in the city of Ghagni in the north and the other in Jalalabad in the east. It is common practice to back up seed stores by depositing duplicates elsewhere. But in war-ravaged countries, such practices often go undone.

What makes this loss particularly tragic to the people of Afghanistan is that these seeds had evolved over years to be drought-, blight-, or pest-resistant. Seed banks serve as "genetic reservoirs of adaptive traits,"[7] designed to keep the best of the best. The looters weren't even after the seeds but rather the airtight plastic and glass jars they were stored in. The jars were upended, their contents spilled and exposed to the elements. Among the seeds lost were varieties of wheat, barley, chickpeas, lentils, melons, pistachios, almonds, and pomegranates. When scientists from Kabul examined the piles of commingled, scattered seed, they knew immediately there was no way to separate or identify them.

In countries like Afghanistan, where only 12 percent of the arable land is suitable for agriculture and only one-third of that land is irrigated, wide seed diversity is mandatory, because the topography is so varied. After decades of war and years of drought, how does a country begin to feed itself again? By importing seed, preferably its own, and if it has been able to archive its seed in a seed vault, far from the sites and sources of conflict, starting over again is at least possible.

But even existing seed banks don't always guarantee sanctuary for a culture's heirloom seeds. Peru's National Agricultural Institute was raided in 1985 and their entire sweet potato collection was stolen by a starving mob. In 2007, the seed bank in the Philippines washed away in a typhoon, taking untold varieties of sweet potato, taro, and banana with it.

Prior to the 2003 bombing and invasion of Iraq by American armed forces, scientists who worked at seed storage facilities in the Baghdad suburb of Abu Ghraib risked their lives to smuggle a "black box" of seeds out of the country. While scientists from ICARDA (International Center for Agricultural Research in the Dry Areas) plan to use the contents of the box to restart Iraq's agricultural future, it is feared that many seed archives, some strains dating back 4,000 years, were lost forever.

Besides Fort Collins and the Svalbard's so-called "doomsday vault," large banks exist in Mexico, Colombia, India, Ivory Coast, Syria, Philippines, and Nigeria. Approximately 1460 seed banks dot the world, each dedicated to keeping seed strains alive and safe. But of those only about 35 meet the necessary security, refrigeration, and sanitation standards required for long-term seed storage. According to a 2005 report by the U.S. Department of Agriculture and the University of California, many are in a very dilapidated condition.[8]

The Svalbard Vault is a joint mission of the country of Norway and the Global Crop Diversity Trust to reclaim and safeguard as many samples of seed as possible. Their mission is one they intend to continue until they are satisfied that samples of all food and grass life across the globe are safeguarded.

SITES OF THE WORLD'S MAJOR SEED VAULTS

Seed archive location	Archive contents*
Mexico City, Mexico	150,000 unique samples of wheat from more than 100 countries (90 percent of the world's diversity); 10,000 types of maize
Lima, Peru	7,000 samples of wild and cultivated potatoes; 6,000 sweet potato
Los Banos, the Philippines	Nearly 110,000 samples of cultivated and wild Asian rice
Palmira, Colombia	64,000 samples of beans, cassava, tropical forages (legumes and grasses)-- the world's largest and most diverse collections
Ibadan, Nigeria	More than 15,000 varieties of cowpea from 88 countries, a key cash crop and one of the region's main protein sources; composes about half the global cowpea diversity and 70 percent of Africa's traditional landraces.**

* The samples from these archives began moving to the Svalbard Vault in stages, in February 2008.
** Table from CGIAR Website, January 2008. http://www.cgiar.org/newsroom/releases/news.asp?idnews=715

At a time when more crops than ever before are being grown on the earth's 1.7 billion acres of arable soil, why all the concern about saving seeds? The seed bankers believe they have reason to be concerned. The world's seeds do not seem able to take care of themselves, not with all the havoc—much of it manmade—being wreaked upon them: global warming, drought, lack of foresight, poor resource management, failed crops, war, pestilence, natural disaster, not to mention genetic manipulation. Just considering global warming, what complications might ensue when those 1.7 billion acres of arable soil begin to shrink and turn saline because of the swelling of the oceans from the melting of the Arctic, Antarctic and Greenland ice masses? The remaining land will have to bear the burden of feeding more people with less crop space. In India alone, its arable landmass will have to produce 30 percent more grain in 2025 than it did in 2000.[9]

In addition, say scientists and seed activists, today's agribusiness stresses monoculture and mass production, and this flattening and uniformity, coupled with the ocean of pesticides that have been dumped on our soils in the last 50 years, weakens not only the soil but the genetic diversity of seeds.

Much of our soil no longer contains any of the necessary web of nutrients and organisms (sometimes referred to as pests) that nurtures it, and therefore, us. The soil has been poisoned, stressed, ignored, exhausted for decades, often in the service of monoculture crops. Rachel Carson observed this nearly half a century ago: "Single crop farming does not take advantage of the principles by which nature works. It is agriculture as an engineer might conceive it to be. Nature has introduced great variety into the landscape, but man has displayed a passion for simplifying it."[10]

Engineering, indeed. Agribusiness assures us that simplifying and homogenizing are efficient ways to allow more food to be grown on fewer acres. We need that to feed the world. Simple, right?

The experts disagree on all counts, saying that monocultures threaten our food supply, harm the soil by leaching it of essential nutrients, and ultimately impede the feeding of Third World populations by running their own farmers out of business. More than 60 percent of the 4 billion people in developing nations of the world still subsist on farming and most simply cannot compete with big American agribusiness efficiency, its lower prices, thinner margins and ever-present subsidies.

Monocultures also mean a lack of seed diversity because they celebrate the uniformity of sameness. As the climate warms, this lack of hardy, differentiated seed stock will become ever more alarming. "Maintaining the genetic diversity that exists among the wild plant population is absolutely essential if we are to have any chance of mitigating the effects of climate change," says Emile Frison, Director General of the International Plant Genetic Resources Institute (IPGRI).[11]

The wild plant population is what keeps food strains strong. It is common in Mexico, for example, for small farmers to plant their corn near wild varieties to encourage cross pollination from wild plants that have proven their rigor just by surviving. If climate change removes these wild relatives from the gene pool, the threat to the genetic diversity that helps crops adapt is clear.

Since 1900 the world has lost much of its agricultural diversity. The UN Food and Agriculture Organization estimates that 75 percent of the world's seeds have gone extinct.[12] Other estimates run as high as 90 percent.[13] In the U.S. alone, the variety of apples grown has dwindled by more than 85 percent from 7100 to about 1,000. Between 1903 and 1983 we lost 80 percent of our tomato variety, nearly 93 percent of lettuces, more than 90 percent of our field and sweet corn varieties, more than 98 percent of asparagus varieties. Just two varieties of apple account for more than 50 percent of the apples marketed,[14] and half of the broccoli grown commercially in the U.S. comes from a single variety: Marathon.[15] In India, where now only a handful of rice varieties are grown, there were once 200,000 types.

So what? Who needs that much variety? According to plant geneticists and seed savers, we do. Frison agrees. As the global weather patterns change, she says, "We're going to need this diversity to breed new varieties that can adapt to climate change, new diseases, and other rapidly emerging threats."[16]

Look no further than current wheat crop yields to see potential threats when diversity is limited. The outbreak of the wheat rust fungus called UG99 (named for the country of origin, Uganda, and the year of its outbreak) concerns agronomists worldwide, and not just because it is hard to control. The cost of pest control (fungicide application runs $100 for less than half an acre) is well beyond the small farmer's means. And the blight is virulent and hardy, able to travel thousands of miles, from Africa to the Caribbean, on air currents in a matter of days. It's not hard to see how it can spread from there and wreak global havoc in a matter of weeks. The effect on crop yields at a time when demand for wheat is increasing with an ever-rising population is sobering.[17]

THE DANGERS OF LOST SEED DIVERSITY

The calamity that can ensue when that rich diversity is lost became painfully obvious in the 1840s when Ireland lost from one to two million people (of a total population of nine million) to a protracted potato famine brought on by potato late blight. Potatoes were a major staple of the Irish diet. It's estimated that the average person ate as much as 14 pounds of the tubers *per day*.[18] Because Ireland's agriculture depended mostly on potato varieties that were very similar, when the microorganism that caused the blight hit one strain, it quickly spread, turning much of the potato crop into shrunken, rotted mush.

Although Irish farmers grew a number of other crops, a majority of those were regularly exported to England. What remained at home was beyond the budget of farmers who could not even afford to eat their own grain after paying the rent on their farms. Many of the poor who depended on the potato for food were doubly affected. With no crop diversity, no other hardy or wild potato varieties to step in and fill the gap, and no new seed to plant because the crop had perished, farmers had to spend what little money they did have to buy food. Many struggled with the remnants of the killed crop and replanted what they could. The blight returned for another terrible season for a total of five long years. Without money to pay rent, many were turned out of their tenant farms, and with no way to grow or buy food, they starved.

The potato famine in Ireland marked the first time in history that a crop had failed not just because of bad weather or the ravages of war, but because of a lack of variety. There was no Plan B. Having originated in the Andes and been brought back from the New World in the late 16th century, the tuber came first to Spain and later to England and Ireland; for the next two and a half centuries, all the potatoes grown in Europe came from those earlier descendants.

More than a century later, that lesson had to be learned again by both U.S. and Soviet farmers and the outcome changed agriculture and world economies in ways no one could have foreseen. In the early 1960s, southern corn leaf blight had begun to get the attention of agronomists in places as far flung as the Philippines and Mexico. By 1968 it was showing up in seeds in the Midwest. By the spring of 1970 it was in the Florida corn crop and by summer's end, with production losses becoming obvious in the nation's supermarkets, corn prices had skyrocketed. The cost to American agriculture exceeded a billion bushels—a full 15 percent of the nation's most important crop—and over a billion dollars in lost revenue. The main reason for the failure? Virtually all of America's corn crop was genetically identical. Just as in Ireland, an undiversified crop had to carry all the production weight. Like a single throw of dice, it was all or nothing.[19]

A year later in the fall of 1971, as farmers in the Ukraine, the USSR's breadbasket, faced winter, they felt confident that they would have a record wheat harvest the following summer. Their fields were seeded with the wildly successful, high-yielding strain called Besostaja. But what they hadn't counted on was the fickleness of weather. January temperatures were too cold for the snow cover the crop needed and spring rains didn't materialize.

As the fears of drought became reality, Russian farmers faced bleak harvest prospects while politicians were alarmed by the implications of perceived weaknesses in their food production system. Meanwhile, a Canadian economist had been keeping tabs on weather data and Soviet media reports and read between the lines. She determined that 30 to 40 percent of the Russian winter wheat crop—at least 20 million tons— would be lost to the harsh winter. Knowing how sensitive Besostaja was and that it was widely planted across nearly 100 million acres spanning different temperate zones, she sent a report to the Canadian Wheat Board. What resulted was a secret deal between Russians and Canadians that sent 27 million tons of grain to Russia to bail it out of its food crisis. At stake was not just a shortage of food for its people, but also stock feed for its vast populations of cows and hogs.

As the Canadians scored this trade coup under American noses at a hotel in New York City, an historic change began to take effect. By October a metric ton of wheat had risen from $65 to $90. American farmers got the message. Then-Secretary of Agriculture Earl Butz sounded a call to arms. His "get big or get out" and "plant hedgerow to hedgerow" resounded in their ears. The age of bigger and bigger farming was underway. Farmers went into debt buying more land, more seed, bigger and better machinery to plant and harvest, "and all the fertilizers, center-pivot irrigation pumps, and pesticides their land could absorb."[20]

This boom in wheat prices produced other consequences. As Butz extolled the virtues of bigger farming, he crowed about American abundance by referring to food as a weapon: a sort of "we have it, you don't" schoolyard taunt that did not go over well in some of the less agriculturally abundant corners of the globe. Some say that the first oil crisis in 1973 was in part a strategically pointed reminder to Americans that they didn't have the only natural resource worth coveting. Just in case we'd forgotten, two other conditions were now in play. Those shiny new combines wouldn't run on anything but the black crude that had suddenly gotten a lot more expensive. And our own domestic production capacities were quickly approaching peak and decline, making us oil shoppers rather than suppliers for the first time in a hundred years as we permanently moved into first place as the globe's biggest per capita user of fossil fuels.

The harsh winters that had decimated the Russian summer wheat crop also hit vast areas of the Third World as their import costs for grain doubled to $6 billion. Resources had entered world politics with hard realities as the 1970s began to unfold. Lost in the excitement of agricultural profit motive was another troubling truth. A lack of genetic diversity had gutted the Russian summer wheat harvest of 1972. While the Besostaja strain did well in the mild regions of Kuban, it perished in the harsher winters of its sister state, the Ukraine. What worked in one part of the Russian breadbasket did not work in another.

Nor did American farmers fare well. By the mid 1980s, the glut of grain on the world markets sent prices into a freefall. Farmers faced rising debts in times of inflation and bloated interest rates. In record numbers, they went out of business. Between 1987 and 1992 alone, an average of 32,500 farms—most of them family run —were lost each year. The "hedgerow to hedgerow" planting continued in an effort to increase output to make up for lost revenue. Increasingly, failed farms were bought up and folded into bigger and bigger farms. In some cases, the farmhouses themselves were burned to the ground and plowed over to create more space for planting.[21]

This same scene played out again years later as the 2008 growing season approached and farmers across America began demolishing old outbuildings to make way for more land to grow wheat, corn, and soybeans—all in response to rising demands for crops from abroad as well as the growing drive for biofuels.[22] Agriculture, it seems, no longer has much appetite for sitting still.

Stabilizing agriculture, it could be said, was a long time coming.[23] The idea of staying put and gathering in stationary places rather than wandering as nomadic hunters took about two million years to develop. In the roughly 12,000 years since the dawn of agriculture, civilization as we now know it—from written language and monumental architecture to trade and, yes, armed conflict—came into being. During much of that time, the most common practice for farmers was to save and share seed, thereby creating hybrids that were heartier and more prolific. As centuries passed and the descendants of hunters and gatherers moved to the cities and suburbs and population increased exponentially, more farmland had to be converted to accommodate this growth, and less land was then available to produce more food. The variety of food being grown slowly narrowed to a handful of crops, and those crops further decreased in diversity, with the result that the food supply became more vulnerable to drought and pests.[24]

"As the first link in the food chain, seed is a central factor in any nation's strategy for food security and self-sufficiency."[25] As long as the markets remained local, the cultures could provide a broad enough diversity to allow farmers to evolve new breeds and conserve seeds and plant varieties. But as agribusiness has become more and more prominent worldwide, this diversity has been winnowed down to very few varieties. Using seed, says physicist and seed activist Vandana Shiva, "is the best way to conserve them; whichever economic system determines how plant species are used also influences which species will survive and which will be pushed to extinction."[26] In other words, use them or lose them.

Seeds have a resilience, a capacity to live and regenerate that is one of nature's safeguards. "When a fire destroys a forest, the species and plants that were lost will reassert themselves over time. Seeds that have lain dormant for decades and that germinate only when subjected to intense heat will come to life, burst into foliage, and bloom in the spring."[27] This was seen recently in the regrowth in Griffith Park in Los Angeles. Less than a year after a fire devastated one-fifth of the park's hundreds of acres in May of 2007, the undergrowth so vital to preventing erosion in the hilly park side had begun to regenerate itself and create a pelt of green.

We can count on the natural wisdom of seeds. What threatens us is the lack of wisdom of those who believe they have figured out a way to permanently alter nature by making it predictable and controllable.

THE SEED CHANGERS

In 1971 a General Electric engineer named Ananda Chakrabarty applied for a patent on a genetically engineered Pseudomonas bacteria to be used as an oil-eating microbe. GE saw it as a boon to cleaning up the crude oil spills that were becoming all too common as oil tanker traffic to and from the U.S. began to increase. The U.S. patent office, operating on a longtime bias against patenting animate life forms, refused the application. General Electric and Chakrabarty persisted and eventually appealed the case to the Supreme Court. In 1980 a landmark 5-4 majority broke a long-term ban on patenting animate life forms and the application was granted.

The situation was not without irony. "They had genetically engineered a micro-organism which could eat oil," says Frank Chapelle, a hydrologist for the U.S. Geological Survey. "As it turns out, all that became superfluous, even though the genetic engineering was brilliant. It turns out that natural micro-organisms were capable of doing the same thing."[28] As it turned out, the microbe, which also snacked on lots of other things besides oil, was never used. Nevertheless, this case had enormous repercussions not for the oil industry but for our food supply. The floodgates to biotechnology burst open, and what happened in less than a decade changed the way both man and beast would sustain themselves. The era of GMO food had begun.[29]

Floodgates of creative activism burst at the same time. Scientists like Vandana Shiva took issue with the technology on several levels. She argued that nothing new was being produced but that existing material was merely being manipulated. "All that genetic engineers really do is 'shuffle genes around'; they do not create life," Shiva said. "Therefore, literally speaking, no life forms should be patentable. However, patent offices and courts have interpreted modification as creation. This allows the ownership of any altered biological material."[30] (Chakrabarty himself described the process thusly: "I simply shuffled genes, changing bacteria that already existed."[31])

The second was summarized by lawyer and executive director of the Center for Food Safety, Andrew Kimbrell: "The (U.S.) Supreme Court's Chakrabarty decision has been extended and continues to be extended, up the chain of life. The patenting of microbes has led inexorably to the patenting of plants, and then animals." In other words it gave corporations the right and power to own and control all the species of life on earth. By 1987, that included human cells, cell lines and genes. And seeds.

According to Wangari Mathai, the 2004 Nobel Peace prize winning Coordinator of The Green Belt Movement, this is the plan of the multinationals whose vested interests are at stake. "This distortion has been deliberately created by blurring the meaning of invention so that corporations can obtain private monopolies on mere 'discoveries' of biological materials and their properties, such as umbilical cord blood cells and basmati rice."[32]

GMOs are foods that have had one or more elements of DNA altered. Every cellular organism has DNA molecules. Within the molecules of higher organisms are genes whose job is to carry our traits, like hair and eye color, height, the facial features that make us look like our parents and siblings. These traits are passed on by reproduction. That's also the way they are passed on in the plant and animal world. Farmers and agricultural pioneers and botanists dating back to Luther Burbank learned to crossbreed crops or animals to develop the most desirable characteristics possible. That is not what genetic engineering does. Author Jeffrey Smith describes the difference in *Seeds of Deception*:

With genetic engineering, breeders have a whole new bag of tricks. Instead of relying on species to pass on genes through mating, biologists cut the gene out of one species' DNA, modify it, and then insert it directly into another species' DNA. And since virtually all organisms have DNA, scientists don't have to limit the source of their genes to members of the same species. They can search anywhere in the plant, animal, bacteria, even human world to find genes with desired traits, or even synthesize genes in the laboratory that don't exist in nature.[33]

For the first time in history, science is intentionally breeding across species. The results include:

- corn and soy crops that grow with pesticide genes inserted in them to resist insects;
- cotton grown to resist the common boll weevil;
- using human growth hormones to increase the size of cows, pigs and even salmon;
- placing the Arctic flounder gene in tomatoes to help them withstand cold temperatures;
- injecting cows with genetically engineered recombinant bovine growth hormone (rBGH) to increase their milk production

Fish like Rainbow trout, Coho salmon, mud loach, and common carp can now be engineered with human growth hormone genes. Antifreeze genes can be harvested from goldfish, oysters, and Arctic flatfish. Insulin producing genes can be engineered from tilapia.[34] If a scientist wanted to breed cold weather tolerance into a tomato, he or she would not have to "wait for the unlikely event of the fish mating with the tomato. Instead, he figured out which gene in the fish keeps it from freezing and then inserted that gene into the tomato's DNA." A gene that had never existed in anything but that particular organism in the Atlantic Salmon from which it was extracted now lives in that tomato. And not just in that tomato, but in every tomato grown from it.[35]

Fortunately, some of these examples have never evolved beyond laboratories. But bovine growth hormone is widely used in the U.S. milk supply, and much of the corn, cotton, canola and soy crops grown in the

United States are genetically engineered and show up in the multitude of genetically enhanced molecules that give our processed foods flavor and long shelf life. Although most corn that reaches the tables of American families is not genetically engineered, many of the animals whose meat and by-products we eat (eggs, butter, milk, beef, pork and chicken, for example) spend their lives eating grains like corn that are genetically modified.[36] Author Michael Pollan's definitive books on the origins of the modern meal, *Omnivore's Dilemma* and *In Defense of Food*, describe the lifecycle of agribusiness corn and farm animals and remind us that not only do we eat GMOs ourselves (most processed food, artificial sweeteners and soft drinks include high-fructose corn syrup, which is derived from GMO'd corn), they are eaten by what we eat. "We are what we eat eats," Pollan reminds us. The growth hormones and genetically modified bits of corn and soy that feed our food also ultimately feed us and reside somewhere in our cell tissue.

So what's the big deal? Corporations that have patented their science, as well as our own FDA have validated Monsanto's promise that this is safe, abundant food. To that end the FDA passed language in 1991 that said in effect that:

- GM'd food was GRAS (generally regarded as safe) and substantially equivalent to non-GM food.
- No testing had proved otherwise.
- Years of having GM'd food in our diets without apparent side effects is proof that it's safe.

These assumptions, however, present a jumble of catch-22s. Opponents of GM food, including scientists, political activists, consumers and farmers alike point out some glaring issues. First, the FDA failed to mention that there is no standard for comparison, because no testing has ever been done except by interested parties who have invested large sums of money in engineering and selling these products. They also failed to mention that independent and even FDA testing (that was not made public for many years) proved that the products were anything but safe. In addition, because it was deemed substantially equivalent to non-GM food, neither testing nor labeling was required.

Citing food slander laws that went into effect after Amarillo cattlemen failed to secure a judgment against talk-show host Oprah

Winfrey for saying on the air that she wouldn't be eating any more hamburgers after she found out about Mad Cow disease, corporations can sue food suppliers in some states for labeling their products "GMO free," "no rBGH" or "no rBST."

It may be the corporations' dogged resistance to labeling that has caused the rush to judgment on GM foods. Polls taken in 2008 show that as many as 90 percent of those asked said they preferred labeling for GM foods. Who can blame them? The truth is that there is no sure way to tell whether food that has had its DNA moved around and altered is safe at all. There is much about this food that is inherently unpredictable. As Dr. Ignacio Chapela, a Microbial Ecologist at the University of California, Berkeley, said, "I think this is probably the largest biological experiment humanity has ever entered into."[37]

This gets to the heart of the issue that repeatedly arises with GMOs: we don't even know what we don't know. To paraphrase former Secretary of Defense Donald Rumsfeld, there aren't just the known unknowns but lots of unknown unknowns. We simply can't understand an issue whose breadth we cannot conceive.

In 1959, Dr. David Price of the U.S. Public Health Service said, "We all live under the haunting fear that something may corrupt the environment to the point where man joins the dinosaurs as an obsolete form of life. And what makes these thoughts all the more disturbing is the knowledge that our fate could perhaps be sealed twenty or more years before the development of symptoms."[38] Price was speaking at a time when the idea of atomic weaponry and its threats were growing but still new. However, the anxiety he spoke of could easily apply today. We do not know what GM foods have done to us already, or when or even if we are ingesting them.

Another troubling issue surrounding GMOs centers on the possible cumulative effects that might manifest in our systems in decades to come, precisely because there has been no mandatory testing to track these effects over time. The breadth of potential risks to our health and genetic contamination may never be known. "We are confronted with the most powerful technology the world has ever known," said Suzanne Wuerthele, EPA toxicologist, "and it is being rapidly deployed with almost no thought whatsoever to its consequences."[39] Going even further, HRH Charles, Prince of Wales, has called GMOs the "biggest environmental disaster of all time."

Monsanto should not have to vouchsafe the safety of biotech food. Our interest is in selling as much of it as possible. Assuring its safety is the F.D.A.'s job.
— Phil Angell, Director of Corporate Communications, Monsanto[45]

KNOWN GMO HEALTH DANGERS

In the 1980s an epidemic of unknown origin had doctors perplexed. People were showing up complaining of paralysis, mouth ulcers, shortness of breath, nausea, hair loss and a host of other seemingly unrelated symptoms. Doctors were baffled and could find no common thread. The only shared complaint was severe, debilitating muscle pain, often coupled with a skyrocketing white cell count, a sure signal of a severe disruption to the immune system. The cases came and went without most doctors knowing the other cases existed. Then in 1989 a surge of cases in New Mexico got the attention of two doctors who sent their queries to the Center for Disease Control in Atlanta. The common complaints suddenly presented a pattern and after some detective work, the common thread emerged. Each of the patients had taken supplements containing L-Tryptophan, an essential amino acid that is found in turkey, milk and other foods, often used to combat insomnia and depression. (Think of drinking warm milk before bedtime to help you sleep.) Each also had skyrocketing white cell counts.

The brand each patient used had been manufactured by a Japanese company called Showa Denko KK, the only U.S. supplier that had genetically engineered the bacteria to create L-Tryptophan. (L-Tryptophan does not naturally cause these symptoms.) The company's reason for using genetic engineering: it saved money. As explained in harrowing detail in Jeffrey Smith's *Seeds of Deception*, the only reason medical experts were able to determine the origin of the problem was the surge in symptoms, finally identified as an illness called EMS (eosinophilia-myalgia syndrome). Otherwise, the epidemic could have spread and its genesis would have remained out of anyone's awareness. An estimated 5,000 to 10,000 people became sick or physically disabled. It is suspected that many more people suffered from the outbreak before it was identified but either they failed to report their symptoms or their cases remained mysteries to their doctors who lacked enough information to be able to connect the dots.

Testifying before a Congressional committee in July of 1991, Douglas Archer, deputy director of the FDA's Center for Food Safety and Applied Nutrition, sidestepped the genetic engineering aspect of Showa Denko's L-Tryptophan and instead used the moment to deride over-the-counter food supplements that the FDA had wanted to ban for years. L-Tryptophan is now available only by prescription, but the issue surrounding the fact that the only version of the supplement that caused any of the symptoms was the genetically modified one were not raised by the FDA or questioned by Congress or the media, with one exception. *Albuquerque Journal* reporter Tamar Stieber who had four friends stricken by the disease, followed the thread back to its origin, and won a 1990 Pulitzer Prize for her reporting.[40]

THE FLAVR SAVR TOMATO

Approved by the FDA against the advice of many scientists, a product named Flavr Savr tomatoes, created by Calgene, a Monsanto subsidiary, was the first genetically engineered food offered to the public. However, it turned out to have a short shelf life and consumers did not like the way it tasted. It was soon removed from the market. In tests done before its product launch, some lab rats that ate the tomato developed stomach lesions, often seen as a precursor to cancer. Seven of the 40 rats died inexplicably.

PIONEER HI-BRED

In 1995 a Dupont-owned seed company took a single protein from a Brazil nut and genetically engineered it to enhance the protein nutrition of a new soybean to be sold as cattle feed. Because the animals would eventually be consumed by humans and some humans have nut allergies, Pioneer ran tests to ensure that the protein they had used would not create allergic reactions in humans. To their surprise, it did in three separate tests. This underscores an issue that is still problematic today. According to FDA toxicologist Louis Pribyl, "There are very few allergens that have been identified at the protein or gene level." He recommended that there be much closer scrutiny by companies who genetically engineer any plant that causes allergic reactions. His recommendations were ignored.[41]

To this day, testing is voluntary. The FDA offers only guidelines, allowing GM manufacturers to create their own test scenarios and conclusions.

STARLINK

In the fall of 2000, StarLink, a brand of corn genetically bred for animal feed and engineered with a mild form of pesticide in it, was inadvertently mixed into the nation's corn supply and showed up in multiple corn-based food products including tortillas, corn meal, and taco shells. Unknown numbers of people experienced anaphylactic shock and more than 300 food products were recalled. It is estimated that the cost to manufacturer Aventis was $1 billion. The FDA allowed Aventis to conduct its own tests and despite a double test conducted and paid for by a public interest group that confirmed contamination by Starlink,[42] Aventis eventually tried to get the ban lifted so they could keep selling the product. Although it was sold as yellow feed corn, USDA tests at the time showed traces of StarLink in 71 of the 288 companies they contacted, and concluded that it "may linger in the human food chain forever."[43]

Coming as it did in the early days of the move to sell GM to foreign markets, the StarLink debacle started a grass roots movement against GM food in England and then the European continent. Labeling for genetically engineered food, still not available in the U.S. despite polls indicating that most Americans want it, has been mandatory in Europe since 2000. Europeans have wavered between being lukewarm to hostile about buying U.S. GM food, not only for human but also for livestock consumption. In the spring of 2001, USDA reports showed that "European demand for non-GM feed jumped from near zero to 20-25 percent within twelve months."

NEW LEAF POTATO

Although the New Leaf never constituted more than three percent of the nation's potato crop, Monsanto engineered it to contain several attractive traits: It promised to be disease- and bruise-resistant, herbicide-tolerant, to grow to a hefty size, and, with its own pesticide in residence, be able to ward off annoyances like the Colorado potato beetle. By 1998 the New Leaf was in the American diet, but that summer a distinguished biologist working for Scotland's Rowlett Institute, Dr. Arpad Pusztai, upset the apple cart. Asked to give a perfunctory okay to plans for a genetically engineered potato that the Scottish Ministry had high hopes to produce commercially, Pusztai was already aware via his own research that there were issues with the potatoes. Identical batches were giving differing results. Nutrition levels were not even and substances in the potato that should have been safe for humans were damaging the immune systems of lab rats.

Since the accepted basic premise of GM foods was that they were stable, Pusztai knew something was wrong. Having created the model for testing GM foods two years before, he was disturbed by the patchy and slipshod testing protocols he was being asked to approve, and he declined. His concerns were overridden and he was fired. A subsequent investigation exonerated Pusztai but the controversy surrounding his firing created a storm of protest. For the first time Europeans found out they had already been eating GM foods for the previous two years. Now they also knew how poorly these products had been tested prior to being introduced into their food supply. In the United States, food manufacturers including McDonalds and Pringles yielded to consumer requests not to use the New Leaf and declined to incorporate the potatoes into their products. Monsanto took the New Leaf off the market in 2001.

Later, when 80 percent of U.S. and Canadian wheat buyers informed Monsanto they would not buy GM wheat and more than 200 U.S. and Canadian groups representing farmers, corn growers, and wheat interests lobbied against it, Monsanto shelved plans to develop GM wheat in the short term.[44] But by 2009 rumors about resurrected plans for GM wheat were back in full swing.

Any politician or scientist who tells you these products are safe is either very stupid or lying. The experiments have simply not been done.
— Geneticist David Suzuki, Professor Emeritus,
University of British Columbia

FARMERS: CROP CONTAMINATION AND FARMER LIABILITY

For his entire life, Percy Schmeiser has lived and farmed in Bruno, Saskatchewan, Canada. In 1998 he found a few tufts of canola (a wheat-like grain also known as rapeseed) growing around telephone poles near the highway bordering his 1400-acre farm. What he did not know at that moment was that the canola he found beside the road was a proprietary patented version of the grain manufactured by Monsanto. Despite the fact that it had blown onto his land and taken root, he soon found himself embroiled in a lawsuit with St. Louis-based Monsanto over patent infringement.

Monsanto alleged that Schmeiser and his wife, Louise, had knowingly grown RoundUp Ready canola on virtually all of their acreage and had not paid the chemical giant the $15 per acre technology fee they claimed was owed them, plus $400,000 in penalties, and additional court costs. Tests revealed not only that more than half of his fields had been contaminated, but also that the entire seed archive that he and his wife had carefully husbanded for five decades was tainted and had to be destroyed. In 2000 the Supreme Court of Canada ruled that Schmeiser had violated Monsanto's patent rights and found that all his profits from his year's worth of crops had to go to Monsanto, even though it was shown that some of his fields were not even contaminated.

The court further ruled that it didn't matter how the seed got into Schmeiser's fields, whether blown in by wind, distributed by passing bees or birds, or dropping off the tires or flatbeds of passing trucks. What was not considered was that Schmeiser and his wife have been long-time seed savers and that because of the Monsanto contamination, their entire life's work was ruined. "You can see what happens now to any farmer in the world who wants to use his own seed," said Schmeiser. "All Monsanto has to do is to contaminate a field. They only have to put their seed into an environment in any country, any region, and if it contaminates a neighbor's crop, that neighbor can no longer grow that crop without a Monsanto license, or permission, or paying a technology charge."[46] In his mind, Monsanto's aim was to bring an end to seed saving and sharing, a way of life for farmers across Canada and the entire world.

In the wake of the court's decision, organic farming of soy and canola in Canada came to an end. It cannot be grown free of GM for the foreseeable future, because the entire crop nation-wide has been cross-pollinated with RoundUp Ready canola and soy. Schmeiser became an anti-GM advocate and activist and tours the world sharing his story. He and his wife continue to farm canola. In 2005 he discovered their fields had again become contaminated with RoundUp Ready canola and this time he took Monsanto to court for damages. On March 19, 2008, in an out-of-court settlement, he prevailed. Monsanto agreed to pay clean-up costs and also agreed not to require a gag order. Most importantly, the company can be sued again if Schmeiser or other farmers discover further contamination.

ENVIRONMENT: FRANKENFISH AND GENE JUMPING

"We know," says Andrew Kimbrell, "how the introduction of a biological species into the wrong ecosystem" can create catastrophe.[47] In the 1950s the Nile perch was introduced into Lake Victoria and since then has devastated its ecosystem, killing to extinction some vital cichlid species and causing mayhem in the world's largest tropical lake and one of Africa's most densely populated shorelines. As detailed in *Darwin's Nightmare*, the grim 2004 documentary about the environmental and social effects of the perch's takeover of the lake, the impact on the local economy has been devastating. The fish has devoured every other lake species and has nearly destroyed the area's ecology. Too poor to afford cooking fuel, the population was forced to cut down the adjoining forests for kindling. The resulting erosion and the voracious appetites of the perch have seriously undermined the size and health of the lake. The perch had originally been introduced to Lake Victoria to add new fish populations and increase fishing opportunities. The only problem was that no one thought about whether the perch belonged in such an environment or what the long-term consequences might be.

The introduction of genetically engineered fish into native fish populations can prove problematic and destructive in many different scenarios. The documentary *Unnatural Selection* looks at the efforts of one company, Aqua Bounty Farms, to establish what are commonly known as Frankenfish—giant salmon cultivated with the help of human growth hormones—in the food chain. The greatest complication is called "gene jumping," a form of species contamination in which a species not intended to be targeted can be disrupted or even eradicated. The giant fish that are created with genetic engineering tend to live shorter lives and be less robust. To make matters worse, the larger fish are more attractive to females, who will choose them over their non-GM, longer living—but smaller—males, thereby short-circuiting the process of natural selection. Because of this tendency to select bigger but weaker partners, it is feared that, should these GM'd salmon escape into the wild salmon population, within as few as six generations only the larger but weaker species would predominate and eventually the entire wild salmon population would be wiped out. This is a particular danger to the Pacific salmon, whose numbers have already been so greatly weakened by overfishing that fishing bans that span an entire season are being enforced along the Pacific coast.

Since most fish farms have to be located near rivers or oceans to ensure fresh influxes of water, mass escapes from the farms into the wild are not unusual. While the best of intentions is to keep these engineered salmon out of the native populations by confining them to these farms, vast numbers of farmed fish have broken free because of flooding—as many as 250,000 at a time—and found their way into native fish populations. Once into the wild, there is no recalling them. There is no repair. It is a Pandora's box that can never be closed again.

Us: GM PRODUCTS WE LIVE WITH TODAY

While most genetically modified crops are used for cattle feed, oils from all of the big four GM products—corn, soy, cotton, and canola—are on the market and are used as ingredients in many processed foods. Even if you don't count corn and soybeans in your daily diet, you're probably ingesting much more of them than you think, from vegetable oils to hidden sweeteners. As Chapter 3 pointed out, one of corn's highest profile byproducts, *high fructose corn syrup*, is one of the most prevalent ingredients in packaged, processed and fast foods—even in so-called low-calorie food—and its ubiquitous presence is frequently cited as one of the culprits in the last decade's uptick in obesity in America. Its presence also signals that a product contains GM corn. Only genetically engineered corn is used for HFCS. If a food is labeled organic, HFCS cannot be an ingredient. Together, GM corn and soy products likely make up 30 percent of your daily calories.[48] In general, the more ingredients on a food label, the more GM corn and soy products are in the food being described.[49]

Recumbent bovine growth hormone (rBGH, also shown as *rBST)*, an additive injected into dairy cows to increase milk production, turns up in many dairy products. While it may increase milk production, it also is a frequent cause of infertility and premature death in cows, and mammary infection in their udders. Unfortunately, some of the pus from these infections often gets into the milk drawn from afflicted cows. Organic milk and milk products certify not only that the cows were not treated with rBGH, but also that the cows were not fed GM corn or soy feed.

GM sugar beets and alfalfa. GM sugar beets were granted USDA approval and were growing by the fall of 2008, and according to one estimate quickly garnered 95 percent of the sugar beet market. But a ruling by a U.S. judge in September 2009 halted their cultivation and put their future on hold, saying the USDA had erred by releasing them before an environmental impact statement had been written. A similar ruling has postponed the release of GE (genetically engineered) alfalfa indefinitely. According to USDA Deputy Secretary, Kathleen Merrigan, final rules would be issued on alfalfa and sugar beets sometime in 2010.

BIOTECH AND INDUSTRIAL AGRICULTURE MYTHS

Industrial agriculture will feed the world

World hunger isn't the result of a lack of food. The UN Food and Agriculture Organization (FAO) estimates that food grows in enough abundance globally each year to provide 4.3 pounds per person per day. "Industrial agriculture actually increases hunger by raising the cost of farming," writes Andrew Kimbrell in an essay in *Fatal Harvest*, "by forcing tens of millions of farmers off the land, and by growing primarily high-profit export and luxury crops."[50] The loss of those farms is often cited as one of the main reasons for the millions of poor in India going hungry each day.

Nor is GM'd seed more productive. According to a report published by the Union of Concerned Scientists in 2009, "The several thousand field trials over the last 20 years for genes aimed at increasing operational or intrinsic yield (of crops) indicate a significant undertaking. Yet none of these field trials has resulted in increased yield in commercialized major food/feed crops, with the exception of Bt corn." The report further explains that even the good news for GM'd corn was more likely due to improved breeding techniques, not genetic engineering.[51]

GMOs will result in less pesticide use

This is a slippery argument for companies like Dow and Monsanto to make, because pesticides are big money makers for them. The truth is that pesticide use with genetically modified seed is frequently just as high and the health risks associated with having seed that has pesticide built into each cell (as is the case with corn and Bt cotton) are unknown because of lack of FDA testing mandates, and the corporations' ability to whitewash the testing process.

A study released in late 2009 confirms that pesticide use actually increased substantially in the first dozen years that GM crops were being used. Farmers used 318 million more pounds of pesticides than they would have used if they had not planted GE seeds. "GE crops are pushing pesticide use upward at a rapidly accelerating pace. In 2008, GE crop acres required over 26 percent more pounds of pesticides per acre than acres planted to conventional varieties. The report projects that this trend will continue as a result of the rapid spread of glyphosate-resistant weeds."[52] RoundUp, the pesticide contained in Monsanto's GM seeds, is a glyphosate. Contrary to its claims, its legacy seems to be bigger toxic bailouts each year to get crops to harvest. And what about all those pesticides being sprayed to kill all those super weeds that became impervious to RoundUp? According to the FDA, at least 53 of the pesticides labeled as carcinogenic are used in massive quantities on today's major food crops.

Farm incomes will increase exponentially using biotechnology

One of the selling points to farmers is that, although GM seeds are more expensive (the cost of Monsanto's RoundUp Ready seed includes a $15 per acre technology fee), the increased output makes the cost worthwhile. Just as lower pesticide use with GE seed proved to be a myth, numerous studies also show that crop yields with GM seed are lower than non-GM seed. As costs for inputs (soil, fertilizer, pesticides) continue to go up and crop prices stagnate or decline, the scenario grows ever less rosy. What is missing from the "high yield" data coming from agribusiness is the "externals" that are often not factored into the bottom-line figures. These factors include health, environmental and social costs—including the loss of farming communities and their wealth of wisdom—and the subsidies that support big agribusiness. The loss from failed crops is at the root of more than 150,000 farmers' suicides in India alone. As one food executive said, "There's money to be made in food unless you're trying to grow it."[53]

Organic crops aren't as productive per acre as conventional crops

This is one of the biggest farces perpetuated by the purveyors of biotechnology and conventional farming. Organic farming is making a huge comeback precisely because of its productivity. Not only do multiple studies demonstrate that organic farming, with its concentration on crop diversity, rotation, and lack of chemical inputs, is more productive and better for the soil, they also show that organic farming—the only kind of farming anybody did until the 1950s—produces healthier food.

The USDA began tracking the nutrient content of foods back in the 1950s, when the Green Revolution was getting a full head of steam. According to their figures the nutrition value of non-organic foods has steadily declined, making it necessary today to eat more food to get the nutrients our bodies need. Increasingly Americans are overweight and undernourished (three out of five Americans are overweight; one in five is obese). On average we are eating 300 calories a day more than we were in 1985. About 90 percent of our calories come from sugars (lots from high fructose syrup made from GM corn) and added fat (much of that from GM'd soybean oil) and refined grains. Less than 10 percent comes from the five servings of fruits and vegetables we're supposed to eat every day.

The effects on children are increasingly alarming. High-calorie, low-nutrient diets are being looked at as the culprits responsible for chronic diseases such as diabetes and cancer. Lacking vitamins C, E, B12, B6, niacin, folic acid, iron or zinc "appears to mimic radiation by causing single- and double-strand DNA breaks, oxidative lesions, or both."[54] All causes are seen as precursors to cancer.

GMOs are safe and their behavior well understood

The stories behind early GM crops like Pioneer Hi-Bred, L-Tryptophan, StarLink, and the Flavr Savr tomato contradict both of those claims. Thanks to the inclusion of unlabeled GMs in our diets, especially processed food, it's difficult for any of us to know exactly what we are eating. Since we are largely unable to know when we are eating GM products or by-products, there is no way to know the genesis of potential illnesses, allergies or worse.

One special item of note: antibiotic resistance marker genes (ARMs). In the process of creating a GM crop strain, when researchers want to get foreign genes into the host DNA, they sometimes use what's called a gene gun, a .22-caliber device that blasts tiny bits of gold- or tungsten-coated genetic material into a dish containing thousands of cells, hoping with this "shotgun" approach to maximize cell penetration. But how can they tell which genes have received the altered DNA? They can't tell, so they attach ARMs to each gene in the shot. Then they wash the blasted cells with antibiotic. If any of the genes was pierced with the ARM-toting gene, it will survive the antibiotic wash. The rest head straight to cellular Boot Hill.

The plot thickens here because it's not a good idea to have genes in the body that are resistant to antibiotics. Biotech scientists insist this is not possible, because ARMs can't survive the human digestive process, so they never reach the gut. The problem is that *they do*.

In a landmark study done in 2002, using test subjects who had colostomy bags, researchers found "a relatively large proportion of genetically modified DNA survived the passage through" the strong acids of the stomach and small intestine. Worse, this meant that the animals that ate the GM'd food that the test subjects ate had transferred them across species, another problem the biotech scientists said was impossible. The danger: that antibiotic-resistant genes could float around in our stomachs and guts for prolonged periods, making us resistant to antibiotics that we might someday need to survive an illness. Another problem: since we don't have food labeling that tells us when we're eating GM food, if anyone contracted a puzzling illness that resisted antibiotics, there would be no way to know if that resistance came from eating something that had ARMS in it.

GMOs are widely successful

Because we don't label or strictly segregate GM from non-GM crops, overseas buyers have a problem with our genetically modified products—corn, soy, canola and cotton. Public distrust of the safety of genetically modified products has driven the United Kingdom and European Union to employ strict rules about labeling and content. Since there is currently no standard that defines a "GMO free" product, France has passed a law requiring that any product containing more than 0.9 percent genetically modified ingredients be labeled as having GM content and a movement is afoot to drop that content to 0.1 percent. Ireland has declared itself a GM-free zone, forbidding import or domestic growing of any genetically modified crops. Egypt has made a similar declaration. Some African countries won't allow our GM'd grain crops or seed on their shores anymore, not even as free food aid, because they fear contamination of heritage grains, a common danger with genetically modified seed. Because crops are open to the winds, once a GM'd crop pollinates, it is impossible to contain. (Virtually all of Canada's canola has been tainted by GM crops for just this reason and GM pollen has contaminated much of their honey, destroying the organic elements of both those markets.) Since much of our corn and soy crops go to feed animals and Europeans don't want GM-fed food animals, many of our beef, pork and dairy markets in Europe have also dwindled. These collapsing markets have in turn increased U.S. farm subsidies by billions annually.

How did GMOs get past the FDA in the first place?

When introduced to the public, GMOs were rated GRAS (generally recognized as safe) and substantially equivalent to non-GMO food; that is, safe simply because there allegedly were no differences between the two food types. For all intents and purposes, the public was told, GM was the same as non-GM food. In May of 1992, the FDA spelled out the direction of its regulatory policy on GM foods: "The agency is not aware of any information showing that foods derived by these new methods differ from other foods in any meaningful or uniform way." And, it said, its scientists agreed.

That didn't turn out to be quite true. The only reason we know otherwise is the diligence of public interest attorney Steven Druker. Suspicious of the FDA claims that its scientists were on board with FDA talking points about the safety of GM foods, Druker filed a lawsuit to get the FDA to release documents proving their contention. During the discovery phase, Druker's office was inundated with 14,000 pages of documentation. "The idea was to flood us with so many documents we would never be able to read them all."[55]

But they read enough of them to find out that there had been many instances of dissension within the ranks of FDA scientists. An attorney named Michael Taylor, whose firm had once represented Monsanto, had become Deputy Commissioner for Policy. According to Druker, during Taylor's tenure, "references to the unintended negative effects of bioengineering were progressively deleted from drafts of the policy statement (over the protests of agency scientists) and a final statement was issued claiming (a) that [GM] foods are no riskier than others and (b) that the agency has no information to the contrary."[56] Taylor would later leave the FDA to become Monsanto's Vice President for Public Policy. In July 2009, he was appointed a senior adviser to the FDA Commissioner on food safety in the Obama administration.

The FDA had some pet ploys, according to scientists within the FDA who tried to warn their superiors of the dangers of not testing. One was that genetic engineering is no different from traditional breeding practices. This, said Linda Kahl, an FDA compliance officer, amounted to the FDA trying to "fit a square peg into a round hole." They were trying to force a conclusion for convenience. Not only were genetic engineering and traditional breeding different, she said, but "they lead to different risks."[57] FDA microbiologist Louis Pribyl agreed, contending that it's not clear that the creators of GM foods "will be able to pick up effects that might not be obvious."[58] Another ploy was to turn this idea of no difference between GM and non-GM food into a broad-based public statement of policy.

THE POLITICIANS AND THE SCIENTISTS

There is general consensus among the scientific community that genetically modified food is no different from conventional food.
— Speaker of the House Dennis Hastert, March 2003[59]

I want to make very clear that it is the position of the United States government that we do not believe there is a difference between GMO commodities and non-GMO commodities.
— Melinda Kimble, U.S. State Department, May, 1999 [60]

Approval of new transgenic organisms for environmental release, and for use as food or feed, should be based on rigorous scientific assessment of their potential for causing harm to the environment or to human health. Such testing should replace the current regulatory reliance on "substantial equivalence" as a decision threshold.
— From the Expert Panel on the Future of Food Biotechnology, January, 2001

The risks in biotechnology are undeniable and they stem from the unknowable in science and commerce. It is prudent to recognize and address these issues, not compound them by overly optimistic or foolhardy behavior.
—Editors, *Nature Biotechnology,* October, 2000

The claim that there is no difference between GM and non-GM food, and therefore no need to label GM foods, continues. In an interview in March 2008, Monsanto spokesperson Lori Hoag used that argument to justify her company's ongoing battle to keep labels like "rBGH-free" off of milk coming from cows not injected with the rBGH hormone. Injecting cows with the hormone helps produce more milk, but the process also creates a number of troubling side effects that have concerned scientists, doctors, farmers, and consumers. These side effects include shorter animal life cycles and increased levels of mastitis, an infection of the udders. Because the mastitis is treated with antibiotics, chances of increased antibiotic resistance as well as increased levels of IGF-1 exist. IGF-1 is a hormone that has been linked to numerous types of cancer.

In several states the labeling bans have been overturned. Not waiting for the bans, Chipotle, Starbucks, and Tillamook have declined to use dairy products derived from rBGH-treated animals and supermarket house brands such as Kroger, Meiers and Publix are now rBGH-free. Kraft is even developing a line of cheese without rBGH.[61]

In August, 2008 Monsanto sold its rBGH division to pharmaceutical giant Eli Lilly. Whether Lilly will bow to consumer will and stop denying GMO labeling, as Monsanto was forced to do because of declining grain markets in the UK and EU, remains to be seen. What is certain is that the opposition won't go away. Monsanto is after all, as writer Jeffrey Smith said, the company "which told us that PCBs, DDT, and Agent Orange were safe." After a decade of rebuffs and reassurances from a company that has betrayed it so many times, a weary and skeptical public is holding its ground. "The obligation to endure," says French biologist and moralist Jean Rostand, "gives us the right to know."

PUBLIC DISTRUST IS DRIVING MORE OPENNESS

Just as polls show that an overwhelming number of U.S consumers want their food labeled so they can know whether food has been genetically modified, some retailers, bowing to public distrust, have simply been opting out of buying them. Whole Foods, Wild Oats and Trader Joe's name brand products are GM-free. Frito-Lay, Gerber, Heinz, Seagram and Hain have declined to use GM ingredients in their products. Citing customer demand, in February 2009 yogurt maker Yoplait (the nation's 19th largest dairy processor) stopped using dairy products that use rGBH.

Farmers, too, have made their voices heard. In August 2009, 1500 U.S. farmers sued Bayer CropScience for releasing an unapproved GM'd rice, apparently in 2006, and not telling farmers, the public or the government about the contamination. That same month thousands of farmers from the southern and central provinces of Pakistan joined forces to ban the trial growth of Bt cotton seeds and GM presence altogether. It is well known from India's experience with Bt cotton that the seed is expensive, it cannot be saved and used for subsequent crops because it is patented by Monsanto, it requires more water than indigenous varieties and, being a monoculture crop, it robs the soil of the benefits of crop rotation. A single bad season can mean devastation and starvation for farming families and whole communities.

In September 2009, a U.S judge rejected the FDA's approval of GM sugar beets, saying the U.S. Department of Agriculture should have written an environmental impact statement. A similar ruling halted the GM'd version of alfalfa which environmentalists, organic farmers and many others decried, as its dissemination via windborne pollination would ensure that virtually all grazing animals would eventually become tainted. Ingesting a genetically modified version of the pollen is inevitable.[62]

It is consumer demand that is shining light on these issues, slowly bringing them into the public eye. A short piece posted in January, 2010 on www.Huffingtonpost.com, describing a report that claimed that three varieties of GMO corn caused deaths in lab rats, caught fire with readers who quickly posted over 1400 comments, more than 6,400 Facebook "share" links and over 1,000 Twitter "tweets."[63] Earlier in 2009, France, Germany, Greece and Luxembourg banned one of the corn varieties mentioned in the study, Mon810, the only GM food grown commercially in Europe. Monsanto currently owns the patents on seeds for 95 percent of all the soybeans grown in the U.S. and 80 percent of all the corn. And every one of those seeds has a genetically modified pedigree.

THE SEED HEALERS

Thomas Jefferson once declared: "Those who labor in the earth are the chosen people of God." Philosopher and farmer Wendell Berry explains how his life's calling hobnobs with infinity.

> *By farming we enact our fundamental connection with energy and matter, light and darkness. In the cycles of farming, which carry the elemental energy again and again through the seasons and the bodies of living things, we recognize the only infinitude within reach of the imagination.*[64]

Since agriculture began, we have counted on farmers to keep that fundamental connection for us, to spend their lives as part of an ancient tapestry woven from a working partnership with the earth. They are the gatekeepers of our survival, the stewards who have been entrusted with keeping us alive with good, healthy food. Ours has been a history of connection. What happened to them affected us.

Today the gatekeepers are largely gone and in their absence, spoiled by decades of cheap, plentiful, accessible food, we have lost our connection with that elemental energy and are mindless of the origin of our nourishment and its impact on our bodies. As modern food eaters disconnected from our nutrition, we are paying for that loss in ways that are outside of our awareness.

Recall for a moment the story in Chapter 1 of Harvard-trained neuroanatomist Dr. Jill Bolte Taylor, who documented her own stroke, and in its midst found her connection to the whole. Each of us is, she said, "the life force power of the universe, with manual dexterity and two cognitive minds." At any given moment we can choose to reside in the connectedness of the right side of that brain and the "50 trillion beautiful molecular geniuses" that we are made of, or the left, where "I become a single individual, a solid, separate from the flow, separate from you." These, she says, make up the "we" inside of each one of us.[65]

What Jefferson and Taylor are talking about is our connection to the whole, to the source of life and, taking it down a notch, to the earth and our food. All around us are examples of both our connectedness and our separation. Borrowing a line from Hindus and Sufis, who believe there are many paths to God because there are many people, so too are there many paths to discovering our relatedness to the whole and to each other. The universe takes care that we have many routes available to accommodate both our need and our capacity to see.

Thomas Jefferson's sense of connectedness to the earth (and to the farmers he admired) was as much a part of his body as his skin and eyes. It was informed and nurtured by his life and times in the playground of his 18th-century consciousness. The connectedness of Dr. Taylor was delivered via her highly educated late-20th-century scientist's receptors. The delivery system was perfectly attuned both to getting her attention and informing her curiosity with new perceptions that forever changed the way she would see herself and others—not merely as beings with brains but spirits in human form.

As Chapter 1 also pointed out, we are not only physical and spiritual beings; we're also energetic beings. Looking at ourselves through what Caroline Myss calls our spiritual anatomy provides another lens that lets us envision our interior, non-physical worlds in ways that most Westerners previously did not, by suggesting that our physical, mental, and spiritual bodies not only are *not* separate entities, but they also speak a mutually reinforcing language. We need only learn some of this "energetic" vocabulary to be able to decipher the meaning of the puzzle that is us, to understand that what registers in one chakra registers in all, as a unique chakra-specific message.

In Dr. Taylor's case, her stroke meant very different things even within a single chakra. It offered her a virtual cornucopia of insights, because it engaged both the linear and analytical left side of her scientist's brain as well as her highly evolved but much quieter, more intuitive right side, the part of her that engaged her spirit. From Taylor's point of view, even though her stroke slowly affected all of her body until she was close to physical and cognitive death, it began as a left-brain, sixth-chakra perception. In chakra parlance, sixth-chakra perceptions don't just sit there. Instead, they ride up and down the energy channels interpenetrating our spines like Paul Revere, alerting our energy system to their findings. We use our left brain to understand them analytically and our right to intuit their symbolic importance.

Dr. Taylor's left brain dutifully recorded what was going on and as its capacity to work broke down, her right brain slowly became the only mode of interpretation; as that began to dominate, a whole world opened up to her. What she experienced in her observation of oneness and how it relates to the whole was something that captured Albert Einstein's imagination, too, when he said, "Our separation from each other is an optical illusion of consciousness"—a statement that neatly sums up the basic teachings of the Buddha. Just as we are not separate from one another, neither are the pieces of us separate from each other; rather they are all just differently labeled parts of our "oneness."

Understanding how the chakras work provides us with a template we can overlay onto our lives to understand our mistaken belief in this separation. Looking at the world through that lens, we can better understand what has happened to the farmers and farmland and the food they've grown for us for the last half-century. We can better see how this break with the earth unfolded, not just on an economic or social level, but also from an energetic, spiritual perspective.

HOW DID THIS BREAK HAPPEN?

Until the middle of the 20th century, we had what Rachel Carson called a "soil community,"[66] an interwoven web of symbiosis between soil and creatures, each fed by the other. Soil is like the earth's digestive system, a supremely efficient mechanism for creation and sustenance. She wrote:

> *The thin layer of soil that forms a patchy covering over the continents controls our own existence and that of every other animal of the land. Without soil, land plants as we know them could not grow, and without plants no animals could survive.*[67]

And since World War II, that thin layer of soil has taken a pounding. Between the post-war era and today, the earth has been subjected to a powerful one-two punch. First came the birth of the so-called Green Revolution, launched on the back of one of the shining chemical luminaries of the war: DDT. In the 1950s, few had begun to question the sincerity of government oversight, and chemical companies were viewed as miracle workers that cured disease and delivered plenty and affluence to the American landscape. The star of the now-infamous pesticide DDT had ascended quickly during the war years, because it had gained a well-deserved reputation as a supreme lice killer, a cheap, quick, easy way to keep GIs free of the vermin that tormented them in the field when they had to endure long periods without clean clothes or baths. By killing lice, DDT was also credited with preventing typhus, which was carried by lice. Prior to World War II, typhus had been responsible for more deaths to soldiers and civilians alike than bombs, bullets and starvation.

This first Green Revolution, by the way, bore no relation to today's movement toward environmental consciousness and sustainability. In fact, they could hardly be more different. In the 50s, green essentially meant go, giving the gas to growth on a massive and unlimited scale. It meant production quantity and economic prosperity. It's no small irony that many of the goals of the modern Green Revolution are to reverse the philosophy and heal the effects of the first one.

With substances like DDT in their arsenals, farmers used and depended on these chemicals to repel bugs and fertilize their crops as never before, with the aim of maximizing farm production to "feed a growing world," the post-war mantra. But slowly it became clear that this new wonderful world of chemicals was having unintended consequences. When Rachel Carson's *Silent Spring* was first serialized in *The New Yorker* in June of 1962, it set off a firestorm of protest from the chemical industry, chiefly from Monsanto, DDT's manufacturer. A public relations and media blitz ensued and Carson was decried as a know-nothing alarmist. Still, her data could not be shaken. Birds had simply stopped singing in many parts of the country. Their corpses were found by the tens of thousands all over American front yards and parks. The culprit was not easy to see. Instead, it was a mystery solved through a chain of evidence that led back to the wholesale spraying of crops and plants to ward off all sorts of pests, from gypsy moths to Dutch Elm beetles. But the chemical played no favorites and its overkill tendencies became clear for the first time. Perhaps one-tenth of one percent of the insecticide sprayed actually prevented an infestation. That left the rest to settle onto leaves, trees, and shrubs, leech into the soil and the water table, into the wildlife, and, of course, into us.

While Carson's book launched the modern environmental movement, its sad prophecy became all too clear. With the unbridled use of these pesticides came more unwanted consequences, among them the vast dead zones created by runoffs teeming down the Mississippi into the Gulf of Mexico, leaving in their wake a destroyed ecosystem affecting the topsoil, the wildlife, and all the area's natural resources. In the Gulf alone these areas span 7,700 square miles—roughly the size of New Jersey—of wetlands, marshes, and water bodies where to this day nothing grows. As more farmers plant corn to meet the growing demand for biofuels, the amount of nitrates leeching into the waterways from fertilizers could increase by another 34 percent by 2022.[68]

The bacteria in the surface foot of one acre of topsoil can weigh half a ton. What happens when the ecosystem in the soil is attacked by chemicals meant to kill one insect but that also destroy much of the microbial life that works in symbiosis with the soil? What was once dark, loamy, rich-smelling soil turns to dusty brown clay. Robbed of their very nature, vegetables grown in such soil have little taste and even less nutritional value.

The second punch was the birth of biotechnology. With the advent of biotech came a new, even greater threat than chemical pesticides, made more troubling because of the extent to which its effects are unknown, unpredictable, and potentially untraceable. Genetically modified food and genetically engineered additives have changed the face of global farming, instituting uniform monoculture where there was once diversity, taxing soil and its nutrients, and, some scientists believe, forever tainting it with genetically modified alterations to its systems. Biotech creates what one critic called "human health havoc."

THE COST IN DESPAIR

In 1910 the farm population of the U.S. accounted for one-third of overall population. By 1969 that number had dwindled to a mere five percent. Today it is estimated than fewer than one percent of our more than 300 million citizens call themselves farmers. And that number doesn't reflect the effects on rural communities when farmers leave. In the mid-1980s, when the U.S. lost 235,000 farmers, an estimated 60,000 other community businesses failed as well. A single farm-centric area, McPherson County, Nebraska, has lost two-thirds of its population since 1920, including 58 school districts and three entire towns.[69]

Between the advent of genetic engineering and the predominance of corporate farming in today's agricultural landscape, it's small wonder that farmers have given up in historic numbers. While many farmers went out of business from the reverses that followed a boom of heavy investments in bigger equipment and larger farms, their exodus in more recent years has been tied to a combination of factors:

Contamination of crops. Four big cash crops have been genetically engineered for commercial use—cotton, soy, corn and canola—and their pollen indiscriminately contaminates organic varieties of the crops, distributed by wind, rain, insects, even trucks driving from a GM field into a non-GM field, rendering them unsuitable for organic markets. This spells ruin for organic farmers and has been the source of many lawsuits in Canada against Monsanto since their RoundUp Ready canola has contaminated virtually all of that country's canola crop.

Loss of natural protection of Bt. Genetic engineering has resulted in the widespread use of an altered form of the natural pesticide Bt (bacillus thuringiensis), making insects more resistant to this strain. The result is that farming without the use of chemical pesticides has become even more problematic. If a farmer wants to grow organic food, using pesticide automatically decertifies their organic status and endangers their livelihood.

Inability to compete: Many small farmers who have tried to compete with agribusiness gave up because of the rising costs of inputs—seed, pesticides, herbicides, fertilizers—and continually lower profit margins. Failed crops wither away seed money. Since globalized trade of the 1990s, farmer suicides in India and China have numbered in the hundreds of thousands. In America after the disintegration of the family farm during the 1980s, suicide was the number one cause of death with farmers, more than three times the rate of the general population.

The first Green Revolution created a divide that has never been repaired: Corporate agribusiness versus individual family farmer. Yield versus quality. Profit versus nurturing. As Wendell Berry said, "The standard of the exploiter is efficiency; the standard of the nurturer is care. The exploiter's goal is money, profit; the nurturer's goal is health—his land's health, his own, his family's, his community's, his country's." [70]

There is no way to measure the total impact on farmers of losing their ability to keep us fed and healthy as land has been turned into a corporate commodity and food into something that no longer nurtures and sustains us. "For the farmer, the field is the mother, which feeds the millions of life forms that are her children." [71]

In Jill Taylor's parlance, our quandary resides in the 6th chakra, the seat of facts and problem solving, of linear thinking and cold science on the left and imagination, inspiration, spirit, and connectedness on the right—two spheres operating with each other's knowledge but not the same interpretative eyeballs. If agriculture is left strictly to business and its bottom-line efficiency, with its endless demands on the soil, the environment and the public's immune system, we are headed away from health and sustainable resources. If we turn to the right, to the spiritual realm most comfortable for the farmer, can we count on connectedness to feed us and keep us healthy?

A number of studies say yes, including a University of Wisconsin-Madison study published in the *Agronomy Journal* in March 2008. Researchers tracked crops grown in various Wisconsin farms for from 8 to 13 years and compared totals grown for alfalfa, wheat, corn, and soybeans. They ranged from 90 percent as productive to equally productive. The beneficial difference: the organic crops were grown without chemicals, either from fertilizers, pesticides or herbicides, making them safer and more nutritious.

A recent UN-FAO study of organic farms revealed that in Bolivia, potato yields went up from 4 to 15 tons per hectare (about 2.5 acres). In Cuba, the vegetable yields of organic urban gardens almost doubled. In Ethiopia, which 20 years ago suffered terrible famine, sweet potato yields went up from 6 to 30 tons per hectare. In Kenya, corn yields increased from 2¼ to 9 tons per hectare. And in Pakistan, mango yields have gone up from 7¼ to 22 tons per hectare. In Japan, a single farmer, using a six-acre plot of land and a species-interdependent system (plants, animals and fish) was measured to be as productive as a typical 600-acre rice farm in Texas.[72]

According to the Organic Trade Association, business for organics is good and getting better. In 1997 the organic food business wasn't exactly keeping big agribusiness up with night sweats. It had a mere .8 percent of the food market. But organic's share of the market has steadily increased each year. By 2006 organic food accounted for $13.8 billion in sales, up 16 percent in a single year, now at 2.48 percent of the market. In 2008 sales were at $24.6 billion. Still not huge, but it is growing consistently and exponentially[73] enjoying growth of 12-20 percent or more annually while conventional food stores are seeing much less, 2-3 percent annual growth.

ORGANICS AS THE NEW NORMAL

We as a nation are physically separated from our food. For the most part, we don't know where it comes from or who grew it. We have grown used to it being cheap and plentiful. That plenty has turned into a potential curse, in part because we've lost track of whether what we are eating is nutritious or harmful. Even the most nutritious food eaten in excessive quantities can create health problems, but much of what is available in our well-stocked stores is downright unhealthful. By now we know that simply eating low-fat or low-calorie foods is not enough. We have to learn to look at the whole picture, including *how* we eat. Busy lives often mean quick meals, and today about one-quarter of the average American's diet is made up of fast food. The concept of eating a nutritious meal at a relaxing pace, preferably in a family or communal setting of some sort, is almost a thing of the past.

For the last five decades conventional agriculture has played an increasingly significant part in our diets. In the early 1970s there were 6,000 to 8,000 items in the typical supermarket, about 40 percent of which were not present in 1960.[74] Today, *17,000* new food products go on the market *every year.*[75] If they are processed, the odds are high that they will have GM components in them, not to mention non-nutritious elements that can cause obesity. And much the same is true of almost all fast food. Because so much fast and/or processed food tricks our taste buds with artificial sweeteners and flavorings, we can no longer count on our senses to tell us what we're eating and whether it's in our health's best interest.[76]

The onslaught on the American public's palate is relentless—and convincing. While the advertising budget for commercial food is $32 billion a year, fresh foods' annual budget is a paltry $2 million. Advertisers love to use children's faces to disarm audiences and imply safety, ethics, trustworthiness, and stewardship. It's no accident that in the film *Michael Clayton*, the spot advertising Monsanto-clone UNorth's product uses the open, trusting hands of a young child to make its toxic blooming plant seem benign. This subtly reinforces the fictional corporation's good aims in the world, even as the film's villains hide the facts about how the corporation's products effectively kill their clients.

While we can't rely on the images that advertisers use to sell us food, we can count on vast resources, from libraries to the Internet, to educate us. Understanding what we eat is not just proactive, it's essential. Knowledge, in the world of hidden food ingredients and altered components, is power. We have to count on ourselves, because for the most part we can no longer count on our former guardians, the farmers. When we lost the connection with farmers, we lost our connection with the soil, with food, what Michael Pollan calls "the circular flow of nutrients through the food chain."

The 2009 CIA World Factbook listed the U.S. as 48th for life expectancy (down from 41 in 2008) at birth.[77] With two-thirds of Americans overweight or obese, it should come as no surprise that diabetes in people over 75 is expected to increase 336 percent by 2050, a grim comment on the health of the first generation to have lived their entire lives in a culture fed by industrial agriculture.[78]

It's important to remember that until the 1950's Green Revolution, organic farming was the *only* farming. It was normal. But that kind of farming is often derided today by proponents of biotechnology as too slow, inefficient, and unproductive even though statistics say otherwise.

At least one study indicates that organic food is simply better for you because of the way it is *not* grown. Using chemical fertilizers makes crops grow faster, so they have less time to accumulate nutrients other than the nitrogen, phosphorus, and potassium that are the fertilizers' hallmark. This in turn means crops don't grow with deep root systems that can reach down to where more mineral nutrients lie. Organically grown crops also contain more phytochemicals, compounds that make them naturally resistant to invasion from diseases and pests. The USDA has discovered that since the 1880s, when improved wheat varieties became common, the nutritional levels have dropped as yields have risen. So, although yields have tripled, iron levels have dropped by 28 percent and zinc and selenium by about 30 percent. To put it simply, we eat more food but get less nutrition. Starved for nutrients, we eat more. Craving but not satisfying the need for nourishment, we get obese.[79]

All of these issues surrounding our food have both physical and symbolic effects. Here again, the human energetic system leaves the clues to a symbolic truth: this is what an energetic heartbreak is all about. As farmers lose their connection to the food they grow for us, to the seed it comes from, and to the consumers to whom they have been connected for thousands of years, we all lose our sense of connection with what nourishes us, the earth from which we came. That loss affects each of us through the other essential fuel of our lives—our food—leaving little aching voids in our bodies, minds and spirits.

It's time for us to demand more of ourselves, to open our eyes, our hearts, minds and spirits, fling the doors of perception off their hinges. We have to do it not because it's fashionable or we need to expiate our sins, but because we want our species to survive. Like the heroes of Leningrad who sacrificed themselves without knowing whether it would even do any good, each of us is called on to step up and do our part.

If the history of the third millennium is ever to be written, then it will be necessary for the people who lived through it to make this time one of a new kind of accountability, of not only individuals, but at the community, country and global level. If you want to see who the new stewards of the earth are, go look in the mirror and at the faces of the people walking down your street and the aisles in your grocery store and on the playgrounds and bully pulpits around the world. It's us, as a body and its billions of component parts, like the countless molecular geniuses that Jill Taylor spoke about. That's us, once shattered into countless pieces, finding our way back to wholeness.

In a time that sees us literally feeding ourselves at the expense of the soil and seed that is the source of our lives—an act that Rachel Carson termed *biocide*, a sacrifice of our own habitat—we must ask ourselves how any sane person can accept this. We can do better than live in a world that ecologist Paul Shepard called "just not quite fatal."[80] And as the last section of this book will demonstrate, doing so is well within both our reach and our capacity for wisdom.

Endnotes

1. Al Gore, *Earth in the Balance,* New York: Houghton Mifflin, 1992, 281-282.
2. *Ibid.*
3. *Blessed Unrest,* 31.
4. See The Svalbard Pages, available at http://links.svalbard.com/index.php?show=pop.
5. Dan Shapley, "Doomsday Seed Bank Opens This Week," *The Daily Green,* February 26, 2008, available at http://www.thedailygreen.com/environmental-news/latest/doomsday-seeds-47022403
6. Hillary Rosner, "Seeds to Save a Species," *Popular Science,* January 4, 2008, *available at* http://www.popsci.com/scitech/article/2008-01/seeds-save-species?page=6
7. Janet Raloff, "Afghanistan's Seed Banks Destroyed," available at http://www.sciencenews.org/articles/20020914/food.asp
8. "Seeds to Save a Species."
9. Bill Lambrecht, *Dinner at the New Gene Cafe: How Genetic Engineering Is Changing What We Eat, How We Live, and the Global Politics of Food,* New York: St. Martin's Press, 2001, 285.
10. Rachel Carson, *Silent Spring,* New York: Houghton Mifflin, 1962, 10.
11. From the People and Biodiversity website, available at http://www.peopleandplanet.net/doc.php?id=2848, September 19, 2006.
12. Alok Jha, "Deep in Permafrost—A Seedbank to Save the World," June 20, 2006, from The Guardian website, available at http://www.guardian.co.uk/science/2006/jun/20/food.frontpagenews
13. *The Future of Food,* a documentary film by Deborah Koons Garcia, director, and Catherine Lynn Butler, producer, a Lily Films Production, 2004.
14. Andrew Kimbrell, Editor, *Fatal Harvest,* Sausalito: The Foundation for Deep Ecology, 2002, 24.
15. Michael Pollan, *In Defense of Food: An Eater's Manifesto,* New York, Penguin Group, 2008, 116.
16. Doug O'Harra, "The World's Best Seeds Head for Arctic Vault," January 25, 2008, from the Far North Science website, available at

http://www.farnorthscience.com/2008/01/25

17. Debora Mackenzie, *"Billions at Risk from Wheat Super-blight,"* New *Scientist*, April 3, 2008, available at http://environment.newscientist.com/channel/earth/mg19425983.700-billions-at-risk-from-wheat-superblight.html

18. Joe Nunez, "History and Lessons of Potato Late Blight," December 21, 2000, from the University of California Cooperative Extension, website, available at http://cekern.ucdavis.edu/Custom_Program573/History_and_Lessons_of_Potato_Late_Blight.htm

19. More detailed descriptions were given in two fine books, *Altered Harvest* by Jack Doyle, New York: Viking, 1985, and *Shattering: Food, Politics and the Loss of Genetic Diversity* by Cary Fowler and Pat Mooney, Tucson: University of Arizona Press, 1990.

20. *Shattering*, x-xi.

21. Tom Philpott, "A reflection on the lasting legacy of 1970s USDA Secretary Earl Butz," February 7, 2008, available at http://www.grist.org/comments/food/2008/02/07

22. Lauren Etter, "Farmers Wonder if Boom In Grain Prices Is a Bubble," January 31, 2008, *Wall Street Journal Online*, available at http://online.wsj.com/public/article/SB120174466249430595-80VjiIeKfXzheSxhrmkWufQ_Y5s_20080301.html?mod=tff_main_tff_top

23. *Shattering*, 8.

24. *"Seeds to Save a Species."*

25. *Shattering*, 116.

26. Vandana Shiva, *Stolen Harvest: The Hijacking of the Global Food Supply*, Cambridge: South End Press, 2000, 80.

27. *Blessed Unrest*, 25.

28. Katharine Mieszkowski, "Superbug to the rescue!" August 28, 2003, available at http://www.salon.com/tech/feature/2003/08/28/bioremediation/

29. Andrew Kimbrell, "High-tech Piracy," *Utne Reader*, March-April 1996, available at http://www.utne.com/1996-03-01/high-tech-piracy.aspx

30. Vandana Shiva, "Ecologists Should Worry About the Dunkel Draft," Sept. 23, 1993, from the SUNS website, available at http://www.sunsonline.org/trade/areas/environm/09230193.htm

31. *Ibid.*

32. Wangari Mathai, "The Linkage between Patenting of Life Forms, Genetic Engineering and Food Insecurity," October 11, 2004, available at http://www.genet-info.org/-documents/AfricaGMOsPatents.pdf (also on http://lists.iatp.org/listarchive/archive.cfm?id=97248).

33. Jeffrey Smith, *Seeds of Deception: Exposing Industry and Government Lies About the Safety of the Genetically Engineered Foods You're Eating*

(Fairfield: Yes! Books, 2003), 50.

34. Andrew Kimbrell, editor. *Your Right to Know: Genetic Engineering and the Secret Changes in Your Food,* San Raphael: Earth Books, 2007, 44-45.

35. *Seeds of Deception,* 50.

36. Exceptions include any food that is certified organic. *Farm-raised, cage-free, free range, hormone- free, natural* and other such designations by themselves do not guarantee that a food is GM free. Likewise, milk that indicates it is "rBGH free" or "rBST free" lacks the bovine growth hormone, but unless it is labeled "organic," it may still come from dairy cows that eat GM grain. Ask your grocer to be sure.

37. *The Future of Food.*

38. *Silent Spring,* 188.

39. *Seeds of Deception,* 145.

40. *Ibid;* condensed from Chapter 4, "Deadly Epidemic."

41. *Ibid,* 162.

42. *Bad Seed: The Truth About Our Food,* a documentary film by Tim Nadudvari and Adam Curry, co-directors and co-producers, Bad Seed Productions, 2006.

43. *Seeds of Deception,* 176.

44. *Seeds of Deception,* 153-155.

45. As quoted in "Playing God in the Garden," by Michael Pollan, *New York Times Magazine,* October 25, 1998

46. Interview with Schmeiser available at http://www.percyschmeiser.com/AcresUSAstory.pdf

47. *Your Right to Know,* 38.

48. *In Defense of Food,* 116-117.

49. *Omnivore's Dilemma,* 91.

50. *Fatal Harvest,* 6.

51. Gurain-Sherman, D. 2009. "Failure to yield: evaluating the performance of genetically engineered crops." Cambridge (MA): Union of Concerned Scientists.

52. Dr. Charles Benbrook, "Impacts of Genetically Engineered Crops on Pesticide Use: The First Thirteen Years," The Organic Center, November, 2009 available at http://www.organic-center.org/science.pest.php?action=view&report_id=159

53. *Omnivore's Dilemma,* 95.

54. *In Defense of Food,* 123.

55. Interview with attorney Steven Druker in *The Future of Food.*

56. *Seeds of Deception,* 131.

57. Document showing comments from Dr. Linda Kahl, FDA compliance officer, to Dr. James Maryanski, FDA Biotechnology Coordinator, about the Federal Register document "Statement of Policy: Foods from

Genetically Modified Plants," January 8, 1992. These and other documents were obtained by Steven Druker as part of discovery resulting from a lawsuit his organization filed to challenge the FDA's claim that most of its scientists approved of the introduction of genetically modified foods into the American marketplace without testing them. This document and others are available at www.biointegrity.org/list.html

58. Louis J. Pribyl, "Biotechnology Draft Document, 2/27/92," March 6, 1992, available at www.biointegrity.org

59. "Speaker Hastert calls for End of European Union's Protectionist, Discriminatory Trade Policies," from *U.S. Newswire*, March 26, 2003.

60. Kimble was acting Assistant U.S. Secretary of State for Oceans and International and Environmental Scientific Affairs in 1999. Reference is from *Dinner at the New Gene Café*, 322.

61. Scott Thill, "Frankenfoods' Giant Monsanto Plays Bully Over Consumer Labeling," March 6, 2008, available at http://www.alternet.org/workplace/78660/

62. "Judge rejects approval of GM sugar beets," September 23, 2009, available at http://current.com/1vcq44c

63. Katherine Goldstein and Gazelle Emami, "Monsanto's GM corn linked to organ failure, study reveals," http://www.huffingtonpost.com/2010/01/12/monsantos-gmo-corn-linked_n_420365.html

64. Wendell Berry, *The Unsettling of America: Culture and Agriculture*, New York: Random House, 1982, 87.

65. Dr. Jill Bolte Taylor lecture, posted March, 2008, available at http://www.ted.com/index.php/talks/view/id/229

66. *Silent Spring*, 56.

67. *Ibid*, 53.

68. David Biello, "Fertilizer Runoff Overwhelms Streams and Rivers--Creating Vast 'Dead Zones' ", March 14, 2008, *Scientific American*, available at http://www.sciam.com/article.cfm?id=fertilizer-runoff-overwhelms-streams

69. ISEC Local Food Toolkit Factsheet, available at http://www.isec.org.uk/toolkit/ustoolkit.html

70. *The Unsettling of America*, 7.

71. *Stolen Harvest*, 8.

72. *Fatal Harvest*, 116.

73. Organic Trade Association's 2006 Manufacturer Survey (from printout), available at http://www.agmrc.org/NR/rdonlyres/6D092BD1-481D-43D1-95CD-B8F1821E2F19/0/AIC_FBIB_3organic.pdf.

74. *The Unsettling of America*, 60.

75. *In Defense of Food*, 133.

76. *Ibid*, 14.

77. https://www.cia.gov/library/publications/the-world-factbook/rankorder/2102rank.html
78. *In Defense of Food*, 73.
79. *Ibid*, 120-121.
80. *Silent Spring*, 12.

PART THREE

Reunion

*The world is a dangerous place to live, not because of the people
who are evil, but because of the people who don't do anything about it.*

— *Albert Einstein*

CHAPTER 5

How to Reconnect to the Earth

*We are bleeding at the roots,
because we are cut off from the earth and the sun and stars.*
— D.H. Lawrence

AS INFANTS WE KNOW NO DIFFERENCE between ourselves and the world in which we wiggle, gurgle and coo. The idea that "all is one" isn't just a catchphrase or a simple mystical truth—it is our nature. It is one of the paradoxes of life that as we individuate and age and separate from what nurtures us, an invisible bit of alchemy is set in motion. Our hearts begin to long for what our minds have forgotten—that sense of oneness, that absolute certainty of connectedness.

The restlessness we feel by midlife may in fact serve us by igniting a need to know what that missing piece is, where life's meaning really resides. As Caroline Myss says, "We often feel a vague sense of meaninglessness long before we acknowledge intellectually that we are spiritually empty."[1] We want to phone home, to mend that spiritual tether to the mother ship. We yearn for reunion with the connection that calls us.

That yearning is what drives us to respond to that sense that something is missing, because it is. We are not meant to feel separate and alone, shattered and distant from our cosmic tribe. On the physical level, we belong to many tribes: family, friends, school, town, nation, ethnic group, political party, planet, and so forth. But on a cosmic plane, we are universal beings. Returning to that sense of our own cosmic identity is part of each person's life quest. And luckily for us, we're designed for that journey of discovery.

Each of us has what Duane Elgin calls a "literacy of consciousness," an innate ability to "know that we know." It is this kind of spiritual intelligence that helps us see and translate the clues that lie strewn throughout our lives. Looking back over the decades, each of us can begin to see the miracle that is our own life unfolding. We need only develop what he calls "the art of attention," to teach ourselves this cosmic vocabulary. "The importance of cultivating this core capacity is recognized by every major wisdom tradition."[2] No matter what belief system we grew up in, there is an avenue that takes us there. Our job is to train ourselves to have a "witnessing consciousness."

It would seem that our time is calling us to awaken from our benumbed and bewitched state to a wonder at and reverence for the astonishing, miraculous and mysterious creation of which we are a part.

—Tielhard de Chardin

And it can feel like a daunting task. How exactly do we go about that? Where do we start? As Jim Garrison, president of the World Forum, said in 2009, "Until now there has been no template for how to do this." The solutions we need won't come just from a government initiative or mandate or from a miracle of technology, a whirlwind of energized business ideas or the creative genius of a new age Bill Gates or Michelangelo. They will also come from what's already in us, from the fierce love and compassionate energies of Jesus, Buddha, Mohammed, and Gandhi and so many others, from all the wisdom of indigenous cultures and all the good souls who have come before us and left their imprint of healing and wisdom on our awakening hearts.

CREATING A TEMPLATE FOR CONNECTING

The job before us is enormous. It involves both re-visioning our place on the Earth and our relationship with her. We will see it reflected in the ways we come to live our lives. As we began to literally rebuild the component parts of our weakened planet, we start not outside ourselves but inside, in the inner landscapes that reflect the chaos and longing created in our outer landscapes. As we strike out to discover all the ways that we can each connect individually and collectively, we will become a species of new Magellans, laying out a healing path as a map for the generations to come.

Along the way, we will begin to re-model what the measure of a lifetime is, how it's about opening our hearts to our own longings, our place and role in a time like no other before in history, when the entire world faces a common and very real danger, the threatened collapse of the very ecosystems that keep each of us alive. This is not a danger that is unique to only a few countries. As Thomas Berry said, "There needs to be a realization that no nation has a future if the planet does not have a future." What we are facing affects every single earthly life form. No one and nothing is unaffected.

How many generations in all of human history have had the opportunity to rise to a challenge that is worthy of our best efforts? A challenge that can pull from us more than we knew we could do? I think we ought to approach this challenge with a sense of profound joy and gratitude that we are the generation about which, a thousand years from now, philharmonic orchestras and poets and singers will celebrate by saying, they were the ones that found it within themselves to solve this crisis and lay the basis for a bright and optimistic human future.

— Vice President Al Gore, speaking at Ted.Com, March 2008[3]

Most of us know by now that CFC bulbs are better than incandescent, that you can put a brick in the back of your toilet to minimize what goes down in a flush, that voice mail uses less electricity than an answering machine, that if the world ate less meat, there would be less methane in the atmosphere, that leaving your grass three inches high when you mow it helps the roots grow deeper and holds in more moisture, that driving a hybrid is better for the planet than driving a Hummer. That much has seeped into the collective consciousness and it's significant that most of the tips and wisdom directed at us about living a greener life have to do with what we consume. They appeal to our quantitative, calculating, how-to side.

But there's much more to us than that. And as Derrick Jensen points out, while it is right for each of us to become more accountable for our own consumer habits, even if we reach the best of all worlds and ratchet down our usage to a bare squeaking minimum, we won't do more than a make a dent in overall CO_2 dumped into the atmosphere. Why? Because more than 80 percent of the pollution going into the atmosphere is directly tied to the big polluters: corporations, industries, government and the military.[4] That's where the real consumption trends have to change.

And that in turn ties in directly with a much deeper issue—what do we value? Within that question floats the issues of our lifestyles, the hungry, many-headed hydra that is a growth-based economy and what our media helps instill in us: a bottomless need to consume. We all know what we like to buy. And so much is built into our culture to keep us from seeing, to keep us anesthetized by the accumulation of stuff, our great pacifier.

One of the ironies today is how much value is placed on artificially enhancing what's "real." As TV viewers, what gets hyped is the screen that has the highest definition, the resolution closest to real life, the ability of a picture to transport us into the middle of the action, to make us feel like we are a part of what we're seeing, because the picture is so vivid and three-dimensional. The same is true with cameras: the higher megabyte resolution, the more pixels, the more true to life the pictures. Recorded music has become so piercingly clear, with the benefit of "noise canceling" headphones, you can close your eyes and believe you actually are sitting in the middle of an orchestra or stage center at a concert. Special effects in movies—like the recent eye-poppingly vivid *Avatar*—are constantly refined to trick our imaginations by bending reality to create action sequences that scare the breath out of our lungs while defying the laws of gravity and human endurance. Reality TV shows consistently draw larger audiences than news programs on what is happening in our physical worlds by drawing us into the stories of people we do not even know who cannot cope with their spouses, children, pets, neighbors, or bosses, struggling under the watchful and intrusive lens of the camera through banal day-to-day routines as they deal with mostly manufactured crises. Why? What is it about our lives that makes us want to crave other realities?

Perhaps our senses have been so tricked by the distracted lives we lead that we cannot count on them to tell us what nurtures our bodies and spirits anymore. We once were keenly aware of where we lived and who lived near us. Not so many generations ago, we could understand weather by looking up and smelling the air, by watching the wind and the sky and the ways the animals behaved. You didn't have to be a farmer to know what the earth was telling you. These sensing skills were "second nature" to us a century ago. We once knew the natural characteristics of the areas we lived in, and had some sense of the human commerce that took place in them from dawn to dawn.

Learning more about where each of us lives is essential to having a sensibility about our surroundings—to be able to perceive that they are not outside of us, but rather we are in the midst of them.

This is not to suggest that we return to the past. As Native American activist Winona LaDuke said, "It is not about going back—*it's about being on your path*—staying on the path that the Creator gave you."[5] Finding our way to that spiritual trailhead is a process, an initiation into our own soul's journey. Each of us learns differently. We hear and see differently. What is meaningful to one of us might never register on another's sonar. That has less to do with our differences than our uniqueness. We are built to receive what is meaningful to us, according to what our individual journeys are. The heavens have trillions of metaphors to hook us with. Nature has the voices of all the billions who have lived before us from the times of our earliest ancestors that whisper to us and nudge us in one direction or another.

The genius of the collective unconsciousness to which we are all permanent subscribers is that it is at once accessible to everyone and individually in a customized form. What gets your attention is as unique as your fingerprints. Learning to *pay* attention and read the information that is always coming into your intuitive receivers takes time. It happens in layers. Layers settle in and attach. More layers follow. Ideas present themselves, new understandings dawn. This is how we awaken, how consciousness is born.

RECONNECTING TO THE EARTH

The rest of this chapter suggests some of the many different ways that you can reconnect to the earth, on ever-deepening levels. Each suggestion is a tool of awakening. As you work through these, note what occurs to you and make your own list.

Before You Start—On Keeping a Journal makes the case for recording what you experience as you work through the practices that follow and why it often becomes a compelling record you'll want to hang onto. Read this first.

Waking Up—Learning About Where You Live is designed to help you familiarize yourself with your surroundings, just as you would get to know a neighborhood you were moving into.

It's All About Dirt describes things you can do that put you physically in touch with the earth. That in turn completes a connection to your heart and your capacity for compassion.

Spiritual Practices—52 ways to reconnect with the Earth gives you a year's worth of weekly practices to keep you reconnected and conscious of the world you live in.

Whichever place you start, what will most likely happen is that as you begin to tick off items, other ideas or questions will occur to you. The universe wastes nothing, especially energy. As the stories in Chapter 6 illustrate, once you invest your energy into listening to your heart and acting on what feels urgent to you, other ideas, other opportunities will present themselves. As you move your perception just a bit, the whole world begins to look different. A layer comes off, then another. That is the nature of grace. It comes as a bonus when your heart is open, your intent is genuine and your attitude is humble.

Try something, then try something else. Start where you are. Honor your limitations, then find ways around them. Demand self growth. Be ruthlessly accountable. Find your way to Yes.

On keeping a journal

In 18th century London, a pair of gentlemen named James Boswell and Samuel Johnson set out to tour Scotland and detailed their separate perspectives on what became the first travelogue, filled with the details of their day-to-day observations and experiences. The reading public was enthralled. In 21st century New York, a young clerk who was a self-described "government drone by day, renegade foodie by night," patiently blogged the nearly daily details of a year in her life as she took a journey through the art of French cooking, doggedly following legendary chef Julia Child's ruminations and recipes into a new wisdom about herself— and a new career.

The word journal comes from the French word for day, *jour.* It is a sip of your life, a tiny picture, a day's view. When joined with countless other tiny bits run into a series, it forms a mosaic you can recognize when you step back. For this reason, journaling your course through this kind of reawakening can be a way to follow the cracking open of your own consciousness. No, you don't need to be a writer and no one but you ever needs to read it. There are many approaches you can try, but the simpler the better.[6] Here's how simple:

- Buy a journal (a ringed notebook is fine)
- Keep handy a pen that you like (you can also use your keyboard)
- Pick a time of day and a timeframe in which to write (10-minutes in the a.m. or p.m., ½ a page, etc.)
- Start tomorrow.

A journal can be multimedia: stick in magazine clippings, draw pictures, add photos or whatever can fit between the pages. Get creative. It's your journal. Do what you want.

What's great about journaling is that it gives you what something like a photo—another version of a captured moment—can't: the history of your growth, not just the visual memory. Uncaptured, it's like the photo that got away. Once the moment has passed, that shaft of wisdom, that kernel of truth, disappears from your memory.

Journaling is a personal form of narrative. Unless it's your preference to be public (today's blogs—we**b**+**log**--are popular alternatives to private journals), your journal doesn't ever need to be read but rather, as journal writing teacher Stephanie Dowrick says, is "simply a vehicle for your inner wise self."

Journaling is particularly helpful when you are undergoing a transformation, a change in your life, a shift in your consciousness. It provides scaffolding, a framework on which you can attach seemingly unrelated meanderings. It is these seemingly miscellaneous pieces that collectively and eventually let you begin to form a new picture of yourself and even some of the ways the universe is trying to get through to you. Recording them creates a link between your mind and heart and gives the pattern a chance to appear. This is part of the gift of the witnessing consciousness. You literally see yourself see yourself.

WAKING UP—LEARNING ABOUT WHERE YOU LIVE

Ecologist and writer Peter Berg first began using the word *bioregion* to describe the areas of land we live in in terms of what he considers interdependent life forms: plant, animal and human. "The bioregional perspective, the one I've worked with for nearly twenty years, recognizes that people simply don't know where they live." One of Berg's goals is to help people "to become inhabitants again." This goes back to the process of naming things to help them have value to us. We cannot value what we do not name.

Once you value something, you never look at it the same way again. It changes you, it becomes a piece of you, however small. And because people today don't know much about where they live, the acreage their building inhabits or where their food, water, and energy come from, they don't feel a sense of kinship with they place they live. That in turn means that they don't know what's healthy for the section of earth they occupy. Most of us don't know our area's history, why the streets, rivers, creeks or parks have the names they have. Like our mountain ranges and old growth forests, our neighborhoods, cities, and states have histories and each region we live in has its own unique story, ancient stories based on countless lives lived right under the spot where you eat your meals, read your newspaper, surf the Internet, and rest your body.

So if you name the components of your neighborhood, if you grow to love it and you grow to feel ownership of it, and you say that in some form "this is my tribe," it's not so easy for you to ignore it, or let it be strewn with trash, sprayed with pesticides, or contaminated by the runoff from a strip mining company that's toxifying the ground water.

That's the first part: get to know where you live. Learn what you can about the space that is providing you with oxygen every day of your life. You don't have to love it, you don't have to live there forever, but find some little thing to cherish about where you live. It has you in it. You have left pieces of yourself behind every time you exhale a breath.

As Berg points out, if we know what is happening in our bioregion that is unhealthy or unsustainable, we can begin to make intelligent decisions about what to do as communities of involved, informed citizens. As resources become more precious and using them wisely and sustainably becomes the new norm, this kind of wisdom is essential. And since 75 percent of Americans live in cities today, "urban consciousness" is only going to become more important.[7] What you are likely to find out is that there are a lot of others in your region who have the same curiosity and concern about the areas they live in. The age of the urban warrior, defending and reinvigorating the health of his bioregion has quietly descended upon us.

Understanding your bioregion is an important piece in the process of establishing a connection to the Earth because it's the part of the Earth where you and people you love are spending your lives, where you dream and work and experience the passage of time. While Socrates admonished his pupils to "Know thyself," more than 2,000 years ago, today's eco-philosophers would more likely say, "Know thy bioregion."

LEARNING YOUR BIOREGION

How much do you really know about where you live? See how many of these questions you can answer without looking them up. If you decide to find out more, this list will take you a long way toward getting a sense of what's going on in your corner of the Earth and how news stories about global warming and the stability of the earth's food, water and air resources may be touching your life. The French philosopher Blaise Pascal said, "The least movement is of importance to all nature. The entire ocean is affected by a pebble." Every effort you make to understand the place you live in nature opens a door. Inside every door lies the gift of insight.

Water

1. Where does your region get most of its water (reservoir, lake, river, aquifer, etc.)? Has this always been your area's source of water? If not, what other sources has your area drawn from? What condition are those former water sources in now?

2. Get a map of your region and trace the water you drink from precipitation to tap.

3. How long has it been since the main water lines in your neighborhood have been replaced? What are they made of (iron, stainless steel, clay, aluminum, PVC, etc.)?

4. Call your local water department to ask what chemicals are in your water. Are there traces of prescription drugs in them?

5. How do you dispose of out-of-date prescriptions and over the counter drugs? What disposal practice does your water department recommend? Ask your friends how they get rid of their outdated pharmaceuticals.

6. How does your town rate the quality of your tap water?

7. What is the state of your area's water table? Healthy? High? Low? How long does your water department consider that your present water source will be sufficient for your town's needs?

8. What was the amount of rainfall in your area last year? (If applicable) What about snowfall?

9. When was the last time your area endured a drought?

10. When was the last time a major fire burned in your area?

11. If there is a wildfire season in the bioregion where you live, how many wildfires have you had in the last five years? How many total acres were burned?

Trash

1. Where does your garbage go? How much of the methane coming off of your city dump or landfill is being captured and recycled? How can you find out?
2. Where do your recyclables go?
3. In your town, is recycling a law or is participation voluntary?
4. What are the rules about how it is to be presented for pickup (separated or not, contained in recyclable plastic, boxes broken down and tied, loose/not loose, etc.)?
5. What day are recyclables picked up in your neighborhood?
6. For one week, weigh your trash—both garbage and recyclables. Make a list of ways you can begin to have less to throw out.

Stuff

1. Look at the clothes, shoes, bedding and towels in your closets. How many come from outside the United States? Consider the travel miles involved.
2. Scientist Jane Poynter spent two years living inside Biosphere 2 outside Oracle, Arizona. After breathing clean unpolluted air the entire time, the first thing she noticed when she emerged into the earth's atmosphere again in 1993 was this: "People stink," she said, from all the chemicals we put on our bodies and clothes.[8] Make a list of the substances that you and members of your family use that contain any chemical additives: deodorant, perfume, hair spray and gel, after shave, mouthwash, fabric softener, room deodorizers, toilet bowl cleaners, carpet fresheners, etc.

Energy

1. What is the source for the electrical power and/or heat for your house or apartment?
2. If it's coal, where does your coal come from? If your coal supply is local, ask your utility company the amount of CO_2 the plant that supplies your energy injects into the atmosphere annually. What is your coal provider's position on when "clean coal" will be available? Which of coal's pollutants will the technology do away with? Which will it have little or no effect on?
3. If it's nuclear energy or you live near a nuclear power plant, where does the radioactive waste go?

GARBAGE OUT GARBAGE IN

Garbage—The Revolution Begins at Home is an 80-minute documentary by filmmaker Andrew Nisker that vividly demonstrates how one family ventured into becoming conscious about how they live and affect the earth. In Ontario, Canada, the McDonald family—a couple and their three children—agreed to save and weigh their garbage for three months. They also wanted to answer a couple of simple questions: how much do we use and where does it go?

Along the way they learned a lot more than they bargained for: that the U.S. alone has 3,000 landfills, that Americans use 500,000 trees each year to enable them to read their favorite newspapers, that worldwide we use 1 trillion plastic bags, for less than five minutes apiece on average (the U.S. uses 100 billion of those annually), so many in fact that some cities have banned their widespread use and some countries have mandated charging for them to reduce their presence in landfills.

As the film attests, the McDonalds faithfully begin to save (they even bring their tossables home from meals out and visits to friends' houses), store and segregate their trash: wet garbage (food, diapers, used cat litter) from recyclables (paper, cardboard, items marked as recyclable) and stuff for landfills that can't be recycled (everything else from plastic food ties to metal, to hard plastic to Styrofoam, broken appliances, etc.). As they save they begin to see just how much one 5-person family throws out over a period of three months. In their case, it's 320 pounds of wet garbage and 83 giant lawn-sized trash bags. But the movie goes into all the other stuff each of us puts back into the atmosphere, by bathing, laundering, cleaning our homes, watering our yards, and using coal to generate the electricity that heats and lights up our homes.

Another key point the film makes: while most of us are beginning to get glimpses of how polluted our air, water and soil are, few realize that the air inside our homes is much more polluted because of the toxic chemicals that surround us and that we use every day and think are safe, from cleaning products to pressure-treated wood to tinned food to porcelain enamel bathtubs and fixtures. Much of this is in the form of the pervasive brominated flame retardants commonly found around the house in everything from the plastics used in computers and small appliances to the back coatings on upholstery. The Toxic Nation studies by Canadian Environmental Defence showed that virtually all Canadians tested carry dozens of toxic chemicals in their bodies. To find out more or to view the film, go to www.garbagerevolution.com.

4. If natural gas, how far does it have to be piped to reach your neighborhood? How old are the gas lines?

5. Is any of your power supplied by solar, wind or geothermal technology? If so, by what percentage has it grown or declined in the last ten years?

6. Where is the closest wind farm or solar array from where you live? How much of your region's power comes from wind or solar?

7. If you own your home or condo, in 2010 prices, what would it cost to install one modern passive solar or PhotoVotaic (PV) solar panel on your roof?

Who speaks for you?

1. What are your local school board's plans on the greening of new or existing school buildings? How about civic buildings (police station, court building, firehouses, etc.)?

2. What are the positions of your U.S. Senators and Congressional members on alternative energy? What are their voting records?

Your little corner of the world: your neighborhood

1. With two days' leeway, how many days since or until the moon has been or will be full?

2. Based on the various soil types, what soil series (sand, clay, etc.) is your home or apartment built on?

3. What is the industrial history of your area?

4. Name five native regional plants and the months that make up their growing season.

5. From what direction do winter storms, tornadoes or hurricanes generally come in your region? Include all storm types that apply.

6. On the longest day of the year, when does the sun set where you live? What about the shortest day of the year?

7. Name five of the grasses that grow in your area. Are any of them native?

8. What spring wildflower is consistently among the first to bloom where you live?

9. Name five resident and five migratory birds in your area. When do they nest and produce young?

10. What primary ecological event or process determined the land

form of your town or city?

11. What species have become extinct in your area?

12. From where you're reading this, point north.

13. What direction does your head point when you sleep?

14. Point to where the sun rises on your residence.

15. How many people live in your city or town? In general, is the population increasing or decreasing?

16. According to EPA standards, what is the air quality in your town on average? How many days last year were environmental alerts issued?

17. What are the local or county regulations regarding the use of pesticides in parks and public areas? In yards? On area farms? Golf courses? Are any warnings required for their use?

18. Do highway departments in your city and county use chemical pesticides and/or fertilizers on the green areas (medians, exits, greenspaces) along public highways and roads? If so, what kind? (If so and you want to do something about it, see the story behind the film *A Chemical Reaction* in Chapter 6.) What do you know about their long-term effects on humans, animals, birds, insects and the soil?

Food

1. What are the main agricultural products of your region?

2. How long is your region's agricultural growing season?

3. If applicable, when are corn and wheat harvested in the summertime?

4. Does your state allow the use of GMO labeling on foods? (How to find out: go to a store that sells organic foods and see if they list "no rGBH" or "no rBST" or "no growth hormone" labeling on containers of milk or cream.)

5. Where are the closest farmers' markets in your area? What months of the year are they open?

6. Do you belong to a CSA or food co-op? Do you know how to find one in your neighborhood or town?

7. Do you know how to plant and tend to a vegetable or herb garden? How to grow one without chemical pesticides or fertilizers?

8. Do you know how to start and maintain an organic compost heap?

9. Can you name at least two farmers who grow organic meat, vegetables or wine grapes near you?

10. Do you know how to shop for fresh, chemical-free produce? To find out the latest news about food being treated by pesticides, go to http://www.foodnews.org/

11. Where did your last purchase of fresh fruit come from? How about the ingredients for your next salad? The last vegetables you served? If your produce came from other countries, what do you know about their food safety laws?

12. Contact the office at a neighborhood school and track the ingredients of a typical lunch. How much of the food is processed or otherwise includes GMOs? How much is fresh and local? Organic?

TEACH YOURSELF THE ART OF LISTENING

"The human heart," says Yale theologian and ecologist Mary Evelyn Tucker, "is waiting to participate in dialogue with the earth. The human soul is poised to recover the language of the sacred that brings us back into contact with the great rhythms of the natural world."[11] In order to hear, we often have to learn to sensitize ourselves to the skill of listening. Here are some suggestions.

1. Watch the movie, *Into Great Silence*. [Note: When you watch it, don't think your TV is muted. As the title suggests, it invites you into a relatively sound-free world, especially in the first half.] If you watch it with someone, agree to not speak during the film. Make sure your phones are turned off. Give yourself the chance to emulate the experience of monastic life. What resistance do you notice? Jot these down in your journal.

2. Find a nearby nature space that you love that you can use in some of the practices listed so that you have a place in mind to go to.

3. Learn to be patient with yourself, not just because it helps slow you down so you can see more clearly but also because it's practical and healthy. Being patient helps keep you grounded and present to your practice. As the Buddhist master Thich Nhat Hahn advises, "In order to understand, you have to take the time to look deeply and to listen deeply." Give yourself time to let things unfold naturally. Otherwise, you can exhaust yourself. Learn the pacing that's best for you. Honor your spiritual "bandwidth."

LEARNING TO LISTEN

Author Sue Monk Kidd was facing a dark period at midlife, feeling constricted by the life she thought she'd always wanted to lead but bereft at the emptiness she felt. Culminating in what she described as "holy quaking" —jarring her into some kind of action— she took a walk one cold winter afternoon, finally settling with dark brooding thoughts on a park bench. As the wind blew, her attention was drawn to a tiny chrysalis hanging at the tip of a dogwood branch. Knowing instinctively this was a sign she should pay attention to, she broke the twig and its prize off and brought it home. As she spent months watching the cocoon go through its stages of transformation, she went through a transformation of her own.[9] She was struck by what writer John Shea said, "When order crumbles, mystery rises."[10]

The caterpillar wraps itself into a cocoon and waits, and while it waits, its transformation includes an absolute metamorphosis into another creature with entirely different DNA. It dissolves into its destiny and what it becomes is nurtured by what it was. The budding butterfly feeds off the goo that the caterpillar dissolves into. At the appointed time it will slice open its own casing, climb out and dry its wings, pump them up and fly away. Within that cocoon the caterpillar dies to its old life to enable its new form. It cannot rush the transformation, nor outguess the wisdom of its timing. If transformation is what we seek in the world we have to begin with ourselves. Mahatma Gandhi understood this when he said, "Be the change you want to see in the world. You can change nothing but yourself, but changing yourself is everything."

4. Learn yoga, tai chi or chi kung to become more attuned to the way your body speaks to you.

5. Set aside a small space that can become your altar. Add things that you cherish, that nurture your spirit: snapshots, icons or statues, likenesses of religious or spiritual figures, stones, shells, crystals, candles, a bundle of sage and a receptacle in which to burn it, a child's baby shoes or graduation photo, a souvenir from a sacred space you visited, a bottle of holy water, a prayer bookmark, books of poetry, prayer or inspiration that you value. The list is a personal one. Prepare it with the reverence appropriate to a sacred space. This will be where you can meditate or pray at the times you choose to do so, a place from which you draw spiritual strength and sustenance. Adorn it with a prayer shawl, a scarf, or a small gong if you wish. Have a CD or MP3 player to play sacred

music if you like. Include a chair and a lamp if space allows.

6. Create a spiritual practice by rotating whichever of these actions are meaningful to you. A spiritual practice is just that: a regular commitment to spend time nurturing your own spiritual life. A regular spiritual practice is a form of ritual that helps ground you and keep you connected to the sacred in your life, to the bigger cosmos of which you and everything else is a part. The amount of time you commit is up to you. What is most important is its regularity. A spiritual practice can be as simple as a pause for prayer at some point in the day. Some find it most meaningful to start each morning with a short inspirational reading followed by a few minutes of prayer or meditation. Others commit to regular neighborhood or global service to others. A spiritual practice is a singular and personal commitment. It must fit your own spiritual needs. Its power is in its regularity and the sincerity of your commitment, not in how much time and energy you put into crafting it. While it's helpful to start with someone else's ideas of what this practice should consist of—like spiritual training wheels—with time and dedication, your own sense of what you need will rise.

7. Begin working with a spiritual director or mentor—someone who is trained to help you learn to listen deeply—to help you recognize and understand the transformations and insights that will begin to unfold in your life. As spiritual director Jim Curtan says, "Enlightenment is an accident. Spiritual direction makes you accident prone." Having a good guide to accompany you is a gift. Each person's need dictates how often you meet but monthly or twice monthly is common. Don't let a director's location deter you from working with him or her. Many spiritual directors work mostly with in-office visits, while other directors live varying distances from their clients and work primarily via phone or even online video consultations (using Skype, for example). Finding a director is an act of faith and involves listening to your own inner guidance. If you have friends who work with a director, see if their director can recommend someone. Also ask at your place of worship or check with local archdioceses, synagogues or churches. You may also inquire at Buddhist centers, yoga centers or clinics that practice alternative and holistic medicine or consider an online search: http://www.sdiworld.org/.

8. As part of your practice, keep books of daily meditations or prayers (even if you prefer an online version or audio versions you keep on an MP3 player) that you spend a few minutes with each day. These help center and ground you. When possible, be out in nature when you read or listen to these.

IT ALL STARTS WITH DIRT

Our cultural stories give us the central clue to why gardens are so key to us. They represent innocence and wholeness, nurturing and security, tranquility and new beginnings, the centrality of life and its cycles of birth and death, stasis and reflection, hope and inspiration. They embody the promise of seed and fertility, the perpetuation of life and even creation itself. Many indigenous cultures have crafted creation stories that describe our true physical origins as earth itself: from wood, cornmeal and seeds, even from mud brought from the bottom of the ocean by a water beetle, or—according to the lore most familiar to Westerners—out of simple garden soil.

With the sweat of thy brow shalt thou eat bread till thou return to the Earth, for out of it wast thou taken, for soil thou art and unto soil shalt thou return.

—Genesis 3:19

As the Bible describes early on, the first inhabitants in this divine creation were Adam (from the Hebrew adama, "earth," or "soil") and the product of his rib, Eve (from the Hebrew hava, or "living"). As geneticist David Suzuki says, "Together they make the eternal connections: life comes from the soil; the soil is alive." So our first identity as an earthling is literally that—a little being of earth. Gardens or nature settings are frequently spots where stories of spiritual unfolding occur. According to legend, it was while he was on his way to the garden of his parents that the young Buddha-to-be was struck by the suffering and fleeting nature of life and dedicated his life to the search for enlightenment. It was in the Garden of Gethsemane that Jesus frequently congregated with his disciples and where Jesus prayed the night before his crucifixion. The garden is often seen as a place to rest and listen for guidance and restore oneself.

Francis Bacon spoke of the divine signature present in the very idea of a garden: "God almighty first planted a garden: and, indeed, it is the purest of human pleasure." A garden is both a sacred undertaking and a source of joy. It's fun to feel the soil on your hands, to stand barefooted on the earth, to lie on the ground at night and look at the stars. There are many different kinds of gardens and they all provide a type of nurturing, some for body, some for soul, some that do both.

DIRT! THE MOVIE

Before you first set hoe to soil, see this film to learn how unique, how alive, how central to our lives the healthy soil of the earth is. Watching this film will demonstrate not only how the world's soil is under attack by industry and commercial agriculture; it will also show how easy it is to make compost and how the simple but powerful recycling of organic matter like leaves and discarded vegetables can become the black gold of nutrient-rich soil.

We are stardust. We are golden.
We've got to get ourselves back to the garden.

— Woodstock by Crosby, Stills, Nash and Young

PLANT A VEGETABLE OR FLOWER GARDEN

It doesn't matter whether you start with a houseplant in your window or a gracious space that surrounds your house—whatever kind of garden you decide to have in your life, begin by blessing the space that you cultivate and invite the spirits of nature to be with you and guide you.

1. Promise to tend to the garden regularly as part of your spiritual practice.
2. Clean the area with reverence as you would tend to the body of a loved one. Ask the earth's blessing.
3. Clean it by spraying a biodynamic detox (see Biodynamics later in this chapter) on it to help it heal from the contamination that has accumulated from chemical fertilizers and pesticides, loss of topsoil and neglect. Note: If you use this detox, you must never use chemical sprays, fertilizers or pesticides on that soil or plant at any time after that. Biodynamics requires the conscious cooperation of the user with

the laws and agreements with nature made by the person who created the mixture and sold it to you. Be sure to verify this with your biodynamics product provider.

4. Prepare the soil with organic cow manure.
5. Plant heirloom seeds that have not been genetically modified.
6. Water daily when needed. Weed as necessary.
7. Minimize what you feel you have to buy to create your garden space. Use what you have, such as old stakes if your plants need support as they mature, and the tools and implements you have used before. Don't waste money on prettifying the process. Spend it buying good quality organic cow manure and unmodified heirloom seeds.
8. Share what you grow.
9. Practice mindfulness and being present. Listen to the earth. Open your mind and heart to its guidance.
10. Keep a garden journal. Take pictures or, even better, shoot short videos to record your progress. Share them on social media sites like Facebook, You Tube or your website.

In the garden more grows than the gardener sows.
— Spanish proverb

Remember that you are tending to the skin of Mother Earth. You are piercing it with an intention of love and healing. When you fall to your knees in the garden to make it ready for the seeds you are about to plant, you are engaging in a form of supplication—the ultimate humble act—and when you dig your hands into the dirt, to turn it over, caress it, expose it to sun and clean it up, you are living your intention and honoring your bond. That act is a hand-to-heart connection that ignites a bond with the earth and begins an alchemical process, a relationship, a partnership of shared healing.

Begin by looking at every little thing as sacred because everything is sacred. In the Talmud, there is a saying: "Every blade of grass has its angel that bends over it and whispers, 'Grow, grow.' " Every stone, every plant, every bird, every tree is sacred. Once you begin to look at nature differently, your entire field of focus shifts. Challenges that seem like roadblocks start to look different.

Here's the divine paradox of the garden: When you work in the garden, the garden works on you.

- Trust this process
- Trust there will be a connection
- Let its influence unfold in you.

This unfolding is the subtle way that the universe gives us direction. Through this process of covenant, of you making a sacred agreement, then honoring it, you show yourself and creation that you can be counted on, that you are sincere. By honoring your agreement, you learn to trust your own spiritual will and its capacity to be dependable and disciplined. This is how you build a spiritual backbone.

Once you set that process in motion—once you put your hands into the earth, give it your sweat and love and attention and nurture what rises out of the soil in response to your care—something will shift in you. The influence of that connection you have reestablished only begins in the contentment you feel or the joy at seeing food or beautiful flowers begin to thrive under your stewardship. Depending on your own capacity to listen, there is no limit to what this process will stir up in you and how it will open your heart and inform you at subterranean levels.

Begin to think of any garden you want to create as an ecosystem. Consider what a natural multi-tasker Mother Nature is. As master gardener Toby Hemenway says, "Nothing in nature does just one thing." A tree once planted solely for shade performs many other services for a yard. It attracts pollinators—butterflies, bees and other essential insects—provides food (nuts and berries) and spaces for bird's nests, pulls rainwater into its roots, cleans the air by absorbing CO_2, and covers the ground with falling leaves and twigs that form soil-enriching compost.

So too, a garden can offer food, herbs for healing and cooking, colorful flowers that lift our spirits and please our eyes (and also draw pollinating insects to continue the cycle of life), fruit arbors that not only give us delectable jams, healthy snack food and wines but serve as beautiful natural borders and accents to our yards. Gardens not only provide edible landscaping and a way to heal the piece of bioregion you live in, they can also be designed to provide a space to spend time in, not just for weeding and tilling but for respite and healing.

Any time that you are participating in any process of creation that involves the earth, you are in a kind of cathedral, a sacred territory. If you are fortunate enough to be able to visit some of our national gardens—our national parks and preserves—these warrant a special kind of respect.

Become personally invested in your bioregion, wherever you live. Each of the 50 states has its own unique beauty, its own secret wonders. Wherever you live, love what is local to you.

On the undersurface of every leaf a million movable lips are engaged in devouring carbon dioxide and expelling oxygen.

— Peter Tompkins

PLANT A MEDITATION AND HEALING GARDEN

Create a meditation garden. Consider the reasons why Zen gardens are so special and in general why gardens tend to be the sought-after sights for the healing that a quiet, peaceful space encourages. Being able to meditate in a natural setting, especially one you have helped to craft yourself, gives you an opportunity to not only connect with your earthly roots but to hear where you are distracted, and to learn discernment as you begin to detect and differentiate the voice of your intuition and spirit.

Depending on how much space you have or whether you support a community garden that also wants this option, a small untrafficked spot can be set aside as a place where visitors can spend quiet time meditating or praying. Fill such a space with healing and aromatic herbs and soft, welcoming plants (for example, lamb's ears, bunny tails, ferns—plants that are soft or willowy—yellows, whites, lavenders, violets and greens). There are hundreds of ways to furnish such a space but typical configurations are built in circles, squares or rectangles, flanked with trees or shrubs, a bird feeder or bath, a fountain or other water element.

Meditation gardens can double as healing spaces. When you surround the space with flowers and healing herbs with a flagstone floor at the center, the person sitting in the middle on a chair or bench can experience the sense of being surrounded by the healing power of nature. To complete the balance of earth's elements, add a piece of metal sculpture and some plants which represent the "fire" element—thistle, yucca, cactus or nettle.

BIODYNAMICS: HOW THE EARTH HEALS ITSELF

To live, we must daily break the body and spill the blood of Creation. When we do this knowingly, lovingly, skillfully, reverently, it is a sacrament. When we do it ignorantly, greedily, clumsily, destructively, it is a desecration.

— Wendell Berry

On a trip back to the family farm of his youth in August, 2009, author Nicholas Kristof wrote about the spiritual downside of modern industrial agriculture. By turning farms into assembly lines of efficiency and its denatured animals into commodities, he said, we have lost something precious. "It's not just that it produces unhealthy food, mishandles waste and overuses antibiotics in ways that harm us all. More fundamentally, it has no soul."

In 1922, a Hungarian-born cultural philosopher, architect, sculptor and mystic named Rudolf Steiner was not only making the same observations but had built a new theory of agriculture around that very thesis. Steiner was a popular lecturer on a wide variety of topics, including those which focused on the ways plant growth is affected by spiritual and cosmic influences. Besieged by requests from farmers concerned about the declining health and viability of their seeds and soils and the declining quality of their food crops, Steiner agreed to help them. In 1924 in Selisia, Germany (now Poland), he delivered a series of eight foundational lectures on a new principle of agriculture he called biodynamics. He talked about how the health of the soil was a key piece in the health of the food chain. Sick soil meant sick food, sick animals, and sick people.

Steiner had been talking about these principles of holism and the importance of practicing them for decades. During the lectures one of his students rose to ask why so many people, even given the specificity of his solutions, find it so hard to stick to the practices.

Steiner responded simply, "This is a problem of nutrition. Nutrition as it is today does not supply the strength necessary for manifesting the spirit in physical life. A bridge can no longer be built from thinking to will and action. Food plants no longer contain the forces people need for this."

To Steiner this was already old stuff. Even then—more than 85 years ago—our food lacked soul, and lacking soul, it failed to nourish us on all the levels critical to our survival—both physical and spiritual. What was true then is radically more true now. What Steiner discovered was the way back from that invisible but potent truth. What we needed was a way to confront our spiritual starvation and heal it. Happily, that path back to health would also reconnect us to the roots of our very life force and what might be called the next step in our spiritual evolution.

Biodynamics comes from the Greek for life (bio) and energy (dynamics). It is a farming technique that employs spiritual and physical farming practices and although it's similar to organic farming in that it does not use any type of chemical fertilizer or pesticide, it has a different philosophy, seeing farming as a closed, self-nurturing system of soil, plants, and animals. It practices the restoration and healing of the earth and working in cooperation with its natural cycles, with the farmer playing a key role as a humble and informed steward. From a posture that sees the Earth as a living organism and a part of an intelligent, living cosmos, biodynamic agriculture observes the celestial rhythms of the moon and sun for planting and harvesting and making what are called the biodynamic preparations.

Each of the nine preparations has a specific healing role, from the specially prepared manure to the finely ground quartz meal of silica powder to ancient medicinals—yarrow blossoms, chamomile blossoms, stinging nettle, oak bark, dandelion flowers, valerian flowers and horsetail. Some are buried in the earth for six months to a year to decompose. Others such as Valerian flowers and horsetail are used as compost sprays. When dug up, each performs a different, significant role in the healthy decomposition of the compost and in the treating of the soil and plants during the growing season.

Biodynamics is designed to work with healing and empowering the immune system in every molecule of soil and plant life, to waste nothing and to be a fully sustainable system. A biodynamic farmer's aim is to understand the laws and forces of nature and work in harmony and cooperation with them to cure the soil naturally of the toxins that have been deposited in it—and heal our own hungry, disconnected spirits in the process.

For more information about biodynamics, contact the Josephine Porter Institute, http://www.jpibiodynamics.org/content/2008calend arrecommendations.html, for detailed listings that show (for the U.S. Eastern time zones) "first choice periods for working the soil, applying the biodynamic preparations, sowing seed, or working with plants in general," or the Pfeiffer Institute, www.pfeiffercenter.org, for information about training in biodynamic agriculture.

Harmony with land is like harmony with a friend;
you cannot cherish his right hand and chop off the left.
That is to say, you cannot love game and hate predators;
you cannot conserve the waters and waste the ranges; you cannot
build the forest and mine the farm. The land is one organism.

— Aldo Leopold

Findhorn: The garden as a community of co-creation

On a snowy November day in 1962, three people in northeast Scotland took a bold step that changed their lives and set the world thinking differently about how man might be able to relate to nature. It was only two months after the publication of *Silent Spring* set the world blinking with disbelief about something called DDT, and only days after the powder keg called the Cuban Missile Crisis had ended in the U.S., introducing more than a decade of revolution and unrest.

The trio, Peter and Eileen Caddy and friend Dorothy Maclean took up residence—with the three Caddy children—in a 30-foot long travel trailer to begin a simpler life, one that connected them not to business and the making of money but to restoring beauty and love to the planet. Although Peter built a tiny annex for Dorothy, for the next seven years the six of them effectively shared this space.

In the five years prior, Peter Caddy, a former RAF squadron leader, had enjoyed the good life as the manager of a large hotel in the Cluny Hills just a few miles from the site of their caravan park. During his tenure, the hotel had prospered and been elevated from a three to a four-star rating. He and his family lived in the lap of luxury, enjoying all the amenities of a resort hotel, complete with a full 5-course dinner each night. Their future seemed secure. Yet by 1962, Caddy was unemployed, living on public assistance—the U.S. equivalent of $20 per week—to feed his wife, children and their friend, on a spot he described as "surrounded by gorse and broom, sitting on sand between a rubbish dump and a dilapidated garage." The area, overlooking the Firth of

Moray, was called Findhorn Bay.

What followed for Peter, Eileen and Dorothy was an adventure in faith. As hard as the next years were, they believed completely, as the deeply spiritual people they were, that their lives were being led purposefully. Each night Eileen rose at midnight and meditated for hours. She faithfully wrote down what came through to her, guidance that told them what they were being called to do—create a garden—and exactly how they were to do that, down to the tasks to be done each day and even to the food and drink it was best for them to consume. The fact that none of them knew anything about gardening didn't seem to bother anyone.

With winter quickly advancing, they spent the next months preparing their garden space. Acting on guidance was nothing miraculous or new to them. They believed that during their years at the hotel that this same guidance had enabled Peter to raise the hotel's standing and triple its yearly income.

Peter was to be the new-world Adam in this Aquarian garden of Eden, creating the structures they would need, procuring the materials and managing their labors. As they worked, preparing the ground for the spring planting, they began to be aware of an energetic and powerful connection to the soil. A few months after they had started their work in the garden, Dorothy, a colleague and the Cluny Hotel secretary who had accompanied them to Findhorn, began to receive impressions in her meditations from the various spirits in her garden. As she learned, there was a different spirit or "deva," for each kind of vegetable and fruit, for the trees, weeds, grass, sand, wind—every single element they were surrounded by. She in turn passed this information along to Peter and Eileen. From these spirits they learned how crucial it was to have complete cooperation and trust between humans and nature.

The soil on their windswept half acre was an impossible mixture of sand, hard grass and rock and seemed a poor host in which to grow anything, much less the vegetable garden they were hoping would supplement their diets through the coming year. Besides the seemingly barren sand, which lacked the mass to hold seeds or absorb water, it appeared unlikely that anything could take root or survive, much less thrive, against the rigors of the wind's constant barrage. Still they tilled their little patch and followed the guidance each was receiving, working the soil over and over, literally willing life into it. As Peter described,

"Every square inch of soil was handled by each of us several times." They built fences and poured concrete walkways, all with raw materials that literally fell into their laps. The first years were hard, busy, and exhausting. There were setbacks and corrections needing to be made but by May the first radishes, turnips and lettuce were appearing. By the end of June, the garden was thriving. Neighbors walking by gawked in disbelief at the appearance of a garden in such a hostile environment. They were witnessing the healing of the soil and the resulting health and vitality of new plant life.

During their second winter Peter got permission from the park owner and began to rebuild the soil in the uneven, sloping area to the south of their garden, planting berry bushes and apples. During that growing season, they grew 65 different types of vegetables, 21 kinds of fruits and 42 different herbs. But what was more significant was the size and vitality of what came out of their garden. During their second summer one of their red cabbages weighed 38 pounds, another 42. A single white sprouting broccoli was so large, the whole family ate cuttings from it for months. When it came time to pull it up, it was almost too heavy to lift out of the ground.

With all visitors coming to Findhorn there was this kind of give and take: our technical knowledge was broadened, their spiritual horizons were extended.

— Peter Caddy

It began to occur to them that there was a bigger reason for their success, beyond their "beginner's luck." Perhaps, Peter thought, "something spectacular was needed to draw attention to our garden, to pave the way for a time when we might openly talk about our conscious cooperation with devas and nature spirits," something they did not yet openly discuss. "People thought us strange enough as it was." With the eye-popping bounty growing out of little more than sand, rumors of this unlikely garden began to draw attention. A soil analysis by the County Horticultural Adviser proved that the thin and unlikely looking soil was in fact perfectly balanced. Support from Sir George Trevelyan and Lady Eve Balfour (author of *The Living Soil*, a groundbreaking book on the interrelatedness of all life and man's need to honor that link) helped begin conversations about topics that people had previously not felt comfortable discussing.

Here were these rank amateurs making plants, vegetables and trees grow where logic said they could not, in size and quantity unmatched before, in soil that was somehow perfectly balanced, in a climate that most believed was forbidding to species that were in fact thriving. All of this was happening in a world just waking to the fact that all was not well with its air, soil and water because of the amount of manmade contamination being dumped upon it. Here was quiet unmistakable proof that man working in cooperation with the forces of nature—instead of trying to make them bend to his will and ideas of productivity—could achieve miracles.

The ancients, of course, accepted the kingdom of nature spirits without question as a fact of direct vision and experience. The organs of perception of the super-sensible world have atrophied in modern man as part of the price to be paid for the evolving of the analytical scientific mind.

— Sir George Trevelyan, writing about the
phenomenon he witnessed at Findhorn.

In 1969, a U.N. agricultural expert and agriculture professor, R. Lindsay Robb, visited Findhorn just before Christmas and quickly realized something besides dedicated gardening was responsible: "the vigor, health and bloom of the plants in the garden at midwinter on land which is almost a barren powdery sand cannot be explained by the moderate dressings of compost, nor indeed by the application of any known cultural methods of organic husbandry. There are other factors and they are vital ones."

Those other vital factors, the communication and cooperation with nature via each participant's intuition or inner guidance continued to make Findhorn a destination for spiritual seekers and garden enthusiasts, drawing horticultural experts and teachers from around the world. In 1970, eight years after Findhorn's humble beginnings, an American spiritual philosopher and teacher named David Spangler arrived and was invited to help envision its future. During the next three years, Findhorn's role would grow from that of garden to an education center, fulfilling the role of the keepers of wisdom—to learn by living and then teach their lessons to others. It was time for Findhorn to move into its next stage of growth, into the education of the human consciousness and what Peter Caddy termed "the transformation of the human soul."

Now, looking back, a clear pattern and plan can be discerned, each apparent challenge seen as teaching the perfect lesson. A man quite untutored in the techniques of gardening was placed in this unpromising terrain and challenged to create a garden. He was provided with all the necessary channels and situations necessary to revive in him the spirit of true cooperation with nature, under the guidance of the God within. And the garden grew.

— Peter Caddy

In the forty years since, as Peter Caddy sensed, Findhorn's identity has continued to evolve, its history and humble beginnings serving as the healing foundation for everything that has been built upon it since. It did evolve into a place of leadership in the teaching of human consciousness and the transformation of the soul. In 1997 Findhorn was given official NGO status by the United Nations. Today, it is a famed source of wisdom and education, an experiential learning center that lives it creed—to discover what it truly means to live an ecological, sustainable and responsible life in the 21st century. Its community has the lowest ecological footprint in the industrialized world (half the average energy usage in the UK). Its onsite Living Machine, the first sewage treatment facility of its kind in the UK, cleans waste water without chemicals by filtering it through a greenhouse of flowering plants, using plant bacteria. It has received a Best Practice designation from the United Nations Centre for Human Settlements.

Having grown way beyond the half-acre garden that its three founders launched, it not only contains the original caravan park, but a campus—the former Cluny Hill Hotel that Peter Caddy once managed— as well as an arts centre, a publication company, and a bakery, among others. It provides 200 classes each year to community members and visitors. Its membership now numbers 300-400 people at any given time.

The Ecovillage contains other similar-minded organizations, including Trees for Life, the nonprofit whose aim is to repopulate the ancient Caledonian Forest in Scotland and the Moray Steiner School (one of 890 Steiner schools in the world), which practices the educational tenets of the philosopher and father of *Biodynamics,* Rudolf Steiner.

"In a period where there is a lot of hand wringing and disempowerment, [Findhorn] is a project where people have moved beyond the politics of protest to actually create something that models what they would really like to see. That is in a sense a model of what the world could look like if we pull all our different images of sustainability into one place."

In the foreword to a book written by the Findhorn Community in 1975, the poet and cultural historian William Irvin Thompson wrote about Findhorn's timely, powerful and gentle legacy, how with patient hands and open hearts and minds, a few people put us back in touch with a deep connection we had forgotten we had:

"Whether we speak of kachinas, devas, djin, angels or sprites, we are invoking a cosmology that is much the same around the world. Industrialization tried to drive that cosmology out of men's minds, but now that the failure of the Green Revolution has dramatized the failure of the industrialization of agriculture, the underground traditions of animism can surface without any sense of embarrassment. It is the proponents of the agro-industry who need to be shame-faced now.

"The landscape of the New Age is not a regressive Crunchy Granola fantasy of nineteenth-century American agrarian life. We are not going back to what Marx called 'the idiocy of rural life'; we are going back to nature with the consciousness of civilization behind us and the adventure of planetization in front of us.

"Modern man knows how to talk back to nature, but he doesn't know how to listen. Archaic man knew how to listen to wind and water, flower and tree, angel and elf. There is a weakness to bigness and power, and all the little cultures have returned to tell us that."

SPIRITUAL PRACTICES—52 WAYS TO RECONNECT WITH THE EARTH

There are as many ways to reconnect with the earth as there are people on the planet. Each of us has a unique link, like an energetic fingerprint. But here's a place to start. Use one practice a week, rotate a few or stick with one you like. Find what works and feels right. There's really no wrong way to do this. This process helps you discern what's comfortable and do-able for you. Add to this list as new ideas or variations that work better for you occur to you.

1. Develop a walking meditation practice. Consider how often in your life you may have solved a problem or received an inspiration just by walking quietly by yourself. Why? Because outside when you are in contact with the earth you are closer to your own life source, a wisdom as old as time itself that waits for you. Whether we can say why, we crave it and feel ourselves calm down and relax when we are within its energetic grasp. Creating a walking meditation allows you to engage this connection, to give your intention to it, to invite it in and be totally present to its healing grace. As the Buddhist master Thich Nhat Hahn affirms, the rules are simple. Have no goal. Just let yourself be happy as you walk. "Each step brings you back to the present moment which is the only moment you can be alive." Suggestion: Google "walking meditation" for YouTube videos or read his book, *The Long Road Turns to Joy: A Guide to Walking Meditation*. Note what rises as you walk. What sorts of things cross your mind? Note these in your journal.

2. Consider how to convert your yard into what author Michael Pollan calls an "edible landscape." Instead of having an ornamental landscape that's merely beautiful to look at, make it earn its keep. Turn it into something that feeds more than the eyes, blending flowers and food. Go to Google Books and search "edible landscape" for book ideas or contact your local university's agricultural extension service for recommendations or classes. Once you have mastered the concept, teach others.

3. Consult a county map and trace where the waste output from a nearby industrial plant (food processing, clothing, bottled water or equipment manufacturer, coal or nuclear plant, etc.) dumps out into a river or stream. If you can, follow it to where it empties. Sit by that site. Close your eyes and concentrate on your breathing. Listen.

4. Native American James Gosling was asked what it was like to go to an area that has had its timber clear-cut: "I couldn't breathe," he

said. "It was as if the earth had been skinned. I couldn't believe anyone would do that to the Earth." Go to an area of a forest or wetland that has been clear-cut. Sit by that site. Close your eyes and concentrate on your breathing. Listen.

5. Scientist David Suzuki says, "From our first cry announcing our arrival on Earth to our very last sigh at the moment of death, our need for air is absolute. Every breath is a sacrament, a sacred ritual." Go to a botanical garden and breathe the oxygen it produces. Think of how the trees in that enclosed space are silently converting carbon dioxide to oxygen, how dependent each of us is on their survival for our own survival.

6. Become a "locavore," someone who eats food that comes from within 50-100 miles of where you live. Begin by taking stock. Examine the contents of your cupboard, refrigerator and freezer. Note how many items do and do not come from within 50 miles of your home and how much of your fresh, frozen and packaged food—cans, bottles, tubes, jars, boxes, etc.—contain HFCS or other GMO'd corn derivatives.

7. Make a plan to restock your pantry, refrigerator and freezer with food that contains no preservatives, chemicals, or processed ingredients (including anything containing HFCS or GMO'd additives). Learn more about where you will find GMOs in the food that fills most grocery store shelves, refrigerator and freezer cases: *Your Right to Know: Genetic engineering and the secret changes in your food,* by Andrew Kimbrell (Earth Aware Books, San Rafael, CA, 2007).

8. If it's not prohibited by state laws that prohibit labeling the GMO ingredients in foods, ask the management at your regular grocery store to stop carrying dairy products that contain rBST or rGBH. If GMO labeling is against the law, call your state and local representatives to register your displeasure and go online to find out where you can join other groups that have helped overturn so-called food libel laws in other states.

9. Plan a pot luck dinner, inviting everyone to bring food that comes within 50 miles of your town, is free of pesticides, chemicals, CAFO-grown (or corn-fed) meat, or genetically modified ingredients of any kind. Keep in mind that before the 1950s, this was the only kind of food that people ate.

10. Contact a local organic farm and volunteer to weed, pick crops or sell produce for part of a day. Industrial agricultural farms

are generously subsidized by the U.S. government. Volunteering offers local farmers a goodwill subsidy that costs the taxpayers nothing while it builds community and offers nonfarmers a way to show gratitude and participate in the process that brings healthy, nourishing food into people's lives. Don't know where to start? Contact http://www.wwoof. org/wwoofaroundtheworld.asp to find out how you can volunteer to work with organic farmers locally or internationally to share knowledge and help create a global consciousness about the benefits of ecological farming. (If you are a farmer, you can also learn how to use your farm to host volunteers.)

TWEET YOUR LITTLE HEART OUT!

Nowdays anything worth sharing can be instantly broadcast to others. Use social networking sites like Twitter and Facebook to raise consciousness about the planet and the hundreds of opportunities to wake up and be of service. Many green, food-related, ecology and earth-friendly sites have fan clubs you can subscribe to on Facebook and on Twitter as well as other sites. You can link to them from Facebook, sign up to get tweets from others, send tweets on your own, gather and follow fans, and generally draw others to your interests. This is an instant way to distribute news, keep tabs on newsworthy stories and help broadcast what others send to you that you would like to share with others.

11. Join an organic CSA (Community Supported Agriculture). When you sign up with a CSA, you pay a farmer an annual subscription for the regular delivery (usually weekly) of fresh produce during the growing season. It's a way to invest in a steady stream of good, organic food from a local farmer and give him or her the security of a regular income. It is a relationship where both benefit. Besides getting good, reliably healthy food, you create a relationship with someone who grows what nourishes you and your family; you in turn help that farmer grow food on one more patch of ground that doesn't pollute the earth with chemical fertilizers or pesticides. To find a CSA near you, go to www.localharvest.org.

12. Find out what farmers markets are near you and patronize them during the harvest months. These markets thrive through community participation. If possible, bring your friends and neighbors and make it a weekly celebration of what's being grown locally for you by people you actually begin to know. Check out http://www.slowfoodusa.org/ to

find out not only where your local farmers markets are but lots more resources available that track the movement away from "fast" processed food to healthier, locally sustainable food.

13. Volunteer to organize an organic community garden in the yard or parking lot of a church, an abandoned lot, a school yard or other open space that is not being utilized. Include edibles and flowers.

14. Go online or call your state parks department and find the closest state park. Spend time sitting in the midst of greenery and trees. Sit under a tree and close your eyes. See how many sounds you can identify. What does the air smell like? What does the wind sound and feel like? Pay attention to how your body feels. What part of your body responds to the experience?

15. When as a young man, the naturalist John Muir first laid eyes on what would become Yosemite National Park, he was so stunned by its beauty, he would spend much of the rest of his life tirelessly working to expand its territory and save it from the encroachment of building developers. His passion about what he called "the heart of the world" would eventually inspire Theodore Roosevelt to create what is now our national park system. If you can, visit one or more of the 62 U.S. national parks. Spanning more than 90 million protected acres, these national sanctuaries are perfect spots in which to immerse yourself in nature, slow down and listen to your life. Many have campgrounds and/or cabins. If you can spend the night, do so. Give yourself time to let the sounds, smells, and rhythms of nature that are unique to each park filter into your consciousness. (If you can't visit one of the parks or you just want to learn more about them, watch the 2009 PBS documentary series by Ken Burns, *The National Parks: America's Best Idea*.)

16. If a state or national park is too inaccessible, sit in a garden, a wooded area, seashore, a porch, a park bench, a dock, or any other place where you can be outside in relative quiet and with your eyes closed, let the sounds you are in the midst of seep into you. Note how your breathing slows and your stress level declines.

17. Plant some trees! Replenish the earth's carbon sinks. Give everyone's lungs the tiniest boost. See www.americanforests.org for ideas. (Plantings are as cheap as $1 per tree.)

18. As weather permits, plan an outing that takes you outside of your house or apartment into fresh air. Stay as long as you can. Make it a gift to yourself that you can look forward to.

19. Take a walk every day that you can. Set aside the time as a discipline. Turn your phone off or leave it at home. Listen instead to the sounds that fill each block as you walk. This is the environment you live in, your bioregion. It keeps you alive. You are part of one another. Feel that.

20. Sit on a porch or under a safe overhang during a rainstorm and feel the power of the electricity in the air, the storm's rhythm, how the earth absorbs the sounds of thunder, how the fury and wind eventually settle into rain, how the air feels afterwards, how the sounds change. Feel how your body responds.

21. If you live where there is snowfall, go outside briefly each hour during a snowstorm to see how slowly the snow turns the world clean and quiet. Notice how it alters the way your landscape appears and sounds, covering the landmarks that are so familiar to you during other times of the year.

22. Have a dawn and sunset practice outside in which you pay homage to your life, to the air you breathe into your lungs and the earth that sustains you. Thomas Merton referred to sunset as a moment in nature that is a kind of Sabbath of the body, a brief period of sustained receptivity. The breaking dawn and sunset of each day are sacred and mystical moments, short and grace-filled. Allow yourself enough time on each end to appreciate the few minutes' duration of each transformation. Thomas Berry said, "Our moments of grace are our moments of transformation." Think of them together as the completion of a cosmic breathing cycle, one inhalation, one exhalation. Allow yourself time to soak up and breathe in their sweetness.

23. At least once a month (when the moon is full or new, for instance), spend time gazing at the night sky, away from the city lights if possible. When the moon is full, watch its trajectory. When it is new, appreciate the darkness of the sky, how regular and dependable life's cycles are. No matter how many times we look at the moon, no matter how many times we look at the stars, we are captivated, in awe, under a spell. Each of us is a little different every 28 days. The moon's placement in the sky is a little bit different too. Even so, it has been the constant through time, through our own lives and the lives of everyone who came before us. The moon and stars have always been there, our tether to the past and the future generation's tether back to us. It's our commonality. That's nature's power.

24. Go to http://hubblesite.org/ or to an observatory and see pictures taken by the Hubble telescope to begin to appreciate how vast the cosmos is. The Greek philosopher Heraclitus once said, "For those who are awake, the cosmos is one." This magnificent creation is what you are a part of.

25. Practice gratitude. Take a gratitude walk in a place that you cherish. Talk to nature. Say thank you. Say a gratitude prayer when you wake up and before you go to sleep. You are breathing and alive. Find the gratitude there. The mystic Meister Eckhart said, "If the only prayer you ever say in your entire life is thank you, that will be enough."

26. Learn about the plight of the many endangered indigenous and healing plants that are being threatened in North America. Offer to work at their 360-acre botanical sanctuary in Ohio as a volunteer. See http://unitedplantsavers.org to learn about interning opportunities and seminars available.

27. Learn the birds indigenous to your area and watch for their comings and goings. As you become more aware of the birds that visit you, you may also want to create a bird sanctuary, matching plants, trees and bird feeders to the bird species that you want to draw to you. Make a daily ritual of putting out food and water for them. Go online and consult your local university agricultural extension service or local nature clubs to find out which trees or plants in your area attract particular types of birds, butterflies and bees. Know that nature yearns to connect to you as you do to it.

28. Find a Buddhist or Catholic monastery that is near you that allows weekend retreats. Arrange for one (they are usually very modestly priced). While there, spend as much quiet time outside as you can. Leave your computer at home. Leave your to-do lists and your work at home. Leave your phone off as much as possible. Honor the healing stillness you have arranged to immerse yourself into. Some monasteries offer spiritual guidance during your time there. Consider arranging an appointment with one of the on-site community members during your visit.

29. Once you are familiar with the seasonal rhythms of the earth in your area, visit a neighborhood elementary school and volunteer to teach them how to cultivate a community garden.

30. If your parks or greenspaces are sprayed or doused with chemical fertilizers or pesticides, petition your park board to forbid their use. This is a form of what Andrew Harvey calls sacred activism. Each

human being on the planet can take personal responsibility for caretaking one piece of the Earth that speaks to his or her heart: one creature, one tree, one piece of a habitat, one part of a vacant lot, one mountain footpath, one bend of a riverbed. Begin there.

31. Cultivate a flower garden that offers a sanctuary for butterflies. Keep in mind that scale is not important. This can be a full-fledged garden whether you have acres of yard or one flower pot on your fire escape.

32. Once you have found a nature spot that you hold dear, go there and practice a meditation in which you ask the Earth's forgiveness. You can create a forgiveness meditation of your own or use this one as a model. Practicing an act of contrition with humility and sincerity in nature is a sacred act of atonement and renewal.

Words have the power to both destroy and heal. When words are both true and kind, they can change our world.
— Buddha

FORGIVENESS MEDITATION

This request for forgiveness is dedicated to all of the Earth, to all living sentient beings as well as to all those no longer alive that we never knew, never mourned and never championed. We ask on behalf of ourselves as well as others who have gone before us or who cannot yet speak for themselves.

Forgive us for our selfishness, for not seeing beyond our own blind sense of entitlement. Replace that with the sense of honor, awe and connection we were born with and have lost. Help us see beyond our own immediate needs to the needs of future generations that are yet unknown to us. Let us be worthy of that stewardship. Help us reconnect and rebuild our own shattered pieces back into a whole that is in union with you.

Forgive us for betraying you, for turning our backs on your anguish, for knowing better and doing the wrong thing anyway. Return us to a sense of integrity and intentionality. We long for a new generosity of spirit. Help us find it.

Forgive us our ego and arrogance, for looking you over and seeing you only for what we wanted for ourselves. We are visitors, guests on this planet. Help us remember to be humble and dependable caretakers.

Forgive us for the grief and loneliness we have caused, the feelings of disenfranchisement, vengeance, the loss of preciousness of what you represent in our lives. Help us find our place again and rekindle those feelings of recognition and joy that we have lost and long for.

Forgive us for our destructive addictions and thoughtless, expedient choices, for feasting carelessly at what we chose to believe was an endless and limitless trough, as if you were ours to devour without thought to anyone but ourselves or any time but ours. Help us gain the gift of wise choice, to be dependable gatekeepers of the gifts you hold ready to share with us.

Forgive us for not seeing clearly, for being unwilling to see or hear what was happening to you and all of our fellow creatures. Help us use our gifted brains in balance to both learn the truth of what we have done and to intuit ways to begin healing. Help us see the way to support and celebrate those who champion you.

Forgive us for waiting so long to see the totality of what is unfolding around us. We have ignored so many voices, derided the wisdom of so many who tried to warn us. We seek now to find a path back to our sacred connection to the energy that is yours, to spend our days working in renewal and rebirth, to pour new healing thinking into the collective, doing our small part in adding to a path that others can follow and then endow to those who follow them.

For all these things we most humbly ask for the courage and wisdom we need to step into our new roles, as we strive to become both spiritually accountable and joyfully responsible in this new world unfolding before us.

As we end this meditation, we are mindful that forgiveness is a process that falls away from us in layers and that it must always begin with us forgiving ourselves.

Peace to each and all.

Forgiveness is the fragrance the violet sheds on the heel that has crushed it.

— Mark Twain

33. Learn about Biodynamics (see the Biodynamics section earlier in this chapter). Find a biodynamic practitioner and obtain some biodynamic compost tea. Then spray your landscaping and garden with the tea to heal the earth from the pesticides and fertilizers it has accumulated on its surface and soil.

34. Join "re-greening" organizations that plant shade trees and fruit orchards to counter CO_2 emissions. While many online sites offer you an opportunity to plant trees to supplement those being lost to tree harvesting or natural disaster (and therefore, help undo oxygen depletion that goes with tree loss), find an organization that lets you do hands-on work, if possible. There is no substitute for the experience of midwifing new growth going into the earth. Become a volunteer and offer to return at regular intervals.

35. Offer your newfound wisdom to others: show children how to plant and tend to a garden.

36. Offer to plant trees or a garden that attracts butterflies or hummingbirds at a senior residence center.

37. Teach dog and cat owners how to fertilize their yards without using pesticides and fertilizers which can injure and kill their animals.

38. According to many indigenous societies, including Native American ones, everyone has a spirit animal. Determine what yours is. Learn about it. Invite that spirit to tell you how it has influenced your life and ask it to be present with you in your daily practices.

39. Bring a heightened awareness of trees into your life. Trees are our carbon sinks. They breathe in CO_2 and breathe out oxygen. They hold water and through their numbers determine what areas will get rainfall. Without them we could not live. Trees have long held sacred connections to spiritual beings. Think of Buddha and the Bodi Tree, Christ being crucified on a cross made of timbers, and the Tree of Life celebrated in the Jewish tradition. Trees are a compound connection with both the roots that dig into the earth and the branches that reach to the heavens. Find a tree in your landscape or nearby park that has caught your eye and visit it often. Speak to it, sit under it, touch it, tune into it, thank it. Enjoy how the sun filters through its branches and leaves. Lean against it while the wind blows and feel it move. Note what it smells like. Learn its branches and crevices. Honor it as a living thing, helping to fill your lungs with clean air.

40. Museums are full of renderings by artists who have tried

to capture the ephemeral changing nature of art on canvases and in sculpture. Nature is so elusive because it never stands still. There is a great tradition of using art in your landscape, of honoring nature's capacity to stir wonder and act as a canvas and backdrop for companion works of art that are manmade. Whether you fill your garden with solar lamps, gazing balls, angels, ornamental iron, sculpture, chimes, shepherd's hooks or ironworks, art is a beautiful way to enhance your landscape. It can add perspective, harmony, balance and charm. More importantly art creates awe in us. "Art," says Matthew Fox, "is the only language we have for awe." The role of the artist, he says is to teach us to "behold being, to go into grief, and show us the intrinsic power of creativity."

41. The geneticist and ecologist David Suzuki says, "One way or another, we are Earthenware." Earth frames our cradle-to-grave lifecycle. It is our life source. Take a pottery class to learn how to throw pots and create with earthen materials. During the wintertime, if you cannot get outside easily or the weather is too inclement, keep some earthen clay on hand to mold. Keep it in an airtight container and save the scraps. Working with clay is a powerful way to help keep you connected to the earth.

42. If these are meaningful for you, find a tool for divining wisdom and learn how to use them: I Ching, Runes, Tarot, Grace cards. All are widely available at bookstores or online. If you want a reading from a good astrologer or numerologist, ask a friend to recommend one or consult public listings at your local health food store.

43. In a nature space you love, practice some form of exercise that stresses mindfulness and regulated breathing, such as tai chi chuan or yoga. Being in nature when you practice such connected body work enhances the experience, bringing you closer to the earth. Tai chi for example, is often called moving meditation. It encourages your body to enter into timeless flow. It is a present time experience. You cannot practice its movements and be thinking about anything else or you will break your rhythm and lose your place. It is a practice that simultaneously inspires deep mindfulness, awareness of your balance and center, the interconnectedness of the parts of your body and the heat of energy, or "chi", moving through your body. This kind of slow purposeful physical exercise done on the earth's surface could be described as mindfulness within mindfulness, or connection within connection and it is a very powerful way to both honor and receive input from the earth.

44. During a nature walk or a time outside by yourself, engage in a practice that Richard Rohr teaches: find something in nature that represents the presence of God to you. Whatever form it takes—tree, bird, rock, wind, rain, animal—just acknowledge its presence and innate sacredness.

45. Make a habit of doing your journaling out of doors in a quiet space whenever possible. If you cannot be outside, try to locate yourself by a window (open if possible) so you can at least look outside.

46. If you live near a cemetery where relatives are buried, visit it and tend to a loved one's grave. Spend time in the stillness and ask your ancestors for guidance. If you do not, find a beautiful graveyard and meditate in its sacredness and stillness.

47. Go hunting with a camera or a tape recorder. Take pictures that record your experience. Set your tape recorder near a lake or a stream and record the surrounding sounds. Share on your website or social networking sites.

48. Teach! Share the gift of wisdom. Find ways to teach others how to do any of these practices—but especially children. Pass along what they can also pass along. This begins anew the creation of traditions that once again honor the earth.

49. Get a massage out in nature. (For example, Esalen, in Big Sur in northern California, is well known for offering massages in a spectacular cliffside setting.)

50. Abraham Joshua Heschel said, "Mankind will not perish for want of information, but for want of appreciation." We are the first generation to be disconnected from the stars and skies that humankind has always turned to in awe. Because of pollution and bright city lights, we are often cut off from the sight of the cosmos to which we belong. Whenever you can, do any of these practices under a full night sky and feel the moon and the stars above you and the earth beneath you. It completes a magical and mystical circle that each of us relates to without knowing why.

51. Find a labyrinth you can walk. Although ancient labyrinths also included square or rectangular shapes, modern labyrinths are most often circle formations composed of parallel paths that slowly wind toward the center and then wind back toward and exit near the entrance. Much like the practice of an internal martial art, which requires reverence, focus and mindfulness, the act of walking a labyrinth takes you out of your day

to day into something of an altered state. Walking a labyrinth is often seen as a symbolic journey inward and many find it a meaningful form of meditation, especially when you walk an ancient labyrinth such as the famous labyrinth on the floor of the Chartres Cathedral in France, on which people have been walking in varying contemplative states since the 13th century. As sacred sites, ancient labyrinths are often the site of mystical insight and revelation and as such represent a potent cosmic force. If you need help finding one, google "find a labyrinth," or go to www.labyrinthlocator.com. This will take you to a site that lets you select a labyrinth you would like to visit based on type, material, category (church, art installation, farm, historic monument, etc.) and proximity to your zip code. If there is no labyrinth near you, contact a Catholic, Episcopal or Unity church near you. They may know of one that is within a reasonable distance. You can also build a small scale labyrinth in your garden or yard. Consult gardening books to help plan how to tier the plants to achieve the height and effect you want.

52. In your favorite nature space, pray. Pray for the healing of yourself, of friends, of the planet. Finish this sentence. "When my life is over, I want my legacy to the earth to be....."

Endnotes

1. *Sacred Contracts*, p. 348.
2. Duane Elgin, *The Living Universe: Where are we? Who are we? Where are we going?* (San Francisco: Berrett-Koehler Publishers, 2009), 148-149.
3. http://www.ted.com/talks/al_gore_s_new_thinking_on_the_climate_crisis.html
4. Derrick Jensen, "Taking Shorter Showers Doesn't Cut It: Why Personal Change Does Not Equal Political Change," *Orion Magazine*, July 13, 2009.
5. Huston Smith, *A Seat at the Table* (Berkeley: University of California Press, 2006), 47.
6. Some journals and their authors:
   On Walden Pond, by Henry David Thoreau
   The Diary of Anne Frank, by Anne Frank
   Travels with Charlie, by John Steinbeck
   A Journey to the Western Islands of Scotland, James Boswell and Samuel Johnson
   The Julie/Julia Project: http://blogs.salon.com/0001399/2002/08/25.html or http://juliepowell.blogspot.com/

Some good how-to books and writers:
Bird by Bird, by Anne Lamott
The Artist's Way, by Julia Cameron
Writing Down the Bones, by Natalie Goldberg
The Writing Life, by Annie Dillard
Journal Writing: the art and heart of reflection, by Stephanie Dowrick
The Story of Your Life: Writing a Spiritual Autobiography, by
Dan Wakefield.

7. Derrick Jensen, *Listening to the Land: Conversations about Nature, Culture and Eros* (White River Junction: Chelsea Green Publishing, 2004), 198-200.

8. Jane Poynter's 16-minute talk can be viewed online at TED.com: http://www.ted.com/talks/jane_poynter_life_in_biosphere_2.html

9. Sue Monk Kidd *When the Heart Waits, Spiritual Direction for Life's Sacred Question*, (San Francisco: Harper and Row, 1990).

10. John Shea *Stories of God: An Unauthorized Biography*, (Chicago: Thomas More Press, 1978), quoted in When the Heart Waits.

11. Mary Evelyn Tucker, *Worldly Wonder: Religions Enter Their Ecological Phase* (Peru (IL): Carus Publishing, 2003), 108.

12. David Suzuki, *The Sacred Balance: Rediscovering Our Place in Nature* (New York: Prometheus Books, 1998), 76.

13. Toby Hemenway, *Gaia's Garden: A Guide to Home-Scale Permaculture* (White River: Chelsea Green Publishing, 2000), 5.

14. Peter Tompkins and Christopher Bird, *The Secret Life of Plants* (New York: Harper and Row, 1973), xiii.

15. Wendell Berry, *The Gift of Good Land* (San Francisco: North Point Press, 1981), 281.

16. Nicholas Kristof, "Food for the Soul," New York Times, August 22, 2009.

17. From the foreword by Dr. Ehrenfried Pfeiffer to Rudolf Steiner, *Agriculture Course: The Birth of the Bio-Dynamic Method* (London: Rudolf Steiner Press, 1958, reprinted 2004).

18. Aldo Leopold, *A Sand County Almanac: with Essays on Conservation from Round River* (New York: Random House, 1966), 189-90.

19. The Findhorn Community, *The Findhorn Garden: Pioneering a New Vision of Man and Nature in Cooperation* (New York: Harper and Row, 1975), 2-3.

20. Peter Tompkins, *The Secret Life of Plants*, "Findhorn and the Garden of Eden," 361-373.

21. *The Findhorn Garden*, 13.

22. The Findhorn Community, *The Findhorn Garden Story* (Findhorn: Findhorn Press, 2008), 23.

23. Quote from Jonathan Dawson, Global Ecovillage Network in *Findhorn Now,* video by the Findhorn Foundation, 2008: http://www.findhorn.org/video

24. William Irvin Thompson, from the foreword to *The Findhorn Garden.*

25. *The Sacred Balance*, 209.

26. *Listening to the Land,* 76.

CHAPTER 6

Individual Acts

*Never doubt that a small group of thoughtful, committed people can change the
world. Indeed, it is the only thing that ever has.*

— Margaret Mead

For six decades, *The New Yorker* featured the work of celebrity caricaturist Al Hirschfeld. Over the years the artist's trademark became a bit of whimsy he played with his viewing public. Into each of his drawings he would carefully etch his daughter's name, Nina. (If there was more than one instance of it, he would add a number next to his familiar boxy signature.) The spidery bits of ink that cleverly composed her name were designed to be elusive, often revealing themselves better in a glance than a methodical search.

As each of us search our hearts to figure out how best to be of service to a planet in serious trouble, we too want to find the strands that hold our name—our Nina—hidden in the lines that make up our lives. That aha moment when we find what we were put on the earth to do is what the mystic and author Andrew Harvey describes as "when your greatest joy collides with the world's greatest hunger." It's known as calling.

One of the wonderful things about a calling is that it's already in you. When you see its strands clearly spell your name, wise sayings make more sense: Know thyself. The truth shall set you free. Become what thou art. While you think you're looking for it, it is already at work claiming you, redirecting your life. The naturalist John Muir said, "When we try to pick out anything by itself, we find that it is bound fast by a thousand invisible cords that cannot be broken, to everything in the universe."

That's because, as the Greek philosopher Plotinus once said, everything breathes together. We are not separate—from one another, from the earth we live on and its countless quadrillion component parts, from the canopy of atmosphere we all stand in, from the earth and cosmos we share.

What is the heaven that you have already discovered? What good thing do you need to share? This is the only work of soul.[1]
— Richard Rohr

THE WORK OF THE SOUL

In the cathedral at Chartres, there is an inscription that quotes the 12th century theologian John of Salisbury: "We are but tiny beings standing on the shoulders of giants." When confronted by the breadth and depth of the world's wounds and the mind numbing list of obstacles to its healing, whatever each of us does springs from a foundation that was provided by the work and vision of those who came before us. They are the answer to the old question, how can any one person make a difference?

Actually, as Margaret Mead said, only individuals can make a difference. This is the only way change happens: one person at a time, then legions. On some level, each of us knows what to do. We each have a mystical fingerprint that identifies our life's calling, and an inner music whose pull we cannot resist. If we would listen—and look around—we'd find ourselves surrounded by others on the same journey of discovery, breathing together with us.

Like the people whose stories follow, that mystical fingerprint is unique and powerful. It beckons in a way that can be soft but is always undeniable. All around us, our brothers and sisters of all ages and economic rank are working quietly and selflessly to make a difference. Why? Because as they looked around their lives and saw a need, for their very own individual reasons—they couldn't not act. This is often how our spirits wake us up, not with a shrill alarm, but with a sudden understanding. These are some of the simple but profound ways that calling shows up in one person's lifetime.

Saving our Forest Elders
Julia Butterfly Hill
www.circleoflife.org

After the 1992 acquittal of three of the four officers accused of the beating of Rodney King a year earlier, parts of Los Angeles erupted. Riots and widespread arson raged around the clock, enveloping several sections of the city for five days, especially in and around the area known as South Central. Before the riots were quelled, more than 800 buildings had been burned, incurring nearly $1 billion in damages and losses to local businesses. The human toll was worse: 53 deaths, more than 2,000 injuries. King's videotaped beating and the verdict had touched off a firestorm of racial unrest that had been smoldering for decades.

As a gesture of reconciliation to a community nearly destroyed by the riots (King himself was awarded $3.8 million in compensation), the city offered a 14-acre plot of land at the corner of 41st and Alameda Streets to local residents in South Central L.A., one of the areas hardest hit economically before, during and after the riots. The idea was to offer 350 low-income families a garden plot to help them grow their own food and wean themselves off of public food assistance. The 14-acre plot of land, a vacant weed and trash-ridden lot that had not been tended in years, came to be known as the South Central Farm. The city erected a fence around the plot, piped in running water and the USDA distributed free seeds to the member families.

In this heavily Hispanic neighborhood, many of the residents who signed on to tend one of the plots were themselves immigrant farmers or campesenos from Mexico and Central America. With them they brought generational knowledge of the land and a wide variety of plants, herbs, heritage seeds, even fruit trees—a cornucopia of biodiversity—that transformed the space, in the middle of a highly trafficked corridor full of rail and truck lines and warehouses, into something magically out of place.

Out of a literal firestorm of the L.A. riots, the South Central Farm rose like a phoenix into a healing enterprise for the many locals who could now supplement their limited incomes with their own food, on land that they tended themselves. But in 2003, the city had a change of heart and sold the plot to the developer with whom they had forced a purchase via eminent domain in 1986. His plan was to bulldoze the spot and build a warehouse development. While much legal wrangling ensued, by 2006 the sale was finalized and the city of Los Angeles issued eviction orders. The new owner wanted the urban farmers out.

Although the farm was eventually bulldozed in June 2006 (as of 2010 it is still a vacant lot), activists from the entertainment, political and spiritual arenas descended on the scene and began to make their voices heard. A tree-sit commenced on the plot's largest tree, a towering walnut. Among the tree's occupants was actress and activist Daryl Hannah. Another was a 32-year old woman named Julia Hill. It was not her first time.

In December 1997, Hill climbed 180 feet to the upper branches of a thousand-year-old redwood in a dwindling grove of old growth trees in northern California and stayed there for 738 days, part of a risky protest to save what she considered a national and natural treasure, a giant redwood nicknamed Luna. Before that first climb, Hill had had no experience as either a tree climber or an activist.

On an August night only a year earlier she had been rear-ended while driving home in her Honda hatchback and badly injured. Although she was wearing a seat belt, the impact snapped her head back, then forward into the steering wheel, slamming her right eye into her skull. Even though she woke up the next morning and was clear-headed enough to remember what had happened, it shortly became evident that she had suffered temporary brain damage. It took her nearly a year to rehabilitate and heal. Like Dr. Jill Bolte Taylor, what happened to Hill's brain not only put her life on hold, it shook her up, changed the way she saw her life, and ignited her with a new sense of purpose.

"Perhaps because I had injured the left, analytical side of my brain, the right, a more creative side, began to take over, and my perspective shifted. It became clear to me that our value as people is not in our stock portfolios and bank accounts but in the legacies we leave behind."[2] Once she had healed, Hill set out from Arkansas with friends to explore the Olympic rain forests in Washington State. While enroute, the group met up with a stranger who recommended that they stop to visit the fabled Lost Coast of northern California, one of the few pristine undeveloped wildernesses left in America and the home of the majestic and ancient—and rapidly disappearing—redwoods.

They drove to northern California's Humboldt County to the Grizzly Creek State Park and stopped. While her friends took a break to walk their dogs, Hill stumbled alone into the forest and became caught up with the quiet, the pull of the woods, and the enormity of the wonder she felt herself surrounded by.

Hill felt herself drawn deeper into the woods. A half mile in and the scale and beauty she found herself in the midst of made her slow, then stop. The sheer size of the trees was startling. "Hundreds of feet high, they were taller than fifteen-, eighteen-, twenty-story buildings. Their trunks were so large that ten individuals holding hands would barely wrap around them."[3]

The farther in she walked, the more the layers of the world she had just walked out of seemed to fall away. Around her was the interior of a world she'd never known. Giant ferns dwarfed anything she had seen before. The forest pelt under her feet included lichens, moss, fungus, and vividly colored mushrooms. Her senses began being fed by the pure, clear output of nature at its own pace and rhythm: silence, sweet clean air, birdsong, wind. She could taste how pure the air was. "For the first time, I really felt what it was like to be alive, to feel the connection of all life and its inherent truth .... the truth that exists within Creation."

Hill returned home to settle her affairs and three months later found herself back in the same area, this time looking for a way to be of service. Within a couple of days she had made her way to a group protesting the cutting of the redwoods and although she had no idea what she was agreeing to, volunteered to do a "tree-sit," a form of nonviolent protest that involves climbing up into a tree slated for cutting and staying as long as possible.

Anytime there is a tree-sit going on, she learned, things are not looking good. It's a last ditch attempt to save a tree—after lawsuits, logic, even the enforcement of laws has failed, "so people go into the trees."[4] Most of the trees get cut down anyway, she learned, but the protest at least slows the process down.

The tree Hill agreed to sit in was in a plot of land owned by Pacific Lumber, the biggest lumber company in the Pacific Northwest. One of the agreements the company had made was to leave certain numbers of trees intact to keep from endangering native species. The tree Hill would sit in was called Luna because activists had scrambled up her sides and in the light of a full moon built the platform for the tree-sit from scraps of wood they had scrounged. Luna had been marked for cutting, in an area that was not supposed to be cut.

Hill quickly made friends with the other activists who at first sat in the tree with her and later with the army of friends who risked arrest to keep her re-supplied over the months she remained aloft. It became a habit to call themselves by nicknames that somehow evoked a spirit they liked and also to protect their real identities: Puck, Zydeco, Almond, Shakespeare, Blue, Sawyer, Nature Boy, Geronimo, Orange, Bird. She chose Butterfly.

Hill's initial assignment quickly turned into a harrowing adventure. In short order, the logging company began cutting very close to where Hill sat, felling trees so close they hit Luna's outer branches as they toppled to the ground. The cutting continued for twelve days. A climber hired by the lumber company came after Hill and her tree sitting partner, Almond, nearly killing him when he intentionally cut a rope Almond was using. Almond fell but luckily landed only a few feet below on a large limb. Less than a month later, Pacific Lumber sent a giant Columbia helicopter to hover over her 6 x 8 foot perch that sat barely 30 feet below the tree top. The noise was deafening and the stench of fuel was nauseating, but even worse was the sucking wind the helicopter generated which threatened to pull Hill and her fellow tree-sitter right off of the treetops. As the helicopter hovered dangerously close, Hill grabbed her video camera and, wrapping her legs around a huge upper branch, lay down directly under the helicopter, pointed up and began shooting footage.

There are strict limits about flying helicopters in forests and no helicopters are allowed by law to fly within 200 feet of people as this one did. When the FAA saw the tape Hill shot, the company was reprimanded and that particular form of intimidation ceased. Other harassments followed including 24-hour marathons of claxon horns sounding and bright lights blaring—whatever would keep her awake and exhausted—but she would not relent. And that didn't include the natural forces that were part of life in a redwood forest: gale force winds and crashing thunderstorms which regularly blew through the tree tops or the wet and bitterly cold winters which gave her painful and dangerous frostbite.

While she sat month after month, ancient trees around her were cut down one by one, including one that was deliberately felled in the direction of several fellow activists in an area near her called Grizzly Creek. A 24-year-old Austin native named David Chain was killed instantly when a tree being cut by an enraged lumberjack who had been threatening the group hit Chain and crushed him. By then Hill had been living in Luna for a year. "Living in a tree made my senses so acute that I was keyed in to all the suffering of life, whether it was the animals or the trees or human beings. Without the distractions of society to numb me, those emotions were overwhelming. I had no immunity for this. So I was completely crushed when Gypsy died."[5]

Hill stayed. On a regular basis the lumber company sent the helicopters back across the tops of the trees to pull the felled lumber out. The blades of the giant machines set 300 mph winds into a spinning updraft which often uprooted trees and if not, managed to break the tree's branches so significantly, the trees often died from the trauma. Aside from that, it meant lots of fast-moving branches flying through the air, any one of which could have torn through her canopy and knocked her from her 180-foot perch.

Halfway through her tree sit, Hill recorded a video essay: "What's happening to our earth is a reflection of what's happening in us," she said, "that our outer landscape is very much a manifestation of our inner landscape. When you rip a plant from its roots, out of the ground, out of what it needs—the minerals, the air, the water—it begins to turn brown and die. We've ripped our roots of connection from the earth and from each other and now we're beginning to die. We must start working our roots of connection back into the earth and into each other and begin remembering how precious and how beautiful and how sacred the earth and our environment is."[6]

On her first visit when she had been so enthralled with Luna's magical neighborhood, as she found out later, if she had walked a little farther, she would have come across a drastically different take on the redwoods. She would have come upon one of the "clear cuts" that the new owners of Pacific Lumber/Maxxam Corporation had become known for. A clear cut is what happens when loggers enter a section of woods and cut down every tree in sight. The previous owners of Pacific Lumber had practiced a type of forest stewardship that was considered more or less sustainable, realizing that if they did nothing but clear-cut, they would quickly put themselves out of business. They had carefully chosen the trees to be felled instead of wiping out whole sections and all their attendant ecosystems. Not so the new owners.

In the case of the woods where Luna stood, the clear-cut process was particularly horrific. After the trees had been cut and removed, the company used the petrochemical napalm to remove any new growth and any slash—the remaining twigs, branches and loose brush that lie on the ground after a clear-cutting.

After the burning, with every nutrient and organism burned out and without the forest canopy to prevent their incursion, invasives sweep in. Since they often grow faster than the monoculture tree farm the lumber company replaces the old growth with, the next step is to spray herbicides on the denuded landscape—using diesel fuel as the delivery device. Then, to speed the progress of the quick-growth trees they plant to replace the redwoods, the lumber company sprays chemical fertilizer. This in turn ensures shallow roots in a grove of trees that lacks any diversity and wildness to make it hardy.

One night in her second year in Luna the lumber company began treating miles of clear cut around her. Although not all of the trees had been cut—the company left a few behind to enable them to claim that they had not clear cut an area—the company napalmed the entire area, incinerating everything left, including the so-called protected trees they had not felled. From her perch Hill could see nothing but fires burning for miles. The expanse of burning was so vast, she said, "it almost looked like a lava flow." The burning went on for six days. Hill sat, smoke thick with the stench of diesel fuel enfolding her the entire time. It was, she said, sheer torture. Breathing through a wet bandana, her small platform open to the whim of wind drifts, her sinuses closed up, her eyes swelled shut, her nose bled uncontrollably.[7]

Hill stayed installed in Luna for a full two years, enduring every attempt by the Pacific Lumber Company to force her down. They finally agreed to the terms of a legal settlement in which they established a three-acre no-cut buffer around the tree. With Luna's safety ensured, in December, 1999, Hill slowly lowered herself to ground.

Seven years later, as the countdown to the eviction from the South Central Farm ticked off, Hill spoke to the crowd gathered to cheer on the protestors, "My passion has always been about connection of issues because I think that's at the root of all the issues facing our world. When we're disconnected from a person, we can destroy their 14-acre oasis … when we're disconnected from the planet, we can cut down a forest for miles and miles and miles and not think anything of it. For me," she said, "the sacred, the movement toward reverence, is about saying no, all of life is connected."[8]

Everyone has been made for some particular work, and the desire for that work has been put in every heart. Let yourself be silently drawn by the stronger pull of what you really love.
— Rumi

Healing Loss
Heather Murphy
www.weicreatechange.org
wei-india.livejournal.com

When Heather Murphy was an Arizona State University college freshman studying accounting, a close friend of hers lost his father. Overnight, her friend's mother became the sole support of their three children. As she struggled to come to grips with her loss, she was also having to try to keep their small business afloat. She began to apply for loans but was repeatedly denied. Eventually, with help from family, a line of credit, a small amount of life insurance from her husband's death and long hours of accounting help from her son's young friend, she was able to restart her life and launch her company. This was Murphy's initiation into working with grieving widows left behind to suddenly face the full responsibility of raising their children alone and without any funds.

It lit a spark within her. A few years later she would credit that experience and the courage and tenacity of her friend's mother as the inspiration for creating Women's Entrepreneurship Initiative, or WEI.

When the time came for her to pick a thesis topic for her accounting degree, Murphy began searching online for widow aid programs and found an article about South Indian farmers who committed suicide and left widows and children behind to support themselves. She decided to write her thesis on creating a micro-financing non-profit for South Indian widows. "I understood right away that the experience from my friend's tragic situation along with my finance and accounting background could potentially change these women's lives." She realized she could not only help teach these widows how to track sales and expenses to create good business practices (and prevent them from making their husband's mistakes), but she could use what she'd learned in finance classes to create sound lending practices for the suicide-prone southern region of India.

But Murphy planned to do more than make this a project for an accounting degree. She intended to action her thesis, by actually creating a non-profit, running it with volunteers and funding it herself.

To augment her knowledge about the culture of the area, she made contact with people who had recently migrated to the U.S. from India, stayed in touch with clergy currently living there and made plans to go there herself. To finance her trip and to help start her foundation, she held fund raisers and solicited donations in lieu of presents when she sent out her graduation announcements. Everything that didn't go toward her ticket would become the seed money for her fledgling initiative.

In June 2008, barely a month after graduating from college, Murphy set off on a three-month trip to southern India. To keep her expenses to a minimum, she slept wherever she could get a bed, often in Hindu, Christian and Catholic orphanages. She spent six weeks doing research, touring the countryside, sitting in on meetings with widows, learning firsthand the details of how in places like the Wayanad district, a huge number of farmers were committing suicide over debt to seed and pesticide providers.

The story of Indian farmer suicides is one that is becoming increasingly familiar, averaging 10,000 per year. Most of the farmers whose widows she proposed to work with were caught in a cycle of poverty and debt. They borrowed money to rent a plot of land, buy seed, provide irrigation, then with a single failed crop, their debt became seemingly unmanageable. Even a debt of $100 or less could turn into a fatal burden, an impossible shame. With lenders' interest rates at 40 percent or higher, no way to buy new seed or feed their families, and facing pressure in the form of beatings and threats from the people they owed, the farmers, many of whom reported that they felt like they were drowning under the pressure of the stress, simply retreated into their barren fields, drank pesticide and lay down to die.

Sadly, the suicides really just shift the burden onto the widows, most of whom now lack any source of income. The catch-22 in which the widows are caught is this: in India government compensation is most often contingent on the dead farmer being the owner of his land, his being indebted at the time of his suicide and the debt being the cause of the suicide. Even if a farmer seemingly qualifies on all counts, the government often gives only a third of the amount to the widow, holding the rest in deposit.

Most families, therefore, are left with no other source of income and no way to continue their farms. Most existing agencies that provide micro-loans are aimed at helping with suicide prevention, rather than its aftermath.

It is this gap within the organizational support structure that Murphy decided to take on. She saw an opportunity to use social entrepreneurship to help these widows get training in business ventures that were culturally and economically suited to them.

She moved on to the states of Andhrapradesh and Maharashtra, living in women's hospitals and in tribal villages. In Wardha (where Gandhi spent his last years), she discovered another region where the suicide rate was very high. She began meeting with women's groups, becoming inspired by an organization called Chetna Vikas which trains people in villages and on community farms how to farm sustainably and naturally without stripping nutrients out of the earth or soaking it with chemical pesticides or fertilizers.

While in Wardha she was attending a meeting at a small civic center hall that gave widows a forum to speak, when she noticed a woman seated about fifteen feet away. Murphy noted the white patches on her neck and arms, discolorations she assumed were birthmarks. Although a widow, she still wore her traditional Hindu wedding necklace. The woman soon stood up to tell her story. A friend translated as she spoke. Before he committed suicide, it seems this woman's husband had poured kerosene on her and struck a match to her. The apparent birthmarks were in fact skin grafts. It is a common practice for women in her culture to be blamed for their husband's failures.

"This woman was awe inspiring," Murphy said, "I learned so much from her about strength and the courage to go on."

The idea behind the WEI program is to create new jobs in a community, break the cycle of debt inheritance by offering micro-loans and grants to applicants and requiring each member who signs up to "pay it forward." That is, each entrepreneur involved in the program must agree to train another person in their same field. This in turn creates a ripple effect: "By giving one person the opportunity to create change in their own life, they will create change in the lives of many."

WEI first provides its applicants with grants that pay for training in a specific skill. After training, the applicants receive micro-loans to purchase assets for their new business. The businesses are often a bit out of the traditional roles assigned to women (bicycle or refrigeration repair, for example). The average microloan is between $75 and $200 and the payoff rate is extremely high. WEI also helps program participants register to vote and brings women together in community meetings where they have a safe environment in which to share their stories.

"Beyond India I would like to eventually start programs in Africa and South America for agrarian widows. Ultimately I want this organization to stay rooted in its goal of helping women to become entrepreneurs but to be able to do it on a much larger scale."

Within the next few years, she hopes to expand into Nigeria to help refugee widows from war-torn families, and eventually into the neediest pockets of South America.

"The main focus is to get quality help for women, to provide them with training, sustainable farming techniques, to free them from working under the burden of a debt collector."

Currently Murphy is working on further fundraisers to provide money that could be funneled into WEI and to secure 503(c) status which will allow her organization to apply for significant grants. They also raise funds by selling bracelets, pashminas, candles and cards made by women worldwide through their online catalog. Murphy, her coworkers and volunteers receive no compensation for what they are doing. But there are other rewards. When it came time for one of her clients in India to name her new baby girl, it was an easy choice: Heather.

The 22-year-old's philosophy: "Giving back to others and working together as one planet will create a consciousness about the environmental, social, and spiritual perspectives that affect us all."

Creating a Space for the Healing of the Spirit
Joyce and Ken Beck
www.thecrossingsaustin.com

When Dell computer executive Ken Beck and his wife Joyce, a psychotherapist, decided to build The Crossings in Austin, Texas, they went about the process slowly and deliberately. Life had been good to the Minnesota transplants. Beck felt he had been blessed through his company's great success and the couple wanted a way to give back to the community they loved. So in 1995, they began to take a very conscious and deliberate approach, talking out loud, day-dreaming, praying, gathering with their friends, brainstorming.

Their key question: what can we responsibly do?

It was a question that would take them eight years to plot out and $25 million of their own money to answer for themselves.

They came up with the idea of a wellness spa and learning center, dedicated to the nurturing of the spirit and created consciously, with sustainability being a key guidepost. "We all have to recognize that we are citizens of the earth and there's a stewardship responsibility attached to that. We had to ask ourselves," said Beck, "how do we continue to evolve as a species but be gentle with this home that we've been given—Mother Earth? The idea of being sustainable grew to mean so much more, not just with the land and its resources but with every aspect of the building and the management practices we began to articulate."

In 1999 they found the piece of land they wanted—210 acres in the Texas Hill Country, nestled in the rugged hills overlooking a wide swath of Lake Travis. Roughly 202 acres was within the federally protected Balcones Canyonland Preserve. Knowing this meant that development would be limited was actually perfect for them. Their plans called for roughly 35 developed acres. They willingly granted a conservation easement on the land, giving up development rights on all but that one parcel.

This had two benefits. It allowed them to protect the area's endangered species—something they were deeply committed to—and it insured that guests would be looking out at and completely surrounded by natural, unspoiled settings. Even though the place they were creating was less than half an hour from downtown Austin, it had a remote, even wild, feel to it that they loved. This in turn ensured that visitors would be immersed by the sights and sounds of nature from the moment they pulled up the long, winding drive.

Because the land had never been developed, it was so overgrown with cedars and ash junipers, it was impossible to get a sense of what the topography looked like. Their first task was to go in with a crew and cut the lower limbs and undergrowth. Once they could see the land on top of the ridge, they spent two weekends camping in a tent, wandering the land, sitting by a firepit at night, looking and listening, getting a sense of where the building sites should be.

One night they heard a mother coyote and her pups calling and running down a remote access road. "You could hear her adult voice and the pups calling back with their little yip yip yip. It was all part of connecting with the land and animals and all that was out there." There were plenty of other sounds and rhythms they began to grow accustomed to. They rose before sunrise to see where the sun came up. At dusk, they watched the sun set, marking where it left the sky. At night, without the intrusion of city lights, they watched the stars and the arcing of the moon. All of these nuances helped them make many of their building decisions.

One of their rules quickly became that the buildings and campus had to sit very gently on the land. The structures needed to look like they belonged there. Because of their experience with the sunrises and sunsets, they decided that all the lodge accommodations would be on the east-facing side of the ridge. Every lodge had a deck or patio and this in turn (along with their in-room coffee or tea service) let people celebrate the rising sun individually in their rooms. The public spaces would all be built on the west side, letting people observe the setting sun collectively, sitting out on the big patio overlooking the lake, with a glass of wine.

Remembering the power and majesty of the star-filled skies they watched from their tents, the Becks also decided to make stargazing easier by using low lighting on the footpaths that honeycomb the area. "The idea is not to have a lightbulb shining in your eyes anywhere. If anyone wants more light to walk through the woods or get to their lodge, we're happy to get them a flashlight."

Another of their aims was to help people reignite their connection to nature and to learning. One key decision was to not include televisions in each room (only two of the seven multi-room lodges have sets in rooms), but to give guests the opportunity to be reflective, to think about what they had learned that day, to spend their time inside being introspective or outside conversing with others.

"That's why there's a porch in front of every lodge so you can sit out there on a rocking chair, meet somebody new, talk about what you're studying, or just enjoy the quiet."

Having a relationship with nature is inescapable and intentional. All the lecturing spaces have windows so you can see outside, watch storms roll through, see the trees blowing in the wind, watch the sun arc across the sky. When you take a break, you only have to go through one door to be outside. Spreading the buildings out also means you have to go outside, whether it's to go to a lecture, to your room, the dining hall or the spa.

"We forget that it's nature that sustains and feeds us, that gives us the energy, the excitement and clarity we need to be creative, to learn, to look at challenges in new ways—we get all of that from the earth."

Their commitment to the ecosystems that the land provides to endangered species eventually resulted in their decision to leave all the hardwood trees intact. One such species that relies on this area is the golden cheeked warbler. The birds migrate into central Texas from Mexico in March, mate and locate a water source. Then, just as it's time to build their nests, these birds begin seeking out the stringy bark of the mature ash junipers. Next they comb the live oak trees on the edges of the ridge, where they find the little oak leaf roller worms that, in concert with the warbler's needs, have begun hanging from the trees by a long silken thread. The worm is perfect food for the warbler and the thread it hangs from is the perfect adhesive to keep its new nest intact. With its food, water and shelter assured, the warbler lays its eggs, raises its young until mid-August—when the long, stifling Texas days make it head back to the mountains of Mexico—where the cycle, and its natural feedback loop, repeats itself the next year.

Keeping all the hardwoods intact required that the architects consider the positions of every building very carefully. Every hardwood tree on the property has a small metal disk attached to it. On that disk was a GPS marking that originally gave the architects a 3D picture to use when laying out the site, so they could determine which cedar trees had to be cut down and where the hardwood trees were. When the time came to dig ditches for the underground utilities, it meant cutting through the Texas limestone with a rock saw and, because of their commitment to keeping the hardwoods, whenever they came upon one, they had to back up or go around them, necessitating some hand cuts and many workarounds.

Many other infrastructure decisions had to be made. With the heavily graded mile-long ribbon of road that led up to the Crossings and circled back down to the road, the classic (and cheapest) choice was to use tar. But tar was not only not sustainable, it was petroleum based and they had already decided not to use oil-based products.

"Besides, in the summer temperatures can climb to 110 degrees and that tar gets very soft. When cars drive down the incline, braking as they go, that creates friction which softens the tar, and that means ongoing repairs. So we chose cement because it's naturally sustainable. That was a hard decision because of the dollars involved in pouring all that cement for a solid mile around the circle, but it's been essentially maintenance free."

For carpeting—which does come from petroleum-based products—the Becks chose Interface Carpeting, knowing that Ray Anderson, the company's former president, pioneered the concept of recyclable carpeting. "We were so impressed with him. You just don't want old carpet to go into a landfill. His idea was to lease carpet. Then if a square becomes torn or ruined, since you're leasing it, you call them up and the local rep comes out, replaces it and sends the bad one back to the factory to be recycled."

In the main hall, they installed bamboo flooring. It's not only a grass, but in a processed form, it's harder than oak and has proved very sustainable. "We haven't had to refinish that floor at all."

They also had to compromise in some spots. They couldn't afford to install central heat and air in all the buildings so they installed the most efficient air conditioning, heating and natural gas-fired water heaters they could find.

When they could, they used native Texas limestone. It's beautiful, durable and local, coming from just 50 miles away. Where they couldn't use stone, they used a cement and wood fiber-based product called Hardy Plank, which is very durable by nature, not susceptible to rot like wood siding. They also used traditional Texas standing seam aluminum roofs where they couldn't use tile, a solution that reflects sunlight in summer, helps keep buildings cool in summer and provides an interface for rainwater collection.

Since they were so far from utility lines, they wanted to be as independent of utility systems as possible. At their primary guest house (the Gatehouse), dining hall and spa, they installed rainwater collection systems, funneling rain into a 5,000-gallon tank that provides gray water that will eventually fan out to irrigate the landscape with environmentally friendly above ground drip pipes.

For potable water, they drilled four wells and found water on three (two became potential backup sites if the first one has a problem) By nature, the preponderance of limestone means Hill Country water will contain a lot of minerals. To purify it, they installed a large commer cial reverse osmosis filtering system. The system works so well, their water is purer than any bottled or city water in the state of Texas. Despite this, visitors arrive every day loaded with bottles of water. "We've spent every day since we opened trying to explain to people why they shouldn't use or even want bottled water, because our tap water is better than anything they can buy bottled and there are so many negative impacts to those plastic bottles of water but that remains a challenge for us."

The water they bring up from the earth and treat not only provides the cleanest of drinking waters, it powers the water sprinklers in the ceilings of all the buildings (fire engines would take a while to get to them if they had a fire), and supplies the retreat's domestic use.

They also installed their own wastewater treatment plant, located halfway down a hillside, so everything drains via gravity, passing through a complicated treatment process with live organisms that purify it. The purified water is then pumped back into another holding tank as treated effluent.

"From there we did something unique that had never been done for a wildlife preserve—we got approval to put in a surface drift irrigation system on the land. We went back into the preserve on 8 acres, lifted up all the trees again, removed all the dead cedar limbs, mulched them all and brought in a treated effluent line. Then we installed computer controlled valves in 16 different sections with sensors so that as we're disposing of that effluent, it goes into a section until the moisture level gets to a certain level, then it switches over to the next and it goes all the way to the next and then start over again, so we're putting all our treated effluent back into the land. It's going back into that whole cycle, the entire water system. You might use a little more technology than nature in the process but you get your water out of the ground, purify it, use it, collect it, purify it again—remove all the bad stuff—then you put it back into the natural systems, so it all eventually goes back into the aquifers."

With water becoming more and more dear in that part of Texas (nearby Lake Travis was so shallow as a result of a 2-year drought, its last boat ramp was closed in August of 2009; it has since reopened thanks to late fall rains), it's a process that pays very precious dividends.

For their decking on all the lodges, they used a product made from recycled wood and woodchip products and recycled plastics, all of which are not only sustainable but unappetizing to insects.

They wanted to compost everything that came out of their dining hall but discovered that turning the compost is a daily—and with their quantities, fulltime—job, so instead they chose a waste hauler who separates everything at their own composting facility, "so everything does get composted, just not here."

In a spot above a sheer natural rock formation with a view perfect for quiet contemplation (and a labyrinth laid out in rocks and pebbles only yards away), they created the Sanctuary, the spiritual locus of the retreat center, a spot you can only get to by walking or being delivered by electric cart. To stay in line with their desire to have buildings merge gently with the landscape, they used the design common to the old Texas missions with walls that look like solid stone. They merged Texas mission with a nuance that paid tribute to their Scandinavian heritage.

"In those old stave churches in Norway, in the main doorway there'd be this little door within a door that was just wide enough for one person at a time. We were told that the design was purposeful, that we all carry spiritual baggage with us, but the little door is only big enough for a person to get through. The baggage must stay outside."

On the little door they mounted the saying that Carl Jung had carved in the lentil over his doorway: Bidden or not bidden, God is present.

Before the foundation for the sanctuary was poured, Beck, his wife Joyce, their extended family, designers, architects and workers wrote down their best wishes, prayers, or memories about the project, read them out loud and laid them throughout the foundation of the floor. When the concrete was added, they became a permanent part of the building's underpinnings.

"And all those wishes are still there."

The latest value they have added to their core set: teaching the world to eat more wisely. With that in mind, they decided to develop menus that are healthier, relying on less meat and more healthy grains. (In 2009 they began pursuing a relationship with a highly regarded food provider well known for its commitment to healthy eating to oversee the preparation of all food on campus, using its nutritionists, menus, and chefs.) Along with that goes the idea to buy locally, using the products of nearby farmers, which includes plans to expand and diversify their own organic herb garden. That will eventually mean fresh gourmet meals served right in the midst of the garden, European style. Along with the benefits of fresh food, there's a lesson. "It all goes to understanding your bioregion because each one is unique—and it's what sustains you."

When it opened in 2003, The Crossings was already pioneering new ways to leave a gentle imprint on the earth. Before the end of 2010, it expects to receive a platinum LEEDs certification. By answering their own question—what can we responsibly do?—the Becks ended up setting a standard.

Teaching the Connection
Jane Presby
www.dimondhillfarm.com

For most of her thirty-four year teaching career, Jane Presby taught physical education, psychology, personal relationships, careers, and health to as many as 150 students each day. When her school day ended she would often join her father to help him farm the land that had been in her family for nearly 200 years. She loved teaching her students and what she called their "raw energy," but the effect her lessons had on them wasn't always readily apparent. On the farm, it was different. She got to see immediate tangible results. When her father died and she had to make a choice about whether to take over the farm she had inherited or keep teaching, however, it was no contest. The farm won.

"I've always been a person who had to ground herself. My hands and feet literally have to be a part of that, so when it came time to decide between teaching or taking over the farm, I had no choice. This has always called me back."

Presby is the owner and most ardent booster of Dimond Hill Farm, in Concord, New Hampshire. She rarely speaks about what she does without a grin spreading across her face. Farming is clearly her joy. In an age when the viable family farm with deep community roots has all but disappeared into history, her 107 acres thrive and hum with activity. "There were probably about 50 farms around here at one time. I think we're the last real farm in Concord." It's no small accomplishment, something recognized locally when Dimond Hill was named a Farm of Distinction in 2009, which in part recognizes the incredibly hard juggling act it is to have a successful farm enterprise in the 21st century.

Presby has figured out how to take her love for her land and its heritage and imbue it with meaningful business values that adapt to the needs of her locale and her customers. She enjoys the way she and her small crew can brainstorm to stay simple, diverse, nimble and receptive to changes in weather, crop prices and public whims. Besides, she still gets to teach. "When you're a teacher, you're a teacher in your soul." The soul will always find an outlet.

The farm is a favorite spot for visiting young children who especially like the job of checking under the hens for eggs. On a warm day in mid-July, the farm is bucolic, almost idyllic—and buzzing with activity. In the clean, remodeled hen house, the air smells like the wood shavings that cover the floor. In the little enclosure behind the nesting area, there's a step stool for the smaller children to stand on so they can reach through the little spring-controlled doors and find the eggs nested in the straw.

"This is an experiential farm," says Presby. "That's what it's all about." Sometimes when the children retrieve the eggs, they're still warm; often they're still beneath a hen. The hens don't seem to mind being robbed.

"They'll usually have three or four eggs under there. They each lay one a day but they share the space. It's a communal laying spot. They jump up, settle in, lay, then they jump down and another jumps up to take the spot, so whichever one's laying there, it's likely the eggs they're sitting on aren't theirs. They don't care if you're taking another hen's eggs, so it all works out."

Presby picks up one of the chicks, then holds one of the hens. "Mostly chickens don't mind being held at all. These guys love it." As she pets and holds them, they cheep and make throaty sounds. Life is good. It's a fate much easier to think about than the all-too familiar pictures of the creatures on the factory farms that have their beaks shorn off and spend their short lives with their heads between metal spokes, eating grain until their slaughter dates.

"The farm used to have everything—all the barnyard animals as well as the crops. That was the typical American farm." Today Dimond Hill Farm is an interesting and evolving adaptation. During the summer months the trough just southeast of the henhouse has several young pigs happily wallowing in the mud. By October when they go to slaughter, each will weigh about 300 pounds. There is always a waiting list for their meat. The dozens of eggs deposited all day by the New Hampshire reds and other breeds—when they aren't hopping down to socialize on the floor of the house or dodging the rooster—are gathered several times a day and taken directly to the refrigerator shelves inside the building which once was the milk room and now serves as part of the sales room and site of the summer market. What's for sale rotates as fresh crops sell out and the seasons progress. She also has partnerships with nearby small fresh food entrepreneurs that allow her to broaden her market offerings to include locally made ice cream, pies, breads, pickles, jams, honey, maple syrup, organic cheeses, and other specialty foods.

Everything at the farm has a job and everything is put to use: the space inside and the space outside. The ridge above the farm offers an ideal setting for weddings with a beautiful overlook of the valley below; the main house's sumptuous large interior ground floor rooms can be rented out for special events like retreats and conferences or even dinner parties. She also puts her rescued animals to good use. The horses can substitute in a pinch in the fields as draft animals and the pet llamas produce manure that makes really good compost (she shaves the animals and donates their highly prized wool to whoever knows how clean and card it and to put it to use). The rest of the animals: chickens, pigs, geese, sheep, and dogs are on hand as farm ambassadors, especially to teach visiting school groups or anybody who happens along just how the modern small farm life works and what it looks like. (The website even includes downloadable farm-themed coloring book pages.)

The farm takes its name from the original owner, Ezekial Dimond, an early Concord settler who fought at Bunker Hill in the Revolutionary War. One of Presby's grandfathers bought the farm in 1827 and eventually it passed down to her. It's a history to which she is well attuned, from the ancient glaciers that carved out a ravine near the ice pond, where the family hacked out ice to keep things cool before the days of refrigeration, to the building across the road which was once the site of the farm's vital metal works and wood shop.

Her house, built in 1882, is a classic 3-story Victorian farmhouse, and is still considered a modern New England farm setup with an ell-shaped shed that connects the house with the original barn. During the harsh New England winters the horse and wagon team could be hooked up without anyone having to go outside into the elements until they were ready to open the doors. All the buildings were constructed with wood that came from the land. Most of the buildings were built by the farm-hands who worked there and lived across the street or down the hill. "The farm provided a lot of food for a lot of people, and a lot of jobs."

Presby uses the story of her own family farm to teach modern and traditional farm history. Just as the old buildings merge with new, old traditions still remain with their wispy clues of how things on the farm used to work, how people lived, what filled their days. The part of the sales area that was once the milk room is a bygone remnant from the days of her grandfather's dairy, when it supplied fresh milk and cream in farm-labeled glass bottles to homes on its route through Concord and several surrounding communities. The huge main barn, corn barn and shed still serve many of the same functions they did when they were built in the late 19th century.

Slowly, as awareness about food security issues grows and food prices rise, Presby sees respect returning for the place agriculture once held in a community's life, for people actually having a sense of and appreciation for where their food is grown and seeing the value in having a relationship with the people who grow it. She walks a line between two worlds, staying competitive enough to keep her business thriving while providing the healthiest food she can in a sustainable way that allows her to be a responsible steward of the land entrusted to her. She follows a tradition now largely gone. "The generation of farmers we're losing now really managed to do things in a natural sequence of time and seeding and going to market."

Presby and her crew are the new wisdom holders of the earth's ways. They are the ones left to teach people about the rhythms of the earth and what should be plainly logical to them—when they are literally out of touch and have no earthly common sense.

"I think there is a spiritual, earthbound, energetic level of feeding that comes from the natural minerals in the land. It's that component in the universe that is fed through what we produce as farmers. So I think places like this—where land is provided to you—sure, you take, but you also have to replace. What's missing in the so-called commercial modern agriculture is the whole feedback loop because it's reap, take, take, take, strip—but nothing is put back anymore. And that whole agricultural looping follows the character of the people and the culture of whatever nation it goes with."

One way she sees this lack of consciousness about the balance the earth needs comes from anecdotal information she gets from nearby suburban gardeners who spent lots of money on seeds and lawn tools and can't understand why things aren't growing well.

"I'll tell them they don't have any topsoil. In New Hampshire you're allowed to remove all of the topsoil except for four inches so if you go into these places that used to be old farms [being converted into housing developments], developers will tear through it and strip everything down to four inches. Then people move into their houses and have to keep watering their lawns because they don't have enough topsoil to hold the moisture. So then they bring in bark mulch which really energetically depletes it faster than the lost topsoil does. The solution is simple: add compost, but they don't want compost because it might spring up weeds and then they bring in Chemlawn. And very soon they wonder why they have skin rashes, burning, runny eyes and sinus trouble and their animals are getting sick."

Her solution for a green yard: "I plant hayseed. It comes up green and if it doesn't, then either there's no topsoil or there's a rock there. It's all about repairing the earth because we've just scraped it to nothing." And besides, the hay helps feed her animals.

Planning at the farm is strategic. There is no waste. They manage to harvest and sell nearly 100 percent of what they grow. And business is good. She and her small crew make the most of it. In a given spring the fields are rich with rows of more than 10,000 plants: a variety of potatoes, onions, heirloom tomatoes, broccoli, cauliflower, Brussels sprouts, carrots, peas, corn, lettuce, Swiss chard, peppers, eggplant, melons, peaches and more with different plants rotating into the fall. Their hothouses give them an early start on the season, growing beets, radishes, Swiss chard, spinach and micro greens that are ready by late May. Through the growing season, they grow ten varieties of tomato plants using their own unique version of hydroponics. Slowly by using greenhouses, they are extending the number of weeks and months they can supply fresh food to their customers.

Everything is planted with conscious awareness of the need to balance production with demand and getting the timing right. They have discovered, as they have moved to growing to a large scale, a key concern is understanding how many of any one item they will need to pick in a day—and who and where their market is. Otherwise, there is waste. By calculating what they need for a year's total harvest, they are very successful in maximizing their output, staying on schedule and growing with maximum productivity, in spite of erratic weather patterns.

Their free and effective technique for pest control includes one of the staff dogs patrolling the rows, urinating once in a while out on the edges. It must work. They have few invasive critters coming in to eat up what's open to the sky.

When it comes to needing modernizing equipment, they don't go buy enormous combines and they don't plant hedgerow to hedgerow. They allow wildness and they think small and efficient.

The lines of vegetables growing on that day peep out neatly through a hole in the thick plastic film that keeps out weeds. How did those evenly spaced holes get in that plastic? After playing hit and miss with augers and drills, they found an Amish craftsman who had created a very economical and practical waterwheel planter. With a tractor (or for the Amish, a horse) pulling it along, all you need do is go up and down the rows with two people seated in the attached bucket seats and pop the plants into the ground through the little holes made by the planter. Presby is always looking for ways to do things more cheaply and efficiently. Anything that costs her less lets her lower her prices without sacrificing a profit. At times like these when people are watching their expenses closely, this is an important tactic.

The farm is a quietly thrumming center of industry, interdependence and co-creation, a balancing act that is at once delicate and sturdy, conscious of possibility and limitation and aware of and respectful of the gifts the land provides. Bounty is recognized. Gratitude is returned. The people who help make this farm hum live with the knowledge that farming involves love of the hard work and ultimately, surrendering to nature's lessons about the natural rhythm of things. There is a quiet understanding here that there is a price we all pay when stewards of the land do otherwise.

"Mother Nature will reclaim herself. She always does."

Living the Connection
Celeste and Bob Longacre
www.yourlovesigns.com
www.bobsfengshui.com

Just outside Walpole, New Hampshire, atop a hill in the Connecticut River Valley, Bob and Celeste Longacre live the promise of what many attempted in the 1960s but abandoned because it got too hard. They mostly live off the land. Celeste grew up in nearby Nashua but had no orientation to nature at all, much less an inkling of what an organic lifestyle looked like.

Then she heard about Adele Davis's bestseller *Let's Eat Right to Keep Fit* and never looked back. "Adele Davis was on Johnny Carson one night and he asked her for one guideline for eating right. She said, 'If they advertise it on TV, it's not good for you.' They cut that from the program."

She crossed paths with *Nourishing Traditions* by Sally Fallon[9] and it funneled her desire to eat right into an altered lifestyle. The cooking techniques Fallon talks about are tied to what's called a traditional diet, one that encourages eating fresh foods healthfully prepared more or less the way our ancestors ate them—basically the antithesis of the modern diet that largely consists of packaged, processed and chemically grown food common to industrialized nations, especially the U.S.[10] Fallon then helped start a foundation that celebrates the work of Dr. Weston Price.

"He was a dentist and nutritionist who retired in 1930 and went all over the world studying native diets. He found one cavity in 200 people, no arthritis, and no diabetes. The one element they all had in common: they ate huge amounts of animal fat."

While vegetarians disagree with Price's findings about animal fat, it's doubtful they would find fault with another of the Longacre's beliefs: today, nobody really knows what's in the food we eat.

"This is what's killing us—the way our food is grown and processed, and the way animals are treated, raised, and killed. What energetic toxins are we taking in as a result? I don't really eat much packaged food. I don't trust our food supply. We pretty much eat healthy food, minus what comes in the wind and gets into the pollen of what's growing in our garden. That's my health insurance and I am an extremely healthy person."

With the exception of the coconut oil she orders, most of what she, Bob and their daughter Crystal eat comes from within ten miles of where they live. They grow their own vegetables and fruit. Their bread comes from a bakery that only does sourdough (so-called hearty grains are too hard for humans to digest, she says, pointing out that all grains are easier to digest if they are soaked overnight and drained before they are added to a bread recipe). She gets her bee pollen from a neighbor. She and her neighbors share and take turns dropping off items. One day a week someone drops off her bread. Another day she drops off everyone's milk. She and Bob buy a one-quarter share of a beef cow every year. Several of her neighbors also raise chickens. She and Bob have a flock of more than two dozen now in their own coop a few yards from the house. One neighbor has a vineyard with over 1,200 plants and when the time is right, everyone congregates for a pick and stomp party.

During the growing season the garden and the food from the shared deliveries sustains them. She cans everything they can't eat and stores it in their in-house cellar, reusing the same jars every year. There is no waste and no packaging. She takes pride in knowing where all her food comes from.

Depending on the season, she augments their income by teaching downhill skiing, selling edible flowers and her incomparable vegetables and fruits from her garden to clients in nearby towns.

For five years she also had a call-in astrology show on a local radio station. She reviewed books, gave astrology readings, and interviewed guests. She's been a highly-regarded astrologer for thirty years and has written two books on the subject. As someone once said, "You weren't named Celeste for nothing."

She preps her beds in the spring with kelp meal, alfalfa meal, azomite powder, green sand and old manure. They plow and shovel everything by hand—no rototillers or tractors.

In July the blueberry bushes are already groaning under the weight of their fruit. The cabbages, Brussels sprouts, onions, chard, carrots, beets, beans, parsnips, kale, tomatoes, fresh herbs and salad greens are dense and brightly colored. There are no invasive insects to be seen. She pulls off corners of tender kale and passes them around. It has a warm, sweet, buttery taste.

"Most kale is bitter at this stage. We eat it when it starts to come up, then we thin, thin, thin and eat the thinnings. We eat kale past the frost."

The garden has a path running through and around it that makes gathering vegetables easy and natural. It has a whimsical, almost magical allure. The air feels good. (All the visitors—and our hostess—walking through have big smiles on their faces.) If a leprechaun suddenly appeared, it would feel perfectly natural. "If I had a healing center, I would definitely make people do gardening. It's so calming."

Inside there is a pot of vegetable soup cooking. Everything in it (except for the corn) comes from the garden or cellar—onions, snow peas, garlic, lettuce, beets and beet greens, carrots—it's all cooked in the broth she makes herself. "It's a nutrient dense meal." She sees soup, especially when it's made from ingredients you can trust, as a highly efficient delivery system for nutrients. Her homemade broth is a kitchen staple.

Everything about the food she grows and cooks is purposeful and conscious. She explains that it only takes six hours for the starch in corn to turn to sugar so when she wants corn, she goes to the farm stand early in the morning, buys and shucks it, gets water boiling, boils it three minutes, plunges it into ice water, then cuts it off the cob, bags and flattens it. "It takes two hours from farmstand to freezer."

Only ten minutes from the quaint town of Walpole, the drive into town passes not only a pastoral river valley but the estate of a Pillsbury heir and the modest home of PBS documentarian Ken Burns. The roads are flanked by groves of maple and birch trees, honeycombed with creeks and river offshoots. Even with its developed wedges of farm and home, Emerson and Thoreau would have recognized its unique New England glory.

She and Bob, a skilled carpenter, married in 1978. A few years before they met, he had decided to build a log cabin on his property. Then he saw an octagon house, came back, and built it from memory. At first that's all it was. There was no running water, no sink, drain, or electricity. Light came from kerosene lamps. The first addition was the kitchen, then the passive refrigerator, a cellar beneath the earth. Then he added a second bigger root cellar and earthbermed it so it never freezes. The couple fill it up in September and October and eat from it until the next spring's crops begin to come in. (They had eaten their last carrot out of the root cellar only two days before.)

Their piecemeal approach was a conscious one. They never had a mortgage on their property and wanted to pay for everything as they went. After three years they added a water pump at the sink, after eight more years, electricity. They centralized all the plumbing in the kitchen. "Not too many people have their bathtub in the kitchen." There is an outhouse out back by the garden. Except for being outside, it has the cheeriness and feel of a regular half bath.

Throughout the house they used sturdy and beautiful recycled products—wood, windows and doors. They heat their home from the wood lying around on the property. The two-story structure is tight and its shape gives it a unique advantage over more squared homes. "There's nothing for wind to grab; it just goes right around it." To take advantage of the warm late morning to mid-afternoon sun, they installed solar panels at the back of the garden in 2008. The panels feed the house usage first, then they top off the batteries. The panels provide more power than the Longacres use in the summer and what they don't use, they sell back to the grid. In the winter when the sun shines less, they are primarily on the grid. It's a system that works well. They use the grid when they need it and sell energy back to it when they don't. It's also fiscally sensible. At the end of the year they installed the panels, they got a tax break from the government and $6,000 from a state rebate program.

As far as pests go, they leave things like mice and moles to their dog and cat. The rest they trust to nature and a little cosmic dialoguing. "I try to be in concert with all living things." She has a deal with the mosquitoes that frequent the property in the summertime: they can have all they want as long as she never knows it: "no itching, bumps, buzzing, landing on my body in front of me, no coming in the house. You break my rules, you die."

She starts each day with a cup of coffee and an hour to herself thinking quietly about her day. "I stay open and look around, listen to the birds and watch the bats go to bed. I love that. I believe the earth knows who you are and I think there's a natural solution to everything. I've sort of made it my business to figure out how."

Unlike his wife, Bob Longacre grew up surrounded by the natural world in the New Jersey Pine Barrens. As a young man he studied history in college, being drawn forever after to the study of sacred traditions. He studied feng shui with His Holiness, Grandmaster Thomas Lin Yun. He helped found the International Feng Shui Guild (IFSG), and helped make its practice popular in the United States. His work at using feng shui to heal and synchronize the energy at sacred places has taken him to 35 countries—from Mayan temples in Central America to the energy network at Beijing's Temple of Heaven. In 1976 he visited the Findhorn community in northern Scotland. Here, he says, his reverence for nature and connection to the earth took a quantum leap.

"It was there I started learning about the inner worlds and the invisible kingdoms, about how each plant has a deva—an angel that overlights that plant—and they in turn overlight what they call the elemental beings in the traditional lore around the world, the fairies and the various beings that build the plants. Celeste and I work consciously with those kingdoms every day. It's not like we have to do some elaborate ceremony; it's just part of our fabric."

Findhorn, he says, was about working with those inner levels. "They told us what the plants wanted for nutrition and location and watering. You'd go into a meditation, image what you want and be connected. That's how simple it is. You don't need any high priests. Anybody is capable of this. When the Christ was in Jesus' body and said 'You will do these miracles and more,' that's the kind of thing he was referring to. He was just an advanced version of what we could be.

"There is a huge movement worldwide right now looking at the quality of our food, and where it comes from. There is a spiritual principle connected to eating local food and when you do that, you are intertwined with the landscape angel. The landscape angel is kind of a generic term for all the devas and angels and elemental beings of all the life forms of that area—and you're part of that. We're not detached, separate observers with this. We're part of it."

When you grow your own food, he says, because it's in the proximity of where you live, "it contains much more vitality in the truest sense of vitality." It's from your bioregion. Your food is connected to you. It's giving you the same nutrients it's getting.

"There are all these horror stories on the news of toxic this and toxic that, synthetic and artificial ingredients, genetic engineering. People are getting much more conscious of where their food comes from and they want it grown locally." The CSAs[11] in their area are selling out memberships for this reason, he says. "It's been shown that people are willing to pay more—even people who are marginally there economically—they are willing to have less to eat, but have it be better quality."

Urban areas, he says, are taking new looks at laws that went on the books in the 1950s when having chickens in your yard was looked down on. "Urban farming is becoming the thing that's happening—rooftop gardens and people having three or four chickens and enough eggs where they can sustain themselves."

He sees that as one more indication of how we're moving toward becoming more decentralized. "One of the things technology did was scale everything up. We're fascinated by everything that's big, so we built these gigantic power plants that lose half of their power just sending it all over the place whereas here we have solar panels that help feed the grid.

All of these things are being decentralized," he says, including the idea of the gigantic factory farm. The antidote: locally grown food.

"I'm not down on tech; I just think it has come too fast. It's overwhelmed us and it's acting to pull us away from our connection to the earth. We wouldn't be alive without the water of the earth and the food that grows. The earth doesn't grow from technology.

"Kids now sit inside doing everything with computers and games and toys and don't get to hear the gurgling of natural water and the wind through the trees. These are important rhythms, in a very subtle way that you can't even verbalize, but they're part of our fabric, part of our intertwining with the earth."

Basically, he says, everything has a spiritual component. "When you build a house, there are spiritual beings that come to get birthed that are guardians of that home. The ancient builders knew that. That's why building ceremonies were so important. We've lost the sense of reverence for the inner aspect of everything because we're like little kids who get over stimulated by the next toy. Gradually the inner worlds have become like fantasy. We don't see them as part of reality. But there are invisible spiritual beings that underlie everything and we're capable of working with them. By their evolution, they're not allowed to just blow in here and fix everything and leave. We have to ask. In this cycle coming up we're going to relearn these inner levels. I think we're on the brink of becoming conscious co-creators with these invisible beings."

*****

Celeste's Best Chicken and Beef Stock
Assemble the following ingredients in a large stockpot:
Beef, chicken, turkey or lamb bones (or a combination)
Small piece of good quality grass-fed organic beef or chicken liver
Beet
Carrot
Swiss chard
Kale
Onion
Chicken or turkey feet (if you can get them)
Cover with water to within two inches of top of pot. Bring to boil and cook on low for 2 days. Strain and separate broth. Add everything remaining to compost.

Action springs not from thought,
but from a readiness for responsibility.
— Dietrich Bonhoeffer, theologian and German
resistance leader during World War II.

Becoming Part of the Solution
Paul Tukey, Brett Plymale and Dr. June Irwin
A Chemical Reaction
www.pfzmedia.com

In 1988, Falmouth Maine native Paul Tukey bought a pickup truck and a lawnmower and went into business as a lawn care professional. He's the first to admit he didn't know what that meant besides walking behind a lawn mower, so he did what he saw others in his field doing. He treated lawns with a four-step process that required that he apply chemical pesticides and fungicides to kill insects and weeds and fertilize the grass throughout the growing season. This was considered state-of-the-art lawn care.

During the third year he was in business, Tukey began to experience blurred vision. Glasses didn't help. Then came the headaches, nausea, and rashes. Finally, a doctor in Boston asked what he did for a living. In short order he found out that the tools of his trade—the chemicals he waded through sixteen hours a day every day—were nerve toxins.

His diagnosis: acute chemical sensitivity. His doctor was blunt. Change jobs or die.

Today he can't go down a pesticide aisle in a store without getting a headache. He can't tolerate his wife's perfume or his son's aftershave. He also has deep concerns that his exposure may be the cause of his teenaged son's severe ADHD, "During the time he was conceived, I was constantly wading through weed killer. I couldn't help but feel I did that to my son."[12]

Tukey changed his business to organic lawn care and eventually began touring the U.S. lecturing on his experiences, promoting his nonprofit, safelawns.org. In 2002, he and the one-time host of PBS's *Victory Garden,* Roger Swain, were at a Portland television station to work on a gardening show where they met Brett Plymale, who would be their cameraman. Tukey and Plymale discovered they shared similar ideas about the wisdom of organics and besides the gardening show, would go on to work on many other projects together.

In 2005, Tukey was doing research on a book about organic lawn care, looking for success stories about how others in his business were treating lawns without chemicals when he stumbled across a story that intrigued him. A little town in Canada had passed a bylaw banning pesticides that ended up going to the Canadian Supreme Court.

"I knew there had to be a much larger back story—a chemical ban that went all the way to the Canadian Supreme Court didn't just happen. Some really motivated person must have taken the bull by the horns, and that's exactly what happened."

In June, 2008 Tukey and Plymale went to the little town, Hudson, Quebec, and attended a talk on the bylaw's story being given by a pair of Canadian politicians. The turnout was huge. The two were able to spend some time with the politicians and began gathering background information. "We asked what the ban meant, what had happened, how they got it passed, and what the political climate was from a politician's point of view," said Plymale. They decided to come back and do some interviews. "I told Paul that maybe this would make a good movie. If you're going to be interviewing these people for a book, why don't we just take a camera along and see what we can get?"

Which is exactly what they did. The result is their 2009 documentary, *A Chemical Reaction* which tells the back story Tukey knew must be there. What Tukey and Plymale had discovered was something of a quiet riot. In September 1984, a Hudson dermatologist named June Irwin was treating a patient who had shown up with a rash on her feet. The normal medications proved worthless. By November the rash had spread all over her body, she had lost her hair and nails, and become delirious. Irwin checked her into Montreal General Hospital. A medical mystery was in full swing. Finally it was determined that the woman's husband had applied a lawn pesticide that contained the chemical 2,4-D. This was the source of her illness. The chemical 2,4-D was widely used all over Canada. Irwin was alarmed at what she saw as a great public health threat—and puzzled at the lack of concern among hospital higher ups.

She became a fixture at the monthly Hudson town council meetings. She would show up and read medical reports into the public record that described what she was seeing—increasing numbers of adults and children presenting with severe reactions to what she now saw was chemical toxicity. Viewed as something of an eccentric, a woman who lived alone with a lot of sheep roaming her property, she would show up in her trademark look: flowing dresses, gothic eye makeup and big floppy hats. The council attendees listened politely.

Irwin persisted. She knew that the key to making her case believable was an accumulation of unshakeable data, tracked over time. So she began measuring the chemicals, herbicides and insecticides that were showing up in the blood, urine and fat tissue of her patients, and in young mothers' breast milk and men's semen. Much of the testing she paid for herself.

Hudson's town council meetings have no time limits on them so Irwin would read and read and people would ask her question after question. Her ultimate goal was not lost on them: she wanted lawn chemicals banned. But accepted perceptions are hard to budge. There was an underlying and unchallenged certainty at work: that chemical companies surely would not allow such toxic chemicals to be sprayed nor would governments see fit to ignore the dangers implicit in their use. But over time Irwin began to make believers out of the council members. One of those, Michael Elliott, became the mayor of Hudson in 1989.

Elliott recalled his own concerns. "One of the questions I asked was, who's really testing this stuff? And of course the pesticide companies would come up with all sorts of PhD documents from such and such a professor and such and such a university who says this is absolutely safe, they've tested it. Why would you trust anything coming from a chemical company? Would you trust the people who made Agent Orange? Why do the chemical companies insist on acid proof rubber boots on their employees? Acid proofing? It means it's going to do you some damage."[13]

On May 6, 1991, six years after June Irwin started her campaign, Hudson, Quebec, population 5,000, became the first municipality in North America to outlaw lawn pesticides on public and private property.

In 1993, two pesticide companies, ChemLawn and SprayTech, sued the town in superior court to try to reverse the ban (farms and golf courses were exempt). They lost. The pesticide companies appealed, saying municipalities didn't have the right to pass the bylaw. They lost again. The chemical companies got very nervous. If this little town could hold such sway, their futures didn't look so good.

South of the Canadian border in the United States, they wasted no time, dispatching lobbyists from coast to coast. By the time they were done, 41 of 50 states had passed state preemption laws. In this case, a preemption law ensures that no town can pass a law that restricts the use of pesticides or fertilizers more than the state law does.

Meanwhile Hudson had tapped into a sentiment that had lain slumbering and was now awake. Other towns all over Canada began their own campaigns to get an anti-pesticide bylaw passed. As one woman in the film working for a pesticide ban put it, "Hudson was the beacon. If they can do it, why can't we?"

"This dermatologist, Dr. June Irwin," says Tukey, "we hold her up as a national community hero in the movie. She starts showing up at every single town meeting for six years facing ridicule, threats, scared for her own safety, not being taken seriously and ultimately, she was the impetus that started a whole national movement. Journalistically, you live for stories like this."

In December 2000, the case went to the Supreme Court of Canada. The day the case opened, the lead attorney for Hudson, Steward Elgie, was shocked. "People camped out hours before the court opened. Media swarmed everywhere. I'd never seen this kind of interest in a case. What hit home for me was that lawns are the places where the environment meets people's lives. What goes on in our municipalities and particularly in our neighborhoods is really the front line of environmental change."

On June 28, 2001, the Supreme Court of Canada ruled 9-0 in favor of Hudson's right to pass its bylaw. Part of Hudson's legal team strategy was to invoke what was known as the precautionary principle, which was defined as, "When an activity could threaten human health or the environment, precaution should be taken, even before there is complete scientific certainty."

Canadian Supreme Court Justice Claire L'Heureux-Dubé defined it this way: "The precautionary principle means you don't have to wait until they're dead to do something." While it must be used wisely, she said, with Hudson, it had been. "With this, it was a health problem."

Thomas Mulcair, Deputy Leader of the New Democratic Party was one of the speakers Tukey and Plymale had heard on their first visit to Hudson. "If there's a lingering doubt about the health risks to you and your kids and your neighbors, how can you ethically, morally continue to use that product or permit its use as long as that doubt is there? That's the precautionary principle. The burden of proof isn't on society to hire reams of experts to produce an absolutely airtight case about the problems that the chemicals can pose."

And if they're wrong? "If down the road science shows we were wrong," says Chris Wilkins, who was a Hudson Town Councilor in 1991, the year of the ban, "then all that's happened because of our actions is a few more dandelions. But if in fact we're right, how many people did we save? Who's got that number?"

The precautionary principle is now a compulsory part of the law in Europe and Canada. It is not in the U.S. and the filmmakers say that in 2009 there will be more of the pesticide 2,4-D used domestically than ever before.

When Tukey asks Irwin during an interview why she did what she did, she says, "I saw an injustice. If you let it happen, you're part of the problem." At one point, he visits her office. She clips his hair, takes his blood and looks at the report on all the chemicals that were detected in his body 15 years ago. They're still there. What Tukey's own poisoning represents is the kind of legacy Irwin was trying to prevent from afflicting the people of her town. About his own condition Tukey is philosophical. There is clearly no way to know what lays in wait in his own tissues. "What motivates me now is creating a safe environment for my children and everybody else's children."

Both filmmakers made huge personal sacrifices to finish the film, digging deep and cutting costs to the bone. They managed to complete it for a fraction of their original $300,000 budget. Plymale's skills as filmmaker were expanded to include many other roles, but as he said, "The most important thing is that we were able to get it done. People get so disillusioned and think that they can't do anything. But this was a story of how you can do something and how you can believe in the system and take action and how that does have an effect. This was my first feature documentary and the whole time I was shooting and editing and showing it, I just felt humbled and honored that it came across my path."

"When you get older and have children," says Tukey, "you start worrying about the world that you're leaving behind. People will tell you how bad it is but they don't tell you what to do about it, so inherent in the message we're spreading is what you can do. Like June Irwin says in the movie, if you hear about a problem and you don't talk about it, you're part of the problem."

Since the Supreme Court ruling, there has been a cascading effect across Canada, something Steward Elgie calls follow the leader. "You get one jurisdiction that breaks from the pack and tries to get out ahead and experiment with a bold new approach and if they have some success, others kind of follow in behind. And this was a prototype example of a follow the leader approach."

By 2004 all of Quebec had joined in the ban. In 2008 most Canadian retailers voluntarily removed synthetic lawn and garden pesticides from garden shelves. And on Earth Day in 2009, the province of Ontario passed an even stricter ban on lawn and garden products. Across Canada green initiatives continue to be passed to ban pesticides in other provinces.

And Dr. June Irwin still spends thousands of dollars of her own money each year to test her patients for pesticide residue.

There is a reason David and Goliath stories like this lift people's hearts and why people like Tukey and Plymale feel compelled to find ways to tell them, regardless of the personal sacrifice, inconvenience or uncertainty. Perhaps it's because they crave and appreciate clarity and they recognize the quiet and humble deeds of heroes when they see them. When Tukey asks Hudson Town Clerk Louise Villandre why she knew they would win the Supreme Court case, her response is almost matter of fact. "It just made sense," she said. "Why wouldn't you be able to do something to protect the lives of your people?"

Knowing isn't enough; neither is being willing. We must do.

— Johann Wolfgang von Goethe

Leading a World Movement: A Heart on Fire for the Planet
Jim Garrison
www.worldforum.org

Born to Baptist missionaries in the Szechuan province of China in 1951, Jim Garrison graduated from Harvard Divinity School with a double MTS in Christology and History of Religion in 1975 and went on to complete a PhD in Philosophical Theology from Cambridge University in 1982

He is the author of several books on theology, politics and the future of America as a world power. In 1991, he founded the International Foreign Policy Association with Georgian President Edward Shevardnadze and former Secretary of State George Schultz. In 1992, Mikhail Gorbachev made him president of the Gorbachev Foundation/USA and in 1995 the former Soviet leader became convening chairman and Garrison became president of the World Forum, a nonprofit institution which draws leaders across multiple disciplines to promote and achieve a humane and sustainable global civilization. Since 2005 Garrison has also been president of the San Francisco-based Wisdom University. Because of the urgency of the threat of global warming, the focus of the World Forum has shifted to seeking solutions to the global warming/climate change crisis.[14]

Q: Tell me about what in your life prepared you to be where you are right now.

JG: Eighteen months ago in spring of 2008, I read an Op-Ed by Bill McKibben in the *L.A. Times* and he was saying ladies and gentlemen, we're about ready to go off the cliff. We have to do something. I've known about global warming and so forth but I was very happily working with Wisdom University, and doing other things. But when I read that, I just sat there, saying to myself, "Okay this is true. What he's saying is true." So I think the next point for me was, what am I going to do about this? If this is true, this means that I have to do something about this. Not the government. Not the private sector, whoever they are, but I think that what makes an activist is someone who connects an awareness of reality or injustice—or an approaching catastrophe in the case of global warming—with the fact that I, Jim Garrison, personally have to do something about this. So then I began to think, what could I do? Well, I've got Wisdom University. I've got State of the World Forum. I can start talking about it at Wisdom. I went to Lester Brown, an old friend, first. I asked him, if global warming is real, how do we stop it? He said 80/20. We have to reduce carbon emissions by 80 percent by 2020. So I said okay. I can work on that.

Q: This was basically a ten-year campaign to save the planet.

JG: Yes. So we started a conference and now I've launched a global campaign called the 2020 climate leadership campaign and it's predicated on the fact that we're about ready to go off a cliff, that the only way to save civilization as we know it, is to reduce carbon emissions by 80 percent by 2020—and that we are all responsible for global warming. We are all responsible for solving it. We all have to become climate leaders. We all have to take personal responsibility for the climate.

We're the ones who kicked the warming off; now the planet is starting to take over the job. Melt all that Arctic ice, for instance, and suddenly the nice white shield that reflected 80% of incoming solar radiation back into space has turned to blue water that absorbs 80% of the sun's heat. Such feedbacks are beyond history.

— Bill McKibben, from "Civilization's last chance,"
Op-Ed, LA Times, May 11, 2008.

So I started to talk about it and then I was invited down to Brazil [near Rio at Belo Horizonte]. One speech led to another thing and another one and finally I was being invited to meet with all kinds of people in the media and political and business leadership, and all of a sudden I began to realize there was some extraordinary energy that was being catalyzed in Brazil. Then it concluded with President Lula da Silva and the entire Amazonian region of Brazil committing themselves [in October 2009] to reducing deforestation by 80 percent by 2020. This happened because a lot of individuals said simply, "I've got to do something,"

These are some key things for people who want to become activists to remember. I think that the single greatest determinant of who becomes a cultural creative[15] is not geography, it's not race, it's not class, it's not gender, it's not wealth—it's basically people who are paying attention. I think it's actually the capacity to pay attention that is where it all starts. Jesus said, if you know the truth, the truth will set you free. That's a profoundly simple but profoundly incisive observation about what makes human beings different and take steps that separate them from the herd. You can only defy the gravity—as Caroline Myss says—of that unconscious patterning you never examine, if you look back at yourself from a distance and see what's really happening, with a kind of ruthless realism.

So first you pay attention. Secondly, whatever grabs your heart you have to realize that you have to be the proximate causation of whatever change that you have in mind. The third thing—which is where many people drop out—is that the perfect is the enemy of the good. You have to start approaching the problem only from where you are. You can't approach the problem, then write a paper and say the government should do this and we should do that so that ultimately somebody else is responsible. You have to start literally from where you are. For me, I had the World Forum and I had Wisdom University.

If you happen to be a housewife living in Gainesville, Florida and you're part of a church group, then you start with your church group. You talk with your neighbors. If you happen to be the president of Brazil, you can take the whole region of the Amazon and do 80/20 in the Amazon. The point is that what we are calling for in terms of the 2020 campaign is everybody has to claim leadership where they are. In this dynamic of social activism, the center of gravity is where you are, wherever that is.

That leads to a fourth point. That is that I've been absolutely relentless. I do this 24/7. I talk about it with every single person I meet. I leave no prisoners. We're about ready to go off the cliff. You know that and I know that, so it's not a matter of being embarrassed. It's not a matter of pretending you don't know. In every social situation I'm in, at the end of the conversation we're talking about global warming and what that person and I can do together to solve it. And now there are 2020 campaigns all over the United States, in Brazil, in Mexico, in South Africa, in Australia, in the Netherlands. We're now mobilizing a global campaign simply because I paid attention, realized I was the proximate causation, realizing I'm only responsible for what I can do. Barack Obama is responsible for what he can do. And I can jump up and down but I'm not President of the United States. And he's not me.

Q: So each of us has a part to play, whatever that is at whatever level. Every role is unique.

JG: Right. And once you start down that road, don't give up. Just keep going and going and going. If you can't figure it out with Plan A, then go to Plan B. And if Plan B doesn't work, go to Plan C. But the goal becomes a determining factor. Those are the lessons that I've learned over 20-30 years of what I would say is sacred activism as Andrew Harvey calls it, and what Jean Houston calls social artistry. We're all creating something beautiful here.

Q: You talk about going nonstop, 24/7. Obviously you don't help any cause if you burn out. What do you recommend people do to detox and recharge? What about spiritual practice?

JG: In order to maintain momentum over time you have to have a very strong practice and pace yourself. I cannot emphasize spiritual practice enough. It's something I do every single day, no exceptions. It's something that then grounds me. Meditation conserves energy. What works for me is a lot of cross-training. I do a lot of physical exercise. I lift weights, I do a lot of yoga, running, and swimming, I keep my body in good shape. I watch my diet. I have a very strong, committed meditation practice and when you do that on a daily basis, you just become centered about what you're doing—and that gives you the compassion to pace yourself. There's only 24 hours in a day, so I get up at 5:00 o'clock and go to bed around 9:00 or 10:00 o'clock and when I finish, by the time I get tired, I just finish. And then I sleep because I know that the next morning, I'm back at it. And so I think that social activists need to be the tortoise more than the hare. You've got to relax in what you're doing with your life.

Q: Derrick Jensen has written this about the idea of 80/20, that we can go down to zero consumption, zero CO_2 footprint as consumers, but 80 percent of the CO_2 being pumped into the air is actually being caused by what corporations, the military, and industry, including agriculture, are doing. What's your response to that?

JG: It's true that most of the pollution is coming from the corporate sector. Look at the Pentagon. It's the worst polluter on the planet. That's true and the opposite is also true: 25 percent of global warming is produced by how we put food on the table. It's hundreds of millions of Americans eating beef that causes global warming. So 25 percent of CO_2 that goes into the atmosphere comes from the farming and the fertilizing and the transportation and so forth and so on to get that Big Mac in Des Moines, Iowa. When you eat that quarter-pound cheeseburger, 14 pounds of CO_2 has been produced and gone up into the atmosphere by the time you take that first big juicy bite.

Q: Of your genetically modified corn-based cheeseburger.

JG: Yes, and that is corporations but that's also the consumer. So part of what I'm saying is that the toxicity in our relationship with the environment which has produced global warming—global warming is an effect not a cause; it's about ready to be a cause of a huge climactic turbulence—but the CO_2 is all the result of our addiction to the oil economy. Wha

I'd be submitting for people's contemplation is the point actually that David Orr makes in his book *Down to the Wire*, that the toxicity in our relationship to the environment is connected inextricably to the toxicity in our relationships with each other, ourselves. So part of what we're saying in the 2020 campaign is that there needs to be as fundamental a transformation of our lifestyles and the way we are orienting ourselves with each other in the world as there needs to be a fundamental transformation from fossil fuels to clean technology and renewable energy. And in fact, that integral approach of interiors and exteriors is fundamental to the politics that we're beginning to lay out.

Q: What we hear about this is that everything we need to do is related to consumerism—drive a hybrid, recycle your trash, buy fluorescent light bulbs, and so forth—what about going beyond consumerism to this other piece you're talking about, which is basically that it's not just what we buy, but it's also our relationship to the earth.

JG: Global warming is really a gateway. It's the last opportunity of the human species to internalize that we come from the earth, we live on the earth, we return to the earth, we now need to learn to live with the earth. We all need to start mimicking the natural systems—start aligning our individual lives, our politics, our economics, our culture in a sort of biomimicry. If you look at every human endeavor, particularly in industrial culture, it's based on violating nature, exploiting nature, devastating nature. We need to turn that completely on its head. This is the beauty of the fact that the Amazon is the first place in the world to adopt the 80/20 goals. Stopping deforestation is the quickest and most effective way to stop global warming, but the extraordinary things in terms of the gateway is this: the Amazon is not only the place where we have to start, but it's in the Amazon, in the indigenous peoples that [we find] all the wisdom that we need for spiritual transformation. So as we mobilize support for the Amazon in the 2020 campaign, we're very cognizant that we can learn from the Amazon the wisdom that we need for the kinds of personal and cultural transformations that will empower us at the level of cities, states, regions, institutions and schools and hospitals and families, so we can make the transformations that are necessary.

Q: What do you think is the upside to all of this?

JG: I think the human race is either going to go through this gateway and do what needs to be done in the next ten years and discover thereby not only how to navigate through the escalating crisis that is emanating out of the CO_2 that we have already put into the atmosphere—which is nearly two trillion tons and we're putting another 70 million tons every 24 hours into the atmosphere—but we're either going to succumb to it and condemn our descendants to an unspeakable, unimaginable hell or we are going to learn that the earth was here long before we were here, will be here long after we are here and the only way to live durably is in concert with it—and that would bring an economic boom that we have never ever seen. It would bring prosperity. It would bring harmony. I believe if we harmonize our economy and politics with the earth, we would harmonize our social relations. It's not to say evil would disappear or that the shadow would disappear but my God, if you look at what's going on in the world today, it is carnage: bombing of civilians and children in Afghanistan, what we did in Iraq and the 4 million people we displaced, the pornography on the Internet, and the massive exploitation of the fact that the banks and Wall Street conducted the biggest bank heist in the history of the world and got away with it. The level of corruption is at every single level. The world is groaning under the weight of shadow and evil and cynicism. We're in the grip of gangster capitalism. And for the people to say, "Enough! We're not going to wait for the government to lead. We're going to move out at the subnational level and work with cities, states and regions. And we're going to make this happen for the sake of those yet unborn." That's what's galvanizing energy around the 2020 campaign.

Will we succeed? Who knows? It may be that in the divine plan of things, the human race is needing to go through a purgatory for a couple thousand years and be reduced to numbers that are 90 or 95 percent so that a remnant, like in the days of Noah, survives the deluge and recreates the upper edges of Canada, parts of Scandanavia, where the only survivors would reside and the new consciousness is burned into our psyche and soul by the very consequences of our conscious inability to defy gravity.

Q: That brings up an interesting image of a new version of Noah with all the icecaps melting and Greenland—as if the earth will drown once again.

JG: Yes. That's exactly what's happening. If you look at global warming from the point of view of the advent of the Age of Aquarius, Aquarius is an air sign. We're putting CO_2 in massive quantities into the air and it's warming the air. Now global warming is a lot of things but the basic dynamic of global warming is it's changing our relationship with water. So Aquarius is the water carrier and the changes in temperature right at that null point where ice turns into water and water turn into ice—basically we're warming so everything that's now ice—Greenland is currently under two miles of ice—all that's melting. There are parts of Greenland and the Antarctic that are now in runaway melt.

Q: And of course that affects all the methane showing up in Siberia because of the permafrost melting.
JG: Yes, we're releasing 40-50 million tons of methane every 24 hours. And methane is 20 times worse than CO_2. And we can't get the government to pay attention long enough to negotiate seriously at Copenhagen on 80 percent reduction by 2050!

Q: Why do we think somebody outside of us is going to take care of this? Are we just in the grasp of a mass psychosis?
JG: I would say we are in the grip of what Jung called collective neurosis—this is the phenomenon of the Nazis—where everybody as an individual is perfectly normal. They go to church. They have children. They have jobs. But collectively they're engaging in something that can only be described as insane. And that is what we're in the grip of. We're in the grip of a collective hysteria, a collective neurosis. I can't say psychosis—I'm not clinically trained in those words, but it's a mass illusion. We've got to wake up the people like us or the people like Gandhi or Martin Luther King, the ones standing away from the crowd saying, "Hey wait a minute. The deluge is coming."

I slept and dreamt that life was joy. I awoke and found that life was service.
I acted and, behold, service was joy.
— Rabindranath Tagore

EVERYTHING BREATHES TOGETHER

What the environmental activists and the South Central Farm participants and the people interviewed for this chapter are trying to do is fulfill a role that no governmental agency is willing to accept. We cannot count on our governments alone to act on our behalf, to simply enact timid legislation that will offend no one and get us exactly nowhere. Rather we have to be the ones to inspire our leaders and demand their vigor. They cannot do it alone. They must be accountable and so must we—and they must be able to count on us standing with them.

So how do we start? How do we reboot human consciousness? How do we reconnect with our heart's ease? We begin by educating ourselves to what's going on around us, by waking up to our own history—our heroic good hearts, genius imaginations and compassionate natures as well as our shadowy greed and denial. We start by creating a daily practice that each of us can believe in—and commit to—and we learn by listening to the wisdom that begins to rise from that, pointing the way for us.

As Richard Tarnas says, "What we do not know hurts us. Don't fall into spiritual sloth. Instead, fall into spiritual heroism. Do all you can as long as you can."[16] Learn to listen. Trust your gut. Don't despair. Get involved. Open your heart and spirit. Individual acts heal the whole of us. Your earth and your fellow beings need your courage, stamina, sweat, wisdom, passion and your good intentions.

As Tarnas notes, we of the modern era have lost so much connection with our universe that we no longer understand its mystery and don't trust it. By objectifying it we can more easily exploit it on all levels, numbing ourselves to the results that surround us. In the end, reconnecting to the earth gives us back our cosmic birthright—to love the earth and acknowledge our place in the cosmos, to realize it's not us at the center of it all but something deep and mysterious and wonderful that is waiting to welcome us home.

Endnotes

1. Richard Rohr, "What is The Emerging Church," webcast of The Center for Action and Contemplation, www.cac.org, November 8, 2008.

2. Julia Butterfly Hill, *The Legacy of Luna: The Story of a Tree, a Woman and a Struggle to Save the Redwoods* (New York: Harper Collins, 2000), p.5.

3. *Ibid*, 6-7.

4. *Ibid*, 23.

5. *Ibid*, 171.

6. Julia Butterfly Hill video essay from an episode of *Thin Green Line*, produced by San Francisco public television.

7. Hill, 217-218.

8. *Fierce Light*, documentary film written and directed by Velcrow Ripper, an Alive Mind Media productions, 2008.

9. *Nourishing Traditions: The Cookbook That Challenges Politically Correct Nutrition and the Diet Dictocrats*, by Sally Fallon with Mary Enig, PhD.

10. Fallon also helped start the Weston A. Price Foundation to further studies made by the dentist and nutritionist who studied the diets of non-industrialized people in the 1930s to investigate diets and dental health and confirmed the validity of traditional pre-industrial era diets.

11. CSA: Community Supported Agriculture. A way for individuals to sign up with a local farmer for regular boxes of food grown during a given growing season. Usually CSA members pay a flat fee at the beginning of each spring for a designated number of weeks. The contents of a box varies each time during the season.

12. Quotes from Paul Tukey are from on-camera narrative in the film, *A Chemical Reaction*, or from a conversation with the author. All quotes from Brett Plymale are from a conversation with the author.

13. *A Chemical Reaction*, documentary written and directed by Brett Plymale and Paul Tukey, a Pfzmedia production, 2009.

14. For more information about the 2020.org foundation, http://www. worldforum.org/2009conference-overview.htm

15. Refers to a phenomenon described in the book *Cultural Creatives*, by Paul Rey and Sherry Anderson, which defines what the authors believe is a growing number of people—mostly unknown to each other—who "care deeply about ecology and saving the planet, about relationships, peace, social justice, self-actualization, spirituality and self-expression."

16. From a lecture Richard Tarnas gave in Chicago, Illinois, October, 3, 2009.

ACKNOWLEDGEMENTS

AT THE END OF THE DAY, so much of what gets any book out the door is the support and love that comes from others. In that spirit, we have a lot of people to thank, both together and separately. First, our spouses and families, of whom we asked so much again and again, never faltered. Our deepest love and gratitude go to John and Miles Gunter (Ellen's husband and son) and Gregory Bembry (Ted's life partner of 23 years). These were not easy issues to wrestle with day in and day out over more than two years but the love and patience with which they sustained us kept this book breathing and moving forward. Thank you all—John, Miles, and Greg—more than we can say.

Together we both have so much to thank our friend Caroline Myss for. She gave selflessly of her time over and over again as *Reunion* progressed from an evolving idea to the book you hold in your hands. She was unfailingly consistent with her time, patience and insight and this book owes much of its life to her encouragement, wisdom and generosity of spirit. Her Foreword is one of her many gifts to this book.

Our mutual friend Andrew Harvey read every chapter and directed us toward a wide body of literature that supported our claims about earth stewardship in both eastern and western religious traditions. Thank you Andrew for that and for giving us an early opportunity to air some of the book's themes at your Institute for Sacred Activism in the spring of 2009.

Endless gratitude to Julie and Patrick Flaherty. Julie, you were *Reunion's* midwife and there's a bit of you on every page.

Thanks to the production crew who helped put this book to bed: Sharon Mullins for her thorough proofing and editing and Sue Wells and

Charles Wells of Chauncey Park Press for their superb job at laying out the book and moving us forward. You're the best!

A special thanks to Jill Angelo for going to work publicizing *Reunion* before it ever began production and for introducing us to the incomparable Heather Murphy, one of the wonderful beings we interviewed for the book's final chapter. Our deepest gratitude to all of our other interviewees for your patience, willingness and hospitality: Joyce and Ken Beck, Jane Presby and Pam Clark, Brett Plymale and Paul Tukey, Celeste and Bob Longacre, and the wonderful Jim Garrison. Your courage and selflessness in a changing and often hostile world gives all of us hope and confidence in the goodness and wisdom of humans everywhere.

To Jan and Jim Gunter, family Katrina survivors, many thanks for reviewing the chapter dealing with Hurricane Katrina.

Much gratitude to CMED's co-founder, David Smith, and to Lench Archuleta, who has taught us so much about the earth. Thanks to the incomparable Dames of CMED for their encouraging words and deeds: Patt Truman, Martie Hughes, Lorena Williams, Kai Marks, Heath Missner, Elizabeth Brown, Lilly White, Joan Maggiacomo, Elaine Hodgson, and Cornelia Serna. And a special thanks to three additional dames, Cheryl Rogers and Georgia Bailey, for reading an early draft of the book and Bronwyn Boyle who has followed its progress and surely told half the population of Australia about it.

❧

Ellen's personal thanks: I also want to thank Daniel Peralta, Stephanie Sterling, Jose Paleaz and Julnar Rizk, who (along with Ted) are old buddies from the first CMED class we attended that magical February in 2003. I treasure you, your brilliance, and generosity of spirit.

A special thanks goes to my spiritual director, Jim Curtan, who helped inspire me to write this book through the deep and revealing work I did with him. There's no one like you, Jim.

My wise classmates in spiritual direction training in Los Angeles, Marianne Gughis and Harriett Salinger, will always have a special place in my heart, wisdom holders in a category all their own.

No one writes a book without standing on the foundation that wa built with the friendship and memories of the people you have spent you life with. My family has given me endless support, love and appreciatio over the years. Thanks to my brothers John and David Sylvester, sisters Deb Sylvester and Suzanne Hawthorne, cousins Jeannie Schultz, Bev House and Victoria Davenport.

Thank you to long-time friends for being patient as I "went dark" for so long: my oldest friend Susan Clark with whom I've literally grown up and learned the world and *mis amigos* John Clark, Joe Madden, Julia Callaway, Margaret Ryan, Jay Setliff, Charlie and Marcia Smith, Margie Bowles, Ted Debosier, Dennis Luczycki, Dotty Umphress and Diane Tucker. A special thanks to Cecilia Galbraith for relentless encouragement and for giving me the gift of a week of utter silence to bring the book to a close.

Lastly, I want to thank my partner in this endeavor, Ted Carter. His steadfastness, unquestioning support, quiet patience and uncanny sense of how the invisible world of nature works was an essential lifeline for me. The two of us encountered endless sobering truths but we also found wonders together and so many good-hearted, courageous souls who love this planet we live on and live without judgment of those who do not yet have the capacity to see with their clarity. Thank you Ted for the huge part you played in this great life adventure.

⚜

Ted's personal thanks: The people who walk with us in our lives change us forever. My siblings—Abby, Mike and Doug—and their spouses and wonderful children continue to amaze and delight me. I want to give special thanks to my parents, Julie and Bob Carter, for the gift of being allowed to be myself. During my summers as a child I remember a large dump truck load of sand being delivered to our back yard, followed two hours later by a load of 500 bricks. I played with my brother Mike and neighborhood friends creating entire neighborhoods with streets and landscaped yards. We happily sculpted brick houses, walkways and driveways into the sand with our hands. Twigs and broken branches placed upright in the sand became the village trees. With a garden hose, we made lakes and streams. It fascinated me to see the sand move and shift as water poured through our villages undermining our brick structures. Houses were always giving way to the endless cycle of destruction and re-birth. This was how I began to see the earth from different perspectives.

Many years later I was gazing down from 35,000 feet on the earth below on a flight to California, on my way to a three-day workshop with Caroline Myss. I sat marveling at the ancient wrinkled whorls below me, at how a stretch of land could remind me of the thick, crinkly hide of an elephant. As I watched, I became aware of a subtle shift in my perception, as if time stood still. The Earth spoke to me – not with words, but rather a sense of connection, like an open channel. She was bereft. "I am so tired," she said. "No one hears me anymore, no one understands me."

I found myself weeping for the loss of our sacred connection with her and how we have grown numb to her pain. At some point I snapped back into my seat and wiped my face in utter embarrassment, hoping no one had seen me. The seats around me were nearly empty, but a young Native American woman across the aisle was looking at me, smiling.

"Were you speaking to the Earth?" she asked. Struck speechless with surprise, I could only nod. She added, "She hears you." As we began to talk, it turned out that she, too, had experienced such dialogues with the Earth. We parted in the airport in Oakland California and I have never seen her since, but the experience haunted me. That flight was the beginning of the weekend that marked my first time seeing Caroline teach and my initiation into learning about dimensions of the human spirit that had been completely out of my vocabulary. I could never have guessed then that I would attend five years of classes at her institute and travel to distant sacred places with her and fellow classmates, or how the people I met during those years would shape and change my life forever.

One of those people was Ellen Gunter. My dear friend Jim Curtan said to me one time, "Ted, there are people in this lifetime that you climb hills with, and then there are people you climb mountains with – Ellen climbs mountains." I never doubted this for a minute. Ellen worked tirelessly for nearly three years as we pulled this book together. She is a gifted writer with amazing foresight and vision. It has been a privilege and an honor to work by her side.

Bibliography

Books referenced

Abram, David. *The Spell of the Sensuous: Perception and Language in a More-than-Human World.* New York: Vintage, 1996.

Barber, Charles. *Comfortably Numb, How Psychiatry is Medicating a Nation.* New York: Pantheon, 2008.

Bartholomew, Mel. *Square Foot Gardening.* Franklin (TN): Cool Springs Press, 2006.

Benyus, Janine. *Biomimicry: Innovation Inspired by Nature.* New York: Harper Collins, 1997.

Berry, Thomas. *The Dream of the Earth.* San Francisco: Sierra Club Books, 1988.

Berry, Wendell. *Bringing it to the Table: On Farming and Food.* Berkeley: Counterpoint Press, 2009.

_____. *The Gift of Good Land.* San Francisco: North Point Press, 1983.

_____. *The Unsettling of America: Culture & Agriculture.* San Francisco: Sierra Club Books, 1981.

Brinkley, Douglas. *The Great Deluge.* New York: William Morris/Harper Collins, 2005.

Brown, Lester. *Plan B, 2.0: Rescuing a Planet Under Stress and a Civilization in Trouble.* New York: W.W. Norton, 2006.

_____. *Plan B, 3.0: Mobilizing to Save Civilization.* New York: W.W. Norton, 2008.

_____. *Plan B, 4.0 Mobilizing to Save Civilization.* New York: W.W. Norton, 2009.

Campbell, Joseph and Bill Moyers. *The Power of Myth.* New York: Random House, 1991.

Carroll, John, Paul Brockelman, and Mary Westfall, editors. *The Greening of Faith:*

God, the Environment, and the Good Life. Hanover: University Press of New England, 1997.

Carson, Rachel. *Silent Spring*. Boston: Houghton Mifflin, 1962.

Cowan, Eliot. *Plant Spirit Medicine: The Healing Power of Plants*. Mill Spring: Swan Raven & Company, 1995.

Davies, Pete. *American Road: The Story of an Epic Transcontinental Journey at the Dawn of the Motor Age*. New York: Henry Holt, 2002.

Davis, Devra Lee. *When Smoke Ran Like Water: Tales of Environmental Deception and The Battle Against Pollution*. New York: Basic Books, 2002.

Devereux, Paul. *Re-Visioning the Earth: A Guide to Opening the Healing Channels Between Mind and Nature*. New York: Simon & Schuster, 1996.

Diamond, Jared. *Collapse: How Societies Choose to Fair or Succeed*. New York: Penguin Books, 2005.

Doyle, Jack. *Altered Harvest*. New York: Viking, 1985.

Duncan, Dayton and Ken Burns. *America's First Road Trip*. New York: Alfred A. Knopf, 2003.

Dyson, Michael. *Come Hell or High Water: Hurricane Katrina and the Color of Disaster*. New York: Perseus Books, 2006.

Elgin, Duane. *The Living Universe: Where are we? Who are we? Where are we going?* San Francisco: Berrett-Koehler Publishers, 2009.

Findhorn Community. *The Findhorn Garden: Pioneering a New Vision of Man and Nature in Cooperation*. New York: Harper & Row, 1975.

_____. *The Findhorn Garden Story*. Findhorn: Findhorn Press, 2008.

Foer, Jonathan Safran. *Eating Animals*. New York: Little Brown, 2009.

Fowler, Cary and Pat Mooney. *Shattering: Food, Politics and the Loss of Genetic Diversity*. Tucson: University of Arizona Press, 1990.

Friedman, Thomas. *Hot, Flat, and Crowded*. New York: Farrar, Straus and Giroux, 2008.

Garrison, Jim. *America as Empire: Global Leader or Rogue Power?* San Francisco: Berrett-Koehler Publishers, 2004.

Gladwell, Malcolm. *Blink, The Power of Thinking without Thinking*. New York: Little, Brown, 2005.

Gore, Al. *Earth in the Balance: Ecology and the Human Spirit*. Boston: Houghton Mifflin, 1992.

Hahn, Thich Nhat. *The Long Road Turns to Joy: A Guide to Walking Meditation*. Berkeley: Parallax Press, 1996.

Hartmann, Thom. *The Last Hours of Ancient Sunlight*. New York: Three Rivers Press, 2004.

Harvey, Andrew. *Teachings of the Christian Mystics*. Boston: Shambhala, 1998.

——————————. *The Hope: A Guide to Sacred Activism*. New York: Hay House. 2009.

Hawken, Paul. *Blessed Unrest: How the Largest Social Movement in History is Restoring Grace, Justice, and Beauty to the World*. New York: Viking, 2007.

——————————. *The Ecology of Commerce: A Declaration of Sustainability*. New York: HarperCollins, 1993.

——————————, Amory Lovins and L. Hunter Lovins. *Natural Capitalism: Creating the Next Industrial Revolution*. New York: Little Brown, 1999.

Heinberg, Richard. *Peak Everything: Waking up to the Century of Declines*. Gabriola Island: New Society Publishers, 2007.

Helminski, Camille, editor. *The Book of Nature: A Sourcebook of Spiritual Perspectives on Nature and the Environment*. Watsonville (CA): The Book Foundation, 2006.

Hemenway, Toby. *Gaia's Garden: A Guide to Home-Scale Permaculture*. White River Junction: Chelsea Green, 2000 edition.

Hill, Julia Butterfly. *The Legacy of Luna: The Story of a Tree, a Woman and a Struggle to Save the Redwoods*. New York: Harper Collins, 2000.

Hinton, David, translator. *Mencius*. Washington, DC: Counterpoint, 1998.

Isaacson, Walter. *Einstein*. New York: Simon & Schuster, 2007.

Jensen, Derrick. *Listening to the Land: Conversations About Nature, Culture, and Eros*. White River Junction: Chelsea Green, 2004.

Kempton, William, James S. Boster, and Jennifer A. Hartley. *Environmental Values in American Culture*. Cambridge: MIT Press, 1995.

Kessel, Anthony. *Air, the Environment, and Public Health*. New York: Cambridge University Press, 2006.

Kidd, Sue Monk. *When the Heart Waits: Spiritual Direction for Life's Sacred Question*. San Francisco: Harper, 1990.

Kimbrell, Andrew. *Fatal Harvest*. Sausalito: Foundation for Deep Ecology, 2002.

——————————, editor. *Your Right to Know: Genetic Engineering and the Secret Changes in Your Food*. San Raphael: Earth Books, 2007.

Kingsolver, Barbara and Stephen L. Hopp. *Animal, Vegetable, Mineral: A Year of Food Life*. New York: Harper Perennial, 2007.

Klare, Michael T. *Blood and Oil: The Dangers and Consequences of America's Growing Dependency on Imported Petroleum*. New York: Metropolitan Books, 2004.

Lachman, Gary. *Rudolf Steiner: An Introduction to his Life and Work.* New York: Tarcher (Penguin), 2007.

Lambrecht, Bill. *Dinner at the New Gene Café: How Genetic Engineering Is Changing What We Eat, How We Live, and the Global Politics of Food.* New York: Thomas Dunne, 2001.

Laszlo, Ervin. *The Chaos Point: The World at the Crossroads.* Charlottesville: Hampton Roads, 2006.

Leopold, Aldo. *A Sand County Almanac.* London: Random House, 1966.

Louv, Richard. *Last Child in the Woods.* Chapel Hill: Algonquin Books, 2005.

Lynas, Mark. *Six Degrees: Our Future on a Hotter Planet.* Washington, DC: National Geographic, 2008.

Mcgaa, Ed. *Mother Earth Spirituality: Native American Paths to Healing Ourselves and Our World.* New York: HarperCollins, 1990.

McKibben, Bill. *The End of Nature.* New York: Random House, 2006.

Myss, Caroline. *Anatomy of the Spirit: The Seven Stages of Power and Healing.* New York: Random House, 1996.

_____. *Defy Gravity: Healing Beyond the Bounds of Reason.* US: www.hayhouse.com, 2009

_____. *Entering the Castle: An Inner Path to God and Your Soul.* New York: Simon and Schuster, 2007.

_____. *Sacred Contracts: Awakening Your Divine Potential.* New York: Random House, Inc., 2001.

Nepo, Mark. *The Book of Awakening: Having the Life You Want by Being Present to the Life You Have.* York Beach: Conari Press. 2000.

Nestle, Marion. Food *Politics: How the Food Industry Influences Nutrition and Health.* Berkeley: University of California Press, 2007.

Niman, Nicolette Hahn. *Righteous Porkchop: Finding a Life and Good Food Beyond Factory Farms.* New York: Harper Collins, 2009.

Orr, David. *Down to the Wire: Confronting Climate Collapse.* New York: Oxford University Press, 2009.

Participant Media and Karl Weber, editor. *Food, Inc.: A Participant Guide: How Industrial Food is Making Us Sicker, Fatter and Poorer, and What You Can Do About It.* New York: Perseus, 2009.

Pearce, Joseph Chilton. *The Biology of Transcendence: A Blueprint of the Human Spirit.* Rochester: Park Street Press, 2004.

Pfeiffer, David Allen. *Eating Fossil Fuels.* Gabriola Island (BC): New Society Publishers, 2006.

Pollan, Michael. *Food Rules: An Eater's Manual.* New York: Penguin Press, 2009.

—————. *In Defense of Food: An Eater's Manifesto.* New York: Penguin Press, 2008.

—————. *Omnivore's Dilemma: A Natural History of Four Meals.* New York: Penguin Press, 2006.

—————. *The Omnivore's Dilemma (Young Readers edition): The Secrets Behind What You Eat.* New York: Penguin, 2009.

Ray, Paul H. and Sherry Ruth Anderson. *The Cultural Creatives: How 50 Million People Are Changing the World.* New York: Three Rivers Press, 2000.

Rifkin, Jeremy. *The Hydrogen Economy.* New York: Tarcher, 2002.

Roberts, Paul. *The End of Oil: On the Edge of a Perilous New World.* New York: Mariner Books, 2005.

Rohr, Richard. *Everything Belongs: The Gift of Contemplative Prayer.* New York: Crossroad Publishing, 2003.

—————. *The Naked Now: Learning to See as the Mystics See.* New York: Crossroad Publishing, 2009.

Shea, John. *Stories of God: An Unauthorized Biography.* Chicago: Thomas More, 1978.

Shiva, Vandana. *Manifestos on the Future of Food and Seed.* Cambridge: South End Press, 2007.

—————. *Stolen Harvest: The Hijacking of the Global Food Supply.* Cambridge: South End Press, 2000.

Smith, Huston. *A Seat at the Table: Huston Smith in Conversation with Native Americans on Religious Freedom.* Berkeley: University of California, 2006.

Smith, Jeffrey. *Seeds of Deception: Exposing Industry and Government Lies About the Safety of the Genetically Engineered Foods You're Eating.* Portland: Yes! Books, 2003.

Stamets, Paul. *Mycelium Running: How Mushrooms Can Help Save the World.* Berkeley: Ten Speed Press, 2005.

Steffen, Alex, editor. *WorldChanging: A User's Guide for the 21st Century.* New York: Harry A. Abrams, 2006.

Steiner, Rudolf. *Agriculture Course: The Birth of the Bio-Dynamic Method.* London: Rudolf Steiner Press, 1958.

Suzuki, David. *The Sacred Balance: Rediscovering Our Place in Nature.* Vancouver: Greystone, 1997.

Swimme, Brian and Thomas Berry. *The Universe Story: From the Primordial Flaring Forth to the Ecozoic Era, A Celebration of the Unfolding of the Cosmos.* San Francisco: Harper, 2004.

Taleb, Nassim. *The Black Swan: The Impact of the Highly Improbable.* New York: Random House, 2007

Tarnas, Richard. *Cosmos and Psyche: Intimations of a New World View.* New York: Penguin, 2006.

Taylor, Jill Bolte. *My Stroke of Insight: A Brain Scientist's Personal Journey.* New York: Viking, 2008.

Thompson, William Irvin. *The Findhorn Garden: Pioneering a New Vision of Man and Nature in Cooperation (Introduction).* New York: Harper Collins, 1975.

Tompkins, Peter & Christopher Bird. *The Secret Life of Plants.* New York: Harper & Row, 1973.

Tucker, Mary Evelyn. *Worldly Wonder: Religions Enter Their Ecological Phase.* Peru (IL): Carus Publishing, 2003.

Ward, Barbara and others. *Who Speaks For Earth?* New York: W.W. Norton, 1973.

Weisman, Alan. *The World Without Us.* New York: Picador, 2007.

WPA Writers Program in State of Texas. *Texas: A Guide to the Lone Star State.* New York: Hastings House, 1940.

Yergin, Daniel. *The Prize: The Epic Quest for Oil, Money & Power.* New York: Simon & Schuster, 1991 (revised 2009).

ARTICLES

Adams, David. "Ice-free Arctic Could Be Here in 23 Years." *The Guardian*, September 5, 2007, updated January 14, 2008.

Baker, Billy. "Saving 'God's Creation' Unites Scientist, Evangelical Leader." *Boston Globe*, May 1, 2008.

Chandler, Lynn. "Africa's Lake Chad Shrinks by 20 Times Due to Irrigation Demands, Climate Change." GSFC press release (Greenbelt, Maryland: NASA, Goddard Space Flight Center, February 27, 2001).

Fischetti, Mark. "Drowning New Orleans." *Scientific American*, October 2001.

Ford, Richard. "A City Beyond the Reach of Empathy." *New York Times*, September 4, 2005.

Gertner, Jon. "The Future is Drying Up." *New York Times Magazine*, October 21, 2007.

Goodman, Brenda. "Drought-Stricken South Facing Tough Choices." *The New York Times*, October 16, 2007.

_____. "Georgia Loses Federal Case in a Dispute About Water." *The New York Times*, February 6, 2008.

Griffith, Kate. "This Too Shall Passacantando." *Grist*, December 29, 2008.

Higgs, Steven. "Surrounded by Factory Farms: Indiana Environment Revisited." *The Bloomington Alternative*, March 9, 2008.

Jensen, Derrick. "Taking Shorter Showers Doesn't Cut It: Why Personal Change Does Not Equal Political Change." *Orion Magazine,* July 13, 2009.

King, Neil Jr. "A Past President's Advice to Obama: Act with Haste." *Wall Street Journal,* December 11, 2008.

Kluger, Jeffrey. "Global Warming: The Culprit?" *Time*, September 24, 2005.

Kristof, Nicholas. "Food for the Soul." *New York Times*, August 22, 2009.

Manier, Jeremy. "Global Warning to Spark Rise in Kidney Stone Cases, study says." *Chicago Tribune*, July 14, 2008.

Marshall, Bob. "Levee Leaks Reported to S&WB a Year Ago." *New Orleans Times-Picayune*, November 18, 2005.

Martel, Brett. "45 Bodies Found at New Orleans Hospital." *Associated Press*, September 12, 2005.

McKibben, Bill. "Civilization's last chance." Op-Ed, *L.A. Times*, May 11, 2008.

McQuaid, John and Mark Schleifson. "In Harm's Way." part of the 5-part series, "Washing Away." *New Orleans Times-Picayune,* June 23-27, 2002.

Pollan, Michael. "Farmer in Chief." *New York Times Magazine*, October 9, 2008.

Ripley, Amanda. "How Did This Happen?" *Time*, September 4, 2005.

Running, Steven W. "Is Global Warming Causing More, Larger Wildfires?" *Science Magazine*, August 18, 2006.

Shane, Scott and Eric Lipton. "Federal Response: Government Saw Flood Risk but Not Levee Failure." *New York Times,* September 2, 2005.

Smith, Daniel B. "Is There an Ecological Unconscious?" New York Times, January 27, 2010.

"Speaker Hastert Calls for End of European Union's Protectionist, Discriminatory Trade Policies." *U.S. Newswire*, March 26, 2003.

Vega, Cecilia M. "As Bodies Recovered, Reporters told, 'No Photos, No Stories.'" *San Francisco Chronicle,* September 13, 2005.

Walsh, Bryan. "The Secret Life of Trees." *Time*, December 14, 2007.

Williams, Carol J. "Drought yields lake's treasures and trash." *The Nation*, July 19, 2007.

Young, Samantha. "Schwarzenegger Asks Obama for More Auto Emissions Rules." Associated Press, January 22, 2009.

Yovich, Daniel. "Ike's Remnants Blamed for Midwest Deaths, Blackouts." Associated Press, September 15, 2008.

Yue, Pan. Interview from Chinese Ministry of the Environment. "The Chinese Miracle

Will End Soon." *Der Spiegel,* March 7, 2005.

_____. "China's Green Debt." *Daily Times (Pakistan),* December 1, 2006.

Zito, Kelly and Matthew Yi. "Governor Declares Drought in California." *San Francisco Chronicle,* June 5, 2008.

ONLINE ARTICLES, INTERVIEWS AND SPEECHES

Alok, Jha. "Deep in Permafrost—A Seedbank to Save the World" June20, 2006. Available at: http://www.guardian.co.uk/science/2006/jun/20/food. frontpagenews

BBC News, August 3, 2006. "China Hit by Rising Air Pollution." Available at http://news.bbc.co.uk/2/hi/asia-pacific/5241844.stm

Barber, David and Sheila Watt-Cloutier interviews in "The Big Melt: The Arctic Ice Cap." Available at: http://video.on.nytimes.com/?fr_story=aa9ac8c8b71dbc3 e2c55b7e6d51020c29c0cd8e

Biello, David. "Fertilizer Runoff Overwhelms Streams and Rivers—Creating Vast 'Dead Zones'." *Scientific American,* March 14, 2008. Available at: http://www.sciam.com/articloe.cfm?id=fertilizer_runoff-overwhelms-streams

China Statistical Yearbook: National Bureau of Statistics web site: http://www.stats. gov.cn/english and http://www.chinability.com/Population.htm and http://indexmundi.com/china.population.html

Dawson, Jonathon quotation. *Findhorn Now.* By the Findhorn Foundation, 2008. Available at: http://www.findhorn.org/video

Environmental Defense Fund, 2007, Report. "Blown Away, How Global Warming is Eroding the Availability of Insurance Coverage in America's Coastal States." Available at: http://www.edf.org/documents/7301_BlownAway_insurancereport.pdf

Etter, Lauren. "Farmers Wonder if Boom in Grain Prices is a Bubble." *Wall Street Journal Online,* January 31, 2008. Available at: http://online.wsj.com/public/article/SB12017446624943059580VjileKfXzheSxhrmkWufQ_Y5s_20080301.html?mod=tff_main_tff_top

Gore, Al. Text of Speech on challenge of converting to alternative energy forms by 2020: http://www.npr.org/templates/story/story.php?storyId=92638501 or http://blog.algore.com/2008/07/a_generational_challenge_to_re.html

Kimbrell, Andrew. "High-tech Piracy". *Utne Reader,* March-April, 1996. Available at: http://www.utne.com/1996-03-01/high-tech-piracy.aspx

Mackenzie, Debora. "Billions at Risk from Wheat Super-blight." *New Scientist,* April 3, 2008. Available at: http://environment.newscientist.com/earth/mg19425983.700-billions-at-risk-from-wheat-superblight.html

Mathai, Wangari. "The Linkage between Patenting of Life Forms, Genetic

Engineering, and Food Insecurity." October 11, 2004. Available at: http://lists.iatp.org/listarchive/archive.cfm?id+97248

Mazza, Patrick. "Adventures in the Smart Grid, No. 1: Why the Smart Grid is Important." *Grist*, June 10, 2007. Available at: http://www.grist.org/article/adventures-in-the-smart-grid-no-1/

Mieszkowski, Katherine. "Superbug to the Rescue." August 28, 2003. Available at: http://www.salon.com/tech//feature/2003/08/28/bioremediation

Moyers, Bill. "Remarks at the 5th Annual Ron Ridenhour Prizes." Available at: www.huffingtonpost.com/bill-moyers/on-journalism_b_95444.html

National Resources Defense Council. "Dirty Coal is Hazardous to Your Health." Available at: http://www.nrdc.org/health/effects.coal.index.asp (pdf download)

Nunez, Joe. "History and Lessons of Potato Late Blight." December 21, 2000. Available at: http://cekern.ucdavis.edu/Custom_Program573/History_and_Lessons_of_Potato_Late_Blight.htm

O'Hara, Doug. "The World's Best Seeds Head for Arctic Vault." Available at: http://www.farnorthscience.com/2008/01/25

Oliver, Rachel. "All About Food and Fossil Fuels." March 17, 2008. Available at: http://edition.cnn.com/2008/asiapcf/03/16/eco.food.miles

Philpott, Tom. "A Reflection on the Lasting Legacy of 1970s USDA Secretary Earl Butz." February 7, 2008. Available at: http://www.grist.org/article/the-butz-stops-here/

Pope, C.T. "Vanishing Lake Chad—A Water Crisis in Central Africa." Available at: http://www.circleofblue.org/waternews/2008/world/vanishing-lake-chad-a-water-crisis-in-central-africa/

Pribyl, Louis J. "Biotechnology Draft Documents 2/27/92." March 6, 1992. Available at: http://www.biointegrity.com.org

Raloff, Janet. "Afghanistan's Seed Banks Destroyed." Available at: http://www.sciencenews.org/articles/20020914/food.asp

Rohr, Richard. "What is The Emerging Church?" Webcast of November 8, 2008. Available at: http://www.cac.org

Rosner, Hillary. "Seeds to Save a Species." *Popular Science*, January 4, 2008. Available at: http://www.popsci.com/scitech/article/2008-01/seeds-save-species

Sanchez, Pedro. "The Climate Change-Soil Fertility Nexus," Available at: http://ifpri.org/2020conference/PDF/summary_sanchez.pdf

Schmeiser, Percy interview. Available at: http://www.percyschmeiser.com/AcresUSAstory.pdf

Shapley, Dan. "Doomsday Seed Bank Opens This Week." *The Daily Green*, February 26, 2008. Available at: http://www.thedailygreen.com/environmental-news/latest/doomsday-seeds-47022403

Shiva, Vandana. "Ecologists Should Worry About the Dunkel Draft." September 23, 1993. Available at: http://www.sunsonline.org/trade.areas/environm/09230193.htm

Taylor, Jill Bolte. Full video and transcript available at: http://www.ted.com/talks/lang/eng/jill_bolte_taylor_s_powerful_stroke_of_insight.html

Thill, Scott. "Frankenfoods' Giant Monsanto Plays Bully Over Consumer Labeling." March 6, 2008. Available at: http://www.alternet.org/workplace/78860

Documentary Films and CDs

A Chemical Reaction. Written and directed by Brett Plymale and Paul Tukey, a Pfzmedia production, 2009.

Bad Seed: The Truth About Our Food. Co-directed and co-produced by Timo Nadudari and Adam Curry, Scared Crow Productions, 2006.

DIRT! The Movie. Produced and Directed by Bill Benenson and Gene Roscow. Common Ground Media, 2009.

End of Suburbia. Produced by Gregory Green, directed by Barrie Zwicker. Electric Wallpaper Production, 2004.

Fierce Light. Written and directed by Velcrow Ripper. Alive Mind Productions, 2008.

Food, Inc. Produced and directed by Robert Kenner and Eric Schlosser. Magnolia Pictures Production, 2008.

Garbage—The Revolution Begins at Home. Written and directed by Andrew Nisker. Garbageman Productions, 2008 (http://www.garbagerevolution.com/).

Into Great Silence: Inside the Famed Carthusian Monastery. Written and directed by Philip Groning, produced by Philip Groning, Andres Pfaffli and others. Zeitgeist Films, 2008.

King Korn. Produced by Curt Ellis, Ian Cheney and Aaron Wolf. Directed by Aaron Wolf. Mosaic Films and ITVS Production, 2007.

The Corporation. Produced by Mark Achbar and Bart Simpson, directed by Mark Achbar and Jennifer Abbott. Zeitgeist Films, 2005.

The 11th Hour. Produced by Leonardo DiCaprio, directed by Nadia Connors and Leila Connors Peterson. Warner Brothers, 2007.

The Future of Food. Produced by Catherine Lynn Butler, directed by Deborah Koons Garcia. Lily Films Production, 2004.

The GMO Trilogy (3-Disc set). Produced by Jeffrey Smith. *(Unnatural Selection* by

Bertram Verhaag and Gabriele Krober, produced by Bertram Verhaag and
Michel Morales, a DENKmal and Haifisch Films Production, 2004.)
You're Eating What? Audio CD by Jeffrey Smith, http://SeedsofDeception.com

RADIO PROGRAMS

"Morning Edition Interview." National Public Radio. May 25, 2005.
"Residents Say Levee Leaked Months Before Katrina." National Public Radio.
November 22, 2005.

TELEVISION BROADCASTS

"Kuwait Still Recovering from Gulf War Fires," by Ryan Chilcote, CNN, January 3,
2003.

Horatio's Drive. Directed by Ken Burns, co-produced by Dayton Duncan and Ken
Burns, produced by Florentine Films, 2005.
Lewis and Clark: The Journey of the Corps of Discovery. Directed by Ken Burns,
produced by Florentine Films and WETA, 1997.
The Journey of the Corps of Discovery. Directed by Ken Burns, produced by Florentine
Films and WETA, 1997.
The National Parks: America's Best Idea. Directed by Ken Burns, produced by
Florentine Films and WETA, 2009.
"The Silent Spring of Rachel Carson." *CBS Reports.* 1963.

GENERAL WEBSITES REFERENCED

http://www.agmrc.org/NR/rdonlyres/6D092BD1-481D-43D1-95CD-
B8F1821E2F19/0/AIC_FBIB_3organic.pdf (Organic Trade Association's
2006 Manufacturer Survey)
http://fire.ca.gov/index_incidents_overview.php (California wildfire information)
http://www.ca.gov (Oil and Gas Production History in California)
http://www.climateprogress.org (Climate Progress)
http://www.edf.org (Environmental Defense Fund)
http://www.eia.doe.gov/emeu/aer/txt/ptb1105.html (U.S. Dept. of Energy website)
http://hubblesite.org/ (Hubble telescope)
http://hydrogenroadtour08.dot.gov. ("Hydrogen Road Tour "08")
http://www.isec.org.ul/toolkit/ustoolkit/html (ISEC Local Toolkit Factsheet)
http://www.kilgorechamber.com/community.htm (Kilgore, Texas)

http://www.nasa.gov/centers/goddard/news/topstory/2003/0321kuwaitfire.html
(Kuwaiti oil field fires aftermath)

http://www.nytimes.com/interactive/2007/10/01/science/20071002_ ARCTIC_
GRAPHIC.html (Animated photos of disappearing ice masses)

http://www.noaanews.noaa.gov/stories2006/s2656.htm (Hurricane Katrina danger
bulletin)

http://www.nps.gov/yell/naturescience/wildlandfire.htm (20th year anniversary of
1988 fire in Yellowstone)

http://www.peopleandplanet.net/doc.php?id=2848. (People and Diversity website)

GOVERNMENTAL PUBLICATIONS REFERENCED AND AVAILABLE ONLINE

Dooley, Alan. "Sandboils 101: Corps Has Experience Dealing with Common Flood
Danger." http://hq.usace.army.mil/pubs/jun06/story8.htm

http://www.aoml.noaa.gov (Atlantic Oceanographic and Meteorological Laboratory
website)

http://www.blancogovernor.com/index.cfm/?md=newsroom&tmp=detail&articleI
D=1523& ("Response to U.S. Senate Committee on Homeland Security
and Government Affairs and Information Request Dated October 7, 2005,
and to the House of Representatives Select Committee to Investigate the
Preparation for the Response to Hurricane Katrina." December 2, 2005.)

http://www.earth-policy.org/Updates/Update29.htm (Environmental Policy Institute
Bulletin)

http://earthobservatory.nasa.gov/Features/GlobalWarming/ (Facts about and latest
updates on global warming)

http://www.gulflink.osd.mil/owf_ii_tabc.htm (Gulflink, Office of the Special Assistant
for the Gulf War Illness)

http://www.ipcc.ch/ (Report from Intergovernmental Panel on Climate Change,
November 2007. Available as .pdf)

http://www.nass.usda.gov (Annual U.S. crop statistics, including production reports)

SOURCES FOR JOURNALING AND SPIRITUAL AUTOBIOGRAPHY

Boswell, James, Samuel Johnson, with an introduction by Peter Levi. *The Journey to
the Western Islands of Scotland* and *The Journal of a Tour to the Hebrides.* New
York: Penguin, *1984.*

Cameron, Julia. *The Artist's Way.* New York: Tarcher/Putnam, 2002.

Dillard, Annie. *The Writing Life.* New York: Harper, 1990.

Dowrick, Stephanie. *Journal Writing: the Art and Heart of Reflection.* New York: Tarcher/Penguin, 2009.

Frank, Anne. *The Diary of Anne Frank.* New York: Doubleday, 1967.

Goldberg, Natalie. *Writing Down the Bones: Freeing the Writer Within.* Boston: Shambhala, 2005.

Lamott, Anne. *Bird by Bird: Some Instructions on Writing and Life.* New York: Anchor/Random House, 1995.

Least Heat-Moon, William. *Blue Highways: A Journey into America.* New York: Little Brown, 1982.

Occhiogrosso, Peter. Classes on Sacred Journaling at his website: http://www.joyofsects.com/class.shtml and select Sacred Journaling.

Powell, Julie. *The Julie/Julia Project:* http://blogs.salon.com/0001399/2002/08/25.html or http://juliepowell.blogspot.com/ and *Julie and Julia: 365 Days, 524 Recipes, 1 Tiny Apartment,* New York: Little Brown, 2005.

Steinbeck, John. *Travels with Charley in Search of America.* New York: Bantam, 1963.

Thoreau, Henry David. *Walden or a Life in the Woods.* Mineola: Dover Publications, 1995.

Wakefield, Dan. *The Story of Your Life: Writing a Spiritual Autobiography.* Boston: Beacon Press, 1990.

A FEW GREEN-ORIENTED WEBSITES

Note: There are thousands of green websites with more coming online every day. These listings will help you get started.

Some farms and ranches have CSAs devoted exclusively to animal-based foods. Search CSAs nationally at http://Eatwellguide.org and http://Localharvest.org/cas (also check out The Green Fork blog at http://blog.eatwellguide.org/ and join it on Facebook if you want instant updates)

www.americanforests.org to learn how to participate in low-cost tree-planting and forest restoration.

www.biodynamics.com for more about biodynamics, biodynamic CSAs, and sites where you can get biodynamic preps, wines, etc.; also check out The Josephine Porter Institute, a biodynamics learning resource at www.jpibiodynamics.org/content/2008calendarrecommendations.html and www.pfeiffercenter.org for information about the Pfeiffer Institute, which conducts training courses in biodynamic agriculture.

www.foodnews.org/ to find out how to buy organic and what and how to substitute when organic food products are not available.

www.huffingtonpost.com/green for current developments on green things in general.

www.organicfoodinfo.net is a cornucopia of information about eating organic.

www.seedsavers.org for more on for saving, ordering and exchanging many types of non-GMO'd seeds.

www.slowfoodusa.org/ celebrates the "anti-fast food" movement, advocating more conscious attempts to grow good, healthy food the old fashioned way, without all the chemicals that speed it to market at the cost of its nutritional value.

www.soulofthegarden.com/ is an amazing website of spiritual and nature sensibilities updated by an Austin native.

www.TED.com features speakers from all arenas of life, from politics, philosophy, and science to the wonders of new inventions; this website is all about what's next and features a diversity of visionaries from all over the world who share their ideas in short, engaging talks.

www.thedailygreen.com provides hits on all things green going on. Short but to the point.

www.treehugger.com is a good general clearinghouse of information about the environment.

http://truefoodnow.org is the Center for Food Safety's True Food Network website advocating healthy food activism.

unitedplantsavers.org is the site for the 360-acre botanical garden that grows endangered indigenous and healing plants that are being threatened in North America.

www.wwoof.org/wwoofaroundtheworld.asp a clearinghouse for volunteers to work with organic farmers around the world.

worldchanging.com is the website for the award-winning book on sustainability and a multiplicity of resources, *WorldChanging*.

www.youtube.com Look for free videos here that can help you go green in endless ways. You can get tips on gardening, composting, seed saving, creating hybrids, permaculture and biodynamics and even see previews of the latest documentaries tracking the health of our food, the changes happening to the planet and the growing cast of characters who are adding their voices to the daily news. It could be called the personal journal gone global. If you have some green wisdom to share, post it yourself.

5173943R0

Made in the USA
Lexington, KY
11 April 2010